M000112957

Born in Chatham, Kent, **HENRY STEDMAN** has been writing guidebooks for over fifteen years now and is the author or co-author of half a dozen titles, including Trailblazer's guides to *Kilimanjaro*, the *Coast to Coast Path* and *Dolomites Trekking – Alta Via 1 & Alta Via 2*, as well as *The Bradt Guide to Palestine* and the Rough Guides to *Indonesia* and *Southeast Asia*. Travel remains his abiding love, a passion surpassed only by his obsession with Kilimanjaro – an obsession that has seen him climb all the routes, collect books, maps and other paraphernalia about it, and even set up the leading website dedicated to climbing it. He now also leads groups up the mountain.

When not travelling or updating his guidebooks, Henry lives in Hastings editing other people's guidebooks, arranging climbs for clients and putting on weight.

Hadrian's Wall Path
First edition: June 2006; this third edition: June 2011

Publisher
Trailblazer Publications
The Old Manse, Tower Rd, Hindhead, Surrey, GU26 6SU, UK
Fax (+44) 01428-607571; info@trailblazer-guides.com
www.trailblazer-guides.com

British Library Cataloguing in Publication Data
A catalogue record for this book is available from the British Library

ISBN 978-1-905864-37-9

© **Trailblazer 2006, 2008, 2011**
Text and maps

Editor: Anna Jacomb-Hood
Proof-reading: Jim Manthorpe
Layout: Anna Jacomb-Hood
Illustrations: pp62-3 Nick Hill
Photographs (flora): © Bryn Thomas
Photographs (other): © Henry Stedman unless otherwise credited
Cartography: Nick Hill
Index: Anna Jacomb-Hood

All rights reserved. Other than brief extracts for the purposes of review no part of
this publication may be reproduced in any form without the written consent of the
publisher and copyright owner.

The maps in this guide were prepared from out-of-Crown-
copyright Ordnance Survey maps amended and updated by Trailblazer.

Warning: Long-distance walking can be dangerous
Please read the notes on when to go (pp36-9) and on safety (pp72-4). Every effort has
been made by the author and publisher to ensure that the information contained herein is
as accurate and up to date as possible. However, they are unable to accept responsibility
for any inconvenience, loss or injury sustained by anyone as a result of the advice and
information given in this guide.

Printed on chlorine-free paper by
D'Print (☎ +65-6581 3832), Singapore

Hadrian's Wall
PATH

WALLSEND TO BOWNESS-ON-SOLWAY
planning, places to stay, places to eat,
includes 59 large-scale walking maps

HENRY STEDMAN

TRAILBLAZER PUBLICATIONS

Acknowledgements

Thanks, firstly, to Charlie Loram, the first series editor, for all the work he did before I even put pen to paper or foot to path. Also thanks to everyone at Trailblazer for their Herculean efforts in turning my text into this book: Anna Jacomb-Hood for editing and the index; Jim Manthorpe for proof-reading; Nick Hill for the maps and illustrations; and, as ever, to Bryn, for keeping me in work. I'd also like to thank the following readers for contributions: Peter & Yvonne Alderson, Peter Berlich, Denise Collins, Giles Cooper, Brian Harman, Philip Hayden, Jane Johnson, David Kunzle, Monica Nelson, Alan Pitt, John Richardson, Chris Sainty, Chris Turner and Scott Vanderbilt.

On the trail itself, I'd like to thank, first and foremost, my trekking companion Peter Fenner for all his help and companionship and for making the walk such an enjoyable one – thanks Peter! Thanks also to David McGlade, National Trail Officer for Hadrian's Wall, for his usual advice and help; Roderick Leslie for checking the bird text, and of course Paula and family at Houghton North Farm in Heddon and Les at The Old Repeater Station for their hospitality.

A request

The author and publisher have tried to ensure that this guide is as accurate and up to date as possible. However, things change quickly. If you notice any changes or omissions that should be included in the next edition of this guide, please write to Trailblazer (address on p2), or you can email us at ⌨ info@trailblazer-guides.com. Those persons making a significant contribution will be rewarded with a free copy of the next edition.

Updated information will shortly be available on:
⌨ **www.trailblazer-guides.com**

Front cover: Walltown Crags (see p163), many people's favourite section of the Wall.
© Henry Stedman

CONTENTS

INTRODUCTION

Just when you think you are at the world's end, you see a smoke from East to West as far as the eye can turn, and then under it as far as the eye can stretch, houses and temples, shops and theatres, barracks and granaries, trickling along like dice behind – always behind – one long, low, rising and falling, and hiding and showing line of towers. And that is the Wall!
Rudyard Kipling, *Puck of Pook's Hill*

On 23 May 2003, Britain's 13th National Trail, Hadrian's Wall Path, was opened in the border country between England and Scotland. The trail (84 miles/135km from end to end) follows the course of northern Europe's largest surviving Roman monument, a 2nd-century fortification built on the orders of the Emperor Hadrian in AD122. The Wall marked the northern limits of Hadrian's empire – an empire that stretched for 3000 miles across Europe and the Mediterranean all the way to the Euphrates. Such is the archaeological and symbolic importance of the Wall that in April 2006 the original list of 'Icons of Britain' was expanded to include it as representative of Roman Britain, just as Stonehenge is of the Neolithic Age.

To say that creating such a path had been problematic would be something of an understatement. This was the first National Trail to follow the course of a UNESCO World Heritage Site. As such, every time a fencepost, signpost or waymark was driven into the ground, an archaeologist had to be present to ensure that the integrity of the Wall was not in any way compromised. To give you an indication of just how careful they had to be, it took *ten years* before the Hadrian's Wall Path was finally opened to the public. By comparison, it had taken the 2nd and 6th legions of the Roman army only six years to build the actual Wall!

Since its opening many have walked the trail and all seem to agree that the difficulties involved in its creation were well worth it, allowing the walker to follow in the sandal-steps of those who built it – the trail itself rarely diverts from the course of the Romans' barrier by more than a few hundred metres. And, though there's only about ten miles of the Wall left and it hardly ever rises to more than half its original height, it – or at least the route it would have taken – makes for a fascinating trekking companion. Punctuated by forts, milecastles and turrets spaced evenly along its length, the Wall snaked over moor and down dale through Northumberland and Cumbria, between the Roman fort of Segedunum (at the appropriately named Newcastle suburb of Wallsend) in the east and the mouth of the Solway River in the west. It's an incredible feat of engineering, best appreciated in the section from Housesteads to Cawfield Quarry where the landscape is so bleak and wild that human habitation and farming never really took a hold. It is here that the Wall stands most intact, following the bumps and hollows of the undulating countryside – as integral a part of the scenery now as the whinstone cliffs on which it is built. Here, too, are some of the best-preserved fortresses, from the vast archaeological trove at Vindolanda, set just off the Wall to the south, to the subtle charms at Birdoswald and the beautifully situated Housesteads itself.

After the Romans withdrew the Wall fell into disrepair. What we see as a unique, awe-inspiring work of military architecture was to the local landowners a convenient source of ready-worked stones for their own building purposes. The Wall is part of the fabric of many of the major constructions built after the Romans left: the priories and abbeys that lie just off the Wall, such as those at Hexham and Lanercost; the Norman castles at Carlisle and Newcastle; the Military Road which we follow for part of the walk; the stronghouses at Thirlwall and Drumburgh – all beautiful, historically important buildings. And all of them incorporate stones from the Wall. Yet even where its destruction was total, the Wall's legacy continues to echo through the ages in the names of the villages that lie along the route: Wallsend, Wallend, Wallhouses, Walton, Wall village and Oldwall are just some of the place names that celebrate the Wall. The past is inseparable from the present.

Quite apart from the architectural and historical interest, all around the Wall is scenery of breathtaking beauty, from the sophisticated cityscape of Newcastle to the wild, wind-blasted moors of Northumberland, the pastoral delights of Cumbria's appropriately named River Eden and the serenity of Bowness-on-Solway, an Area of Outstanding Natural Beauty and a haven for birdwatchers and those seeking peaceful solitude.

Yet perhaps the best feature of the Wall is that all its treasures are accessible to anyone with enough get-up-and-go to leave their armchair. The path itself is regarded as one of the easiest National Trails, a week-long romp on a grassy path through rolling countryside with the highest point, Green Slack, just 345m above sea level. (That said, there are still a couple of tiring stages.) The waymarking is clear and, with the Wall on one side and a road a little distance away on the other, it's very difficult to lose one's way. There are good facilities, from lively pubs to cosy B&Bs, friendly, well-equipped hostels and idyllic little tearooms. And for those for whom completing the entire trail is over-ambitious, there are good transport connections, including a special Hadrian's Wall Country bus (the AD122). With a little planning, you can arrange a simple stroll along a short section of the trail, maybe take in a fort or museum on the way, then catch the bus back to 'civilisation'. While for those who prefer not to follow any officially recognised National Trail, the path also connects to 43 other walks, details of which are readily available from one of the half-dozen or so tourist offices serving the trail.

So, while the Wall no longer defines the border between Scotland and England (90% of Northumberland, an English county, actually lies to the north of the Wall, and at no point does the wall actually coincide with the modern Anglo-Scottish border), it nevertheless remains an inspiring place and a monument to the breathtaking ambition of both Hadrian, the youthful dynamic emperor, and of Roman civilisation itself. And this trail is a great way to appreciate it.

About this book

This guidebook contains all the information you need. The hard work has been done for you so you can plan your trip from home without the usual pile of books, maps, guides and tourist brochures. Pre-departure planning information includes:

● Descriptions of all kinds of accommodation from campsites to luxurious guesthouses
● Walking companies if you want an organised tour
● A number of suggested itineraries for all types of walkers
● Answers to all your questions: when to go, degree of difficulty, what to pack and how much the whole walking holiday will cost

When you're all packed and ready to go, there's comprehensive information to get you to and from the Hadrian's Wall Path and 59 detailed maps and town plans to help you find your way along it. The route guide section includes:

● Walking times in both directions
● GPS waypoints to aid navigation and for those who want to plot their path on a GPS
● Reviews of campsites, bunkhouses, hostels, B&Bs, guesthouses and hotels
● Cafés, pubs, tearooms, takeaways and restaurants as well as shops for buying supplies
● Rail, bus and taxi information for the villages and towns along the path
● Street plans of the main towns both on and off the Wall: Newcastle, Wylam, Corbridge, Hexham, Haltwhistle, Brampton and Carlisle
● Historical, cultural and geographical background information

PLANNING YOUR WALK

About the Hadrian's Wall Path

THE HISTORY OF THE WALL

Though by far the most famous, Hadrian's Wall was in fact just one of four Roman frontiers built between the subjugated south of what is now called Britain and those tribes living in the northern part of the island, known collectively as the Caledones. Since their invasion in AD43, the Romans had at one time or another conquered just about all the tribes living on the island of Britannia. But the area we now call Scotland, once defeated, proved more difficult to keep under control. Even a potentially decisive victory in AD84 somewhere north of the Tay at a place they called Mons Graupius failed to quell the ongoing insurrection by the Caledones.

Emperors came and went before the pragmatic Domitian (who reigned AD81-96) decided that maintaining a grip over all of the island would ultimately require too many troops; troops that could be more usefully employed in other parts of the empire. It was thus

---

❏ **Hadrian's Wall ... or is it?**
It should be stated here that there are some who believe that the refortification of Trajan's turf-and-timber wall by Hadrian actually took place *before* the latter visited Britain. The history of the Wall is full of minor controversies like this because, as you'll see when you read this book and other accounts, much of the history of Hadrian's Wall is still open to conjecture. Indeed, up until the 19th century or so, the Wall was actually known as **Severus's Wall**, after the emperor who ruled at the beginning of the 3rd century AD. It was just prior to Severus's reign, in AD197, that the Wall was overrun for the first time, leading to an extensive overhaul and rebuilding of the Wall between AD205 and 208 – which explains why, until archaeological discoveries proved conclusively otherwise, the Wall was originally attributed to Severus.

The reason for this uncertainty is that no contemporary accounts of the construction of the Wall have yet been discovered, with the earliest mention having been written by Spartianus, as quoted below, over 150 years later. So with the following account of the Wall's construction and history, it's worth bearing in mind that not all of it should be taken as gospel but merely as a version of events currently accepted by the majority of Wall experts. Furthermore, don't be surprised if some of the 'facts' written here are contradicted by accounts in other books.

decided to draw a line across the island and establish a border to separate the controllable south from those 'lawless' lands to the north. Initially that boundary was drawn to watch over the glens – the main gateways into and out of the Highlands – a border known as the **Gask Frontier**. However, as more and more troops were withdrawn from Britannia to fight in other parts of the Empire, the border by necessity receded south to the area now known, appropriately enough, as the Borders.

Soon after his accession, Emperor Trajan (AD97-117) decided to move the border still further south, choosing as his frontier the **Stanegate** (though this was not what the Romans called it), the east–west road that ran between the Roman settlements of Carlisle and Corbridge. Built during the governorship of Agricola in AD80, the Stanegate was an important trade route that needed protecting. Trajan's troops set about building a line of turf and timber forts to guard the Stanegate, including Vindolanda (see p155) and Corbridge Roman Town (p130).

Hadrian builds his Wall

Having completely transformed the soldiers, in royal fashion, he made for Britain, where he set right many things and – the first to do so – drew a wall along a length of eighty miles to separate barbarians and Romans.   Aelius Spartianus, **The Augustan History**

During Trajan's reign, his fortified border was used less as a defensive barrier than as a launchpad for incursions into Scotland; an *attacking* border, if you like. His successor, Hadrian (AD117-138), however, saw it as more of a traditional border; as both a defensive barrier and a physical marker for the northern limit of his territories. Following a tour of his dominions in AD122, Hadrian ordered the refortification of Trajan's border with the building of a wall to the north along the line of the Whin Sill ridge. This wall was to extend beyond the limits of the Stanegate, to stretch across the entire island. And thus the Hadrian's Wall that we know today began to take shape.

The building of the Wall was something of an organic process, evolving as the geology and political climate dictated. This is best illustrated by the curious size of the foundations, much of which for the first half of the walk (from Newcastle west to the River Irthing) are far too broad for the wall that was eventually built upon them, suggesting, of course, that the Romans initially had plans to construct a much bigger barrier. The materials used in the Wall's construction changed too, depending on where it was built: in the east of the country, for example, a rubble-and-puddled-clay core was used, whereas a limestone mortar core was prevalent in the middle of the country, while in the western half of the country an all-turf wall was built (though this, too, was later converted to stone sometime in the second half of the second century AD as the infrastructure improved and the supply of building materials to the line of the Wall became more efficient).

To carry out all this construction, three legions were employed: the Second Augusta from Caerleon in South Wales, the Twentieth Valeria Victrix from

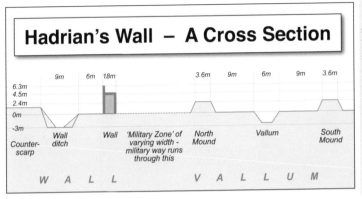

Hadrian's Wall – A Cross Section

| | 9m | 6m | 18m | | 3.6m | 9m | | 6m | 9m | 3.6m |

6.3m
4.5m
2.4m
0m
-3m

Counter-scarp — Wall ditch — Wall — 'Military Zone' of varying width - military way runs through this — North Mound — Vallum — South Mound

W A L L   V A L L U M

Chester and the Sixth Victrix from York. It was their task to clear the ground of trees and scrub where necessary and quarry, transport and organise the estimated 25 million facing stones, each approximately ten inches long, six inches high and twenty inches deep (25cm by 15cm by 50cm respectively). These were then set into the rubble-and-puddled-clay/limestone mortar core of the Wall. As a measure of the legions' efficiency, an experiment was conducted recently in which a section of the Wall was rebuilt using some original facing stones. It concluded that a gang of 80 men needed 32 wagons and 64 oxen to keep it supplied with enough lime, water and stone to build the Wall. Yet despite all the effort required, the original construction took as little as six years to complete.

It's a level of efficiency that becomes even more impressive when one considers the sheer enormity of the Wall, and that an estimated one ton of stone had to be dragged up for every single yard of it. Stretching from the Solway Firth to the North Sea, the Wall was 80 Roman miles long (73 modern miles) and stood at around 6m (20ft) high and just under 3m (10ft) thick. And just to ensure the security of the Wall, a 6m (20ft) **ditch** (Hadrian's ha-ha, perhaps?) was dug on the northern 'Scottish' side along its length (though not, it must be said, around many of the crags, where the crags themselves were considered an adequate defence). A typical Roman defence, this ditch would probably have had a 'false floor' under which sharp spikes would have been concealed.

Such manifold defences are impressive. Yet even so, Hadrian's Wall could act as an effective barrier only if it was sufficiently manned. So while the bulk of the men continued to be stationed in the old forts built by Trajan along the Stanegate road, **milecastles** (see box p112) with a capacity for 32 men were built along the entire length of the Wall at intervals of, as their name suggests, one Roman mile (the equivalent of a thousand paces) – a total of 80 milecastles in all. And evenly spaced between each one were two **turrets** or observation posts, 161 all told along the Wall's entire length and always made of stone,

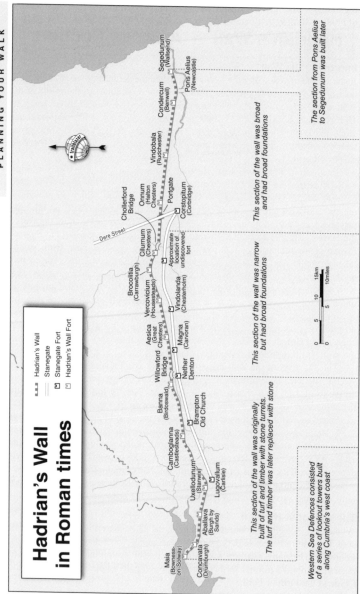

Hadrian's Wall in Roman times

Key:
- Hadrian's Wall
- Stanegate
- Stanegate Fort
- Hadrian's Wall Fort

Maia (Bowness-on-Solway)
Concavata (Drumburgh)
Aballava (Burgh by Sands)
Uxelodunum (Stanwix)
LugoVallum (Carlisle)
Camboglanna (Castlesteads)
Banna (Birdoswald)
Brampton Old Church
Nether Denton
Willowford Bridge
Magna (Carvoran)
Aesica (Great Chesters)
Vindolanda (Chesterholm)
Vercovicium (Housesteads)
Brocolitia (Carrawburgh)
Cilurnum (Chesters)
Chollerford Bridge
Approximate location of undiscovered fort
Dere Street
Onnum (Halton Chesters)
Portgate
Corstopitum (Corbridge)
Vindobala (Rudchester)
Condercum (Benwell)
Pons Aelius (Newcastle)
Segedunum (Wallsend)

This section of the wall was originally built of turf and timber with stone turrets. The turf and timber was later replaced with stone.

This section of the wall was narrow but had broad foundations

This section of the wall was broad and had broad foundations

The section from Pons Aelius to Segedunum was built later

Western Sea Defences consisted of a series of lookout towers built along Cumbria's west coast

0 5 10 15km
0   5   10miles

regardless of the material of the Wall draped between them. Each was capable of holding 10 men. Estimates suggest that it would have taken just $2^1/_2$ minutes to run from one fort to the next, so messages could have been relayed along the Wall speedily.

Improving the Wall

Just a couple of years after the wall was finished the defences were strengthened, possibly in response to pressure from either the Caledones to the north of the Wall or the Brigantes – whose territory the Wall crossed. Specifically, a series of **16 forts**, each housing 500 to 1000 men, was constructed at irregular intervals along the Wall. These, in many cases, replaced the forts along the Stanegate, which were either converted into supply bases or abandoned altogether. The Wall was extended too, beyond Pons Aelius to Segedunum (see p93).

In addition, 50 to 100 yards (46-91m) south of the Wall two 10ft (3m) high walls of earth were constructed, with a 10ft (3m) deep, 120ft (36m) wide ditch between them. This earthwork is known as the **Vallum** which, confusingly, means 'wall' in Latin; the name was given by the Venerable Bede, an 8th-century monk and early English historian who was the first to write about the Wall's dimensions. (Incidentally, Bede wrote his *Ecclesiastical History of the English People* at his monastery in Jarrow, constructed, at least in part, from stones taken from the Wall.) Nobody is completely sure what the Vallum is for; as it is on the south side of the Wall it is unlikely to have been a defensive barrier; nor, with both the Stanegate and Military Way (see p17) nearby, would it have made much sense to construct a road here. Recent theories have suggested that the Vallum marked the border between the civilian territory and a sort of 'military no-go zone' surrounding the Wall. Another suggestion is that it was used to stop conscripted British soldiers, forced against their will to serve the Romans along the Wall, from running away.

The character of the Wall had now changed. From a lengthy but fairly flimsy construction whose primary purpose was a lookout from which to keep an eye on the locals, the Wall now became a defensive, heavily fortified barrier; while the number of soldiers stationed on the Wall went from a relatively measly 3000 to a much more intimidating 15,000 – a 500% increase in manpower.

It should be noted here that, although Roman soldiers built the Wall, it was Rome's auxiliary legions who actually manned it. These soldiers were recruited from various parts of the empire – on the Wall alone you'll come across evidence of auxiliary legions from Belgium, Germany, Spain, Iraq, Syria and elsewhere. These auxiliary soldiers were not officially Roman citizens, at least not until they had served a certain length of time in the army and had retired.

The Wall post-Hadrian

Whatever the original intentions of Hadrian, the defensive obligations of the Wall soon became rather secondary to more mundane yet lucrative financial duties. Following Hadrian's death in AD138 his successor, Antoninus Pius, decided to push the Empire's frontier further north once more, to a line stretching from the Clyde to the Firth of Forth. *(continued on p17)*

❏ THE ROMANS IN BRITAIN

It took the Romans a while to reach Britain. Expanding in every direction from their base on the west coast of what we now call Italy, conquering the cold, windswept island in the top left-hand corner of the known world was never really a priority for them. And even when the Romans did eventually decide to invade, it wasn't the beauty of the land or the treasures it contained that lured them here. Instead, it could be said that the invasion was instigated by the whim of one man who was looking for a way to impress his friends and fellow citizens and strengthen his political position at home.

That man was Julius Caesar, and the year was 55BC. At that time Julius Caesar was one of a triumvirate, along with Pompey and Crassus, vying for supreme power in Rome; and the best way to improve your standing at home at that time was to win a battle abroad. So casting his eye around for a suitably easy yet seemingly impressive land to conquer, Julius hit upon Britannia.

Iron-age Britain was a dynamic society of hillforts and nascent towns characterised by a grid of streets each flanked with houses, places of worship, forges and workshops, and each populated by traders, craftsmen, warriors and druid priests. Metalwork was the Briton's signature craft, whether for vanity and decoration, such as the beautiful brooches that now sit in museums across the land, or for more belligerent purposes, such as horned helmets, swords and spears. The Romans described the country as 'uncivilised', but to them that simply meant that the inhabitants didn't live in cities.

To Caesar, Britain was the perfect victim for his invasion. He knew it wasn't the land of popular imagination, a land peopled by a barbaric yet united race that would fight tooth and nail to defend their homeland. Instead, he knew that it was inhabited by a disparate set of tribes who were too busy with their own internecine squabbles to care too much about foreigners arriving on their shores, and whose squabbling would make them easy to divide, conquer and rule. Unfortunately, things didn't quite pan out the way Caesar had imagined. Firstly, the weather – that most fickle of British characteristics – intervened. Storms across the channel smashed much of Caesar's army before it had even caught sight of land; those troops that did make it across found the locals would not stand and fight, as the Romans had hoped, but preferred instead to engage in guerrilla warfare, which hardly seemed fair at all. Thus their first invasion in 55BC was abandoned almost as soon as it had begun. A second campaign the following year was only slightly more successful: though they managed to get across the Channel in greater numbers this time, the might of the Roman Empire managed to reach only as far as the Thames at Brentford – which, as anybody who's been to Brentford recently will agree, is a poor return for all that effort. Confronted with the might of the Catuvellauni tribe, the Romans were forced to retreat with their imperial tail between their legs, the only trophies they had to show for their invasion being a couple of tributes and taxes paid by a few piddling little tribes in southern England.

Claudius and the conquest

So it was left to one of Julius Caesar's successors, the divine Emperor Claudius, finally to invade and occupy in AD43, using a massive force of some 40,000 men. The disparate tribes of Britain in the 1st century AD were no match for the professionalism and discipline of the Roman legions. The Romans knew this; so, too, did many of the British tribes, or at least the smarter ones who, rather than engaging the imperial legions in battle – a route that could lead only to certain defeat and possible annihilation – opted instead to live in peace and relative freedom, albeit under the rule of Rome, and enjoy the advantages that acquiescence brings.

Thus, for the first decade or two, things went pretty much to plan for the empire. True, the west and north of the island still lay beyond their control. But the tribes in that part which they had conquered seemed to find living under the Romans to be no bad thing, and played the part of meek and obedient subjects rather well. And they probably would have done for much longer too, had Nero not ascended to the imperial throne in AD54. Corrupt and oppressive, Nero's brutal administration caused the Britons to rise up against their rulers. The leader of this revolt was Boudicca (aka Boadicea), queen of the Iceni tribe who rampaged through the province in AD60 destroying key Roman settlements one by one as she went, including Colchester (Camulodunum), London (Londinium, where thousands of Romans were massacred) and St Albans (Verulamium). Though the uprising was soon quashed the entire affair had exhausted both sides. Boudicca, witnessing the slaughter of her own troops at the final battle, took her own life and now lies buried, so it is said, under Platform 10 of London's King's Cross Station.

What's more, further upheaval back in Rome forced the empire to rethink its ambitions, and a halt to its expansionist policy in Britain was called – even though the west and north still remained unconquered and alive with the enemies of Rome and its empire.

The accession of Vespasian in AD68 saw a return to stability and a consequent reinvigoration of Rome's ambitions to subjugate the British Isles; just a decade later Rome was again launching successful campaigns into the lands we now know as Wales, Cumbria and Scotland, under the rule of the new governor, Gnaeus Julius Agricola. Of the three regions, it was Scotland (then called Caledonia) that proved the most stubborn and even after a decisive victory against the Caledones at Mons Graupius (believed by some historians to be Bennachie in Aberdeenshire) the survivors were able to flee and regroup in the relative safety of the Highlands.

Recognising the difficulty of flushing the Caledones out from their remote base, the Emperor Domitian opted instead for a policy of containment, building a line of fortifications known as the **Gask Frontier**, which ran south-west to north-east across Perthshire in Scotland. The idea of the frontier was to watch over the Scottish glens – the main exit and entry points into the Highlands – thereby effectively placing the Caledones under house arrest. Yet even this newer, more realistic strategy was soon deemed to be too ambitious and, as other parts of the empire came under attack from various tribes, the decision was made to withdraw one of the four legions stationed in Scotland and to pull back from the Gask Frontier.

Trajan and expansion

With the death of Domitian (possibly at the hands of his wife) in AD96, and the brief reign of Nerva, who ruled for less than two years, Marcus Ulpius Traianus, or Trajan, a career soldier, was anointed emperor in AD98. As his military background would suggest, Trajan's style was aggressive and focused largely on the continuing expansion of Rome's borders. Indeed, the empire was never larger than it was under his reign, as Armenia, Romania and Mesopotamia were brought under his rule.

Once again, however, in order to achieve these victories Trajan was forced to reduce his army's presence in Scotland, and in order to do this the empire's northern frontier was once again redrawn further south. This time a road known as the Stanegate (Saxon for 'Stone Road') was chosen as the frontier. Built in AD80 to link the towns of Corbridge and Carlisle, the road cut across the two main military routes heading north, one on either side of the Pennines.   (*continued overleaf*)

Trajan and expansion

(continued from p15) To suggest that Trajan ignored Britain, however, is wrong. Indeed, his unquenchable ambition would simply not allow him to be content with only half the island. So, while it is true that under his reign the northernmost border of his empire had receded south into what we now know as England, Trajan did not view the Stanegate Frontier as a defensive border but more of an offensive one, as a base from which to launch further raids into Scotland. Indeed the Stanegate road became an essential military line of communication, enabling the Romans to move troops quickly across the Pennines from one major north–south road to the other. To guard the road, forts and watchtowers were placed at intervals along the Stanegate – the forerunner, of course, to Hadrian's Wall and its forts.

As for the land to the south of the Stanegate, Trajan was content to continue with what was known as the Flavian policy (the Flavians being the imperial dynasty that preceded Trajan and included Emperor Vespasian): allowing Roman culture and society to influence the development of the province, so that in time Britain would come to identify more closely with its masters and therefore, hopefully, be less inclined to rebel.

Hadrian and his Wall

With the death of Trajan in AD117, another Spanish military man and a relative of Trajan, Publius Aelius Hadrianus, was chosen as heir. Though no less competent, militarily speaking, than Trajan, where the latter was consumed by an ambition to push back the frontiers of his empire, Hadrian was content to adopt a more defensive approach and protect all the gains made in his predecessor's reign. This change in policy heralded a period of almost 100 years of continuous peace; it also, of course, led to the building of one of the greatest military constructions of them all: a wall of stone along their northern border, a frontier that up until now had been defended merely by hastily built turf and timber forts and watchtowers.

The end of Roman Britain

The Romans survived in Britain for almost another 400 years after Hadrian, until the start of the 5th century. Indeed, it's fair to say that they did more than just survive: they positively prospered. And so, too, did their subjects, who found that the Roman way of doing things, particularly when it came to matters of architecture, road-building, cooking, drinking, trading, educating and organising society in general, was often the best way (see box p18). Far from an extended swansong, the last 200 years of Roman rule saw some of the empire's greatest achievements in Britain, including Bignor Villa in Sussex. In fact, some historians have even gone as far as to declare that, by the time the Romans departed, Britain was one of the most 'Romanised' of its territories, and its people the most prosperous and peaceful.

So what drove the Romans out from this most compliant of provinces? The truth is that nothing did, or at least nothing within Britain itself. Instead, as the Empire crumbled and its borders were attacked from all sides, the Romans found themselves unable to hold on to all their territories; just as Britain was one of the last places to succumb to Roman rule, so it became one of the first to be dispensed with when the going got tough.

As they withdrew, other invaders filled the vacuum. In particular, the Anglo-Saxons from across the North Sea, Picts from northern Scotland and invaders from Ireland all penetrated Roman Britain's borders. Attempts to restore some sort of Roman law and order went on for the next two centuries or so. But by then, the Golden Age of Roman Britain was well and truly over.

(continued from p13) Not to be outdone, Antoninus fortified his new border with a 'Wall' of his own (AD142-4), the **Antonine Wall**, made of turf. So, just 10 years after the completion of Hadrian's Wall, its primary purpose as a border-cum-defensive-barrier was all but finished. The character of Hadrian's original fortifications changed too. Some forts, such as Housesteads, no longer on the front line, were left to languish and developed more into trading posts than military positions. Others, however, such as Corbridge, two miles south of the Wall, prospered as supply bases for the Roman troops stationed further north along Antoninus's border.

Markets were established near all the forts and the local tribe, the Brigantes, soon set up small villages in the shadow of the Wall to take advantage of the trading opportunities afforded them by having the world's first professional army, staffed by regularly paid, full-time soldiers. The new, non-military character of these forts continued even after the Antonine Wall was abandoned, c AD160, just 20 years after its inception, having been repeatedly overrun. After this, Hadrian's Wall remained the definitive limit of the Roman Empire for the next 200 years. The forts became the business and social centres of the Wall, and villages, called *vici* (singular: *vicus*), grew up around them. In addition, a second road, the **Roman Military Way**, was built around AD160 between the Stanegate and the Wall, often along the northern earthwork of the Vallum (which had by now been largely decommissioned). Such a road would be vital for the rapid transport of troops along the Wall and eventually replaced the Stanegate as the primary artery adorning the neck of Britain.

It would be wrong, therefore, to think of the Wall purely as a means of defence, a place to shelter from the spears of the Barbarians to the north. Because, whatever Hadrian's original intention for his Wall, it had evolved to become more of a checkpoint, a place to watch the comings and goings of the locals as they crossed the border, and to collect tolls and customs duties from the traders.

Severus's restoration
That is not to say that the Wall had entirely forsaken its military duties; indeed, following a successful breach by invaders sometime around the end of the 2nd century AD, it was decided to restore, renovate and refortify Hadrian's Wall. This took place at the beginning of the 3rd century under the reign of Emperor Severus, to whom the Wall was (wrongly) ascribed and after whom it was named for over 1500 years; prior to conclusive proof that the Wall was built during the reign of Hadrian, it had always been assumed that Hadrian had ordered the construction of the Vallum only and that it was Severus who had built the actual Wall; see box on p9.

Amongst Severus's improvements was a rebuilding of the Wall using a super-hard white mortar which allowed it to be much narrower than previously. The Wall had never looked so good, nor so impregnable; it's been estimated that 3,700,000 tons (30,138,000kg) of stone was used in its construction.

❏ Life in Roman Britain

Though the number of Roman troops who occupied Britannia was relatively small compared to the total population, their influence was all-pervasive. Roman cities sprouted on England's green and pleasant land, filled with quintessentially Roman buildings – basilicas, villas, baths and forums – that employed the latest Roman construction methods, exuded an architectural style that was intrinsically Roman, and were all crowded by local people who dressed in the Roman style, spent Roman money, measured distances in Roman miles (the word itself derived from the Latin for 1000 paces, the Roman mile being slightly shorter than the modern one) and ate Roman food. Nor did Roman influence end there, for towards the end of their empire the descendants of many who had prospered under Roman rule even began to worship Roman gods and speak Latin as a first language!

And you can't blame them; without deriding the traditional British culture that had thrived before the invasion, life under the Romans certainly seemed a more comfortable affair. Rough, muddy roads became sleek metalled affairs. Buildings, previously made of timber, thatch and mud now became imposing, stone-made constructions with such novel features as windows and columns, with indoor plumbing and warmth provided by underfloor heating rather than the dangerous and unhealthy open hearth. The Romans brought with them a complete change in the organisation of British society, from the family-based 'clan' system so popular among the 'primitive' tribes to a highly stratified civil and military structure.

Other innovations that were introduced include canals, water mills, factories, new cereals and vegetables. And when they went they took much of their technology with them, including glass-making (the secret of which wasn't rediscovered until the 13th century), lighthouses (reintroduced in the 19th century), lavatories and central heating (commonplace again only in the 20th century).

Indeed, so pervasive was their influence that their currency became the legal tender of Britain just as it was across the rest of the empire, and Latin became the *lingua franca* of traders in this remote northern outpost. Furthermore, as the merchants and traders of Britain learned Latin, so they learned the advantages of literacy and the written record. Nor was that the only benefit reaped by the traders of the occupied provinces. The fact that there were now thousands of foreign troops on their land was in itself a business opportunity and soon local villages were springing up near Roman strongholds to take advantage.

Of course, while Britain enjoyed great prosperity, it was still forced to play the part of the conquered; because while there was some integration and mixing of the two sides – an integration that grew the longer the Romans remained in Britain – there was still very much an 'us and them' mentality on both sides. For the Romans, inevitably, there was a sense of snobbery when it came to discussing the Brits, whom the former frequently came to sneer at as the Britunculli – a translation of which would be something like 'wretched little Brits'.

The Brits, too, while happy to adopt much that was good about the Roman way of life, still identified themselves first and foremost with their tribes. The Brigantes occupied the region that today we think of as northern England (Lancashire, Yorkshire, Westmorland, Cumberland and parts of Derbyshire) while the Hadrian's Wall region was shared with the Carvetii. But the 'independence' of these tribes depended to a large extent on their obedience to Rome: the more supine the tribe, the greater the control they had over their affairs, with the more compliant even allowed to establish their own governing body.

After the Romans
Unfortunately, after the Romans had gone their greatest monument on these shores suffered. Though it had been overrun only three or four times (nobody is 100% sure exactly how many) since its original construction, when the Empire crumbled and the troops were withdrawn in AD409 the Wall was subjected to all manner of depredations and indignities. For one thing, local landowners started to remove the stone for their own purposes. Hexham Abbey (see p134) was just one beneficiary of this pilfering, with the crypt constructed entirely of Wall stone. And where the locals left the Wall untouched, the elements took their toll as wind and rain gradually wore down the remaining structure. Today, only around ten miles of the Wall are still visible.

And so it stood for centuries, forlorn and neglected if not exactly ignored. Soon it even lost its duty as a boundary between countries as the border gradually drifted north and the land to the north, now called 'Scotland' after the Scots tribe from Ireland who migrated centuries after the Romans had left, shrank.

Interest in the Wall was first revived, at least in print, in 1600 with the publication of *Britannia* by William Camden, headmaster of Westminster School in London, who attempted to explain the form, function and construction of the Wall. His work was built on a century later by the Rev John Horsley and the publication of *Britannia Romania*, in which, of course, the Wall featured heavily.

The General wades in
Horsley's work revived great interest in the Wall amongst the reading public but it was not enough to prevent further damage being visited upon it during the Jacobite Uprising. In 1745, Bonnie Prince Charlie smashed his way from Scotland down through Carlisle and on to Derby before turning back. The ease with which he was able to advance so far had much to do with the fact that his adversaries, General Wade and his men, were hunkered down in Newcastle waiting to ambush him there, having assumed that Charlie would choose the eastern road for his advance.

As a result of Charlie's success, Wade's troops constructed the Military Road (the modern B6318) across the Pennines to enable the swift movement of troops from one side of the country to the other. (This Military Road should not be confused with the Roman's Military *Way* – see p17 – though this lies nearby and performed much the same job almost 1700 years earlier.) To build this road, the Royal forces of George II removed sections of the Wall to pave their new highway. In fact, not only did they plunder the Wall for building material, they even built their road on top of it! (It should be noted that, though Wade is most associated with this road, it was actually built three years *after* his death.)

The Wall's modern pioneers
Once peace had returned to Britain, Camden's and Horsley's works encouraged others to look at the Wall anew. Among them was the shopkeeper William Hutton who in 1802 walked from his home in Birmingham to the Wall, walked along it and back, and then walked all the way home again – a total journey of about 600 miles (966km). Taking 35 days to complete, it was an impressive feat by any stan-

dards, particularly when one considers that he was 78 years old at the time and wore the same pair of socks for the entire walk! The product of his adventure was a book, *The History of the Roman Wall which crosses the Island of Britain from the German Ocean to the Irish Sea, Describing its Antient* [sic] *State and its Appearance in the Year 1801* – a title almost as long as the Wall itself – in which his love of Severus's Wall (as it was still called) and his interest in its history shines through. John Hodgson and John Collingwood Bruce (whose *Wallet Book of the Roman Wall*, printed in 1863 and later renamed *Handbook to the Roman Wall*, was still being published over 100 years later) also contributed to our knowledge with books on the history and archaeology of the Wall.

Then there was John Clayton, a Newcastle town clerk in the late 19th century, who bought four of the Wall forts and to whom we owe a great debt of gratitude; without his excavation and restoration work, much of the Wall still extant would have been lost. That's not to say Clayton's work is unanimously admired today. In particular, his attempts to rebuild much of the Wall, taking great liberties and using largely non-Roman methods and materials, make more than one modern archaeologist weep; Clayton preferred to rebuild without mortar, so in effect the sections of Wall he rebuilt resemble a 'modern' drystone wall, still common around northern England, rather than the original Roman Wall. Clayton's efforts may have ensured that there is more of the Wall visible today but it can also be argued that what we are looking at is not really the Roman Wall at all but a 19th-century reconstruction, with almost none of the Wall's original inner core remaining. Nevertheless, to the layman, Clayton's work is vital, the miles he 'reconstructed' helping us to imagine what the Wall must have looked like when first built.

The work of Clayton was continued in the 20th century by individuals such as FG Simpson (of Stead & Simpsons shoeshop fame), Eric Birley and Sir Ian Richmond, and later by bodies such as the National Trust, English Heritage and the Tyne and Wear Museums Service, organisations who concentrated less on the Wall and more on its accompanying forts and other buildings.

A proper survey of the Wall, recording every surviving remain and ruin, was conducted in 1985 to ensure there was a complete record of what exactly the authorities had in their care. And then, in 1987, UNESCO announced that the Wall was to become a World Heritage Site, thereby placing it alongside such wonders as the magnificent ruined city of Petra in Jordan, the awe-inspiring Pyramids of Giza, the mesmerising temples of Angkor Wat, the fabled lost city of Machu Picchu, the architectural dream that is the Taj Mahal and that other Great Wall, the one in northern China. The establishment in 2003 of a national trail running along the entire length of the Wall has once more brought it into the spotlight, and its instant success should ensure that millions more will enjoy the Wall's grandeur for years to come.

HOW DIFFICULT IS THE HADRIAN'S WALL PATH?

The Hadrian's Wall Path is just a long walk. Indeed, many rate this as the easiest of the national trails in the UK. At only four to seven days long, it's one of the shortest too. (Indeed, there's a guy called Elvis who works at Sainsbury's in Haltwhistle who completed it in one 30-hour stretch for charity.)

Age seems to be no barrier to completing the walk either. While updating this edition I walked with a friend, Peter Fenner, who (and I am sure he won't mind my revealing this) was just a month shy of his 78th birthday.

So there's no need for crampons, ropes, ice axes, oxygen bottles or any other climbing paraphernalia, because there's no climbing involved. All you need to complete the walk is some suitable clothing, a bit of money, a rucksack full of determination and a half-decent pair of calf muscles.

That said, it is a fairly wild walk in places. Regarding safety, there are few places on the regular trail where it would be possible to fall from a great height, unless you stray from the path near the crags; and with the Wall on one side and a road on the other, it's difficult to get lost too. Nevertheless, you may find a compass or GPS unit (see below) useful.

Your greatest danger on the walk is from the weather. Thus it is vital that you dress for inclement conditions and always carry a set of dry clothes with you. Not pushing yourself too hard is important too, as over-exertion leads to exhaustion and all its inherent dangers; see pp72-4.

But really, while it is no mean achievement to complete the walk, this is nevertheless a straightforward but fairly exhausting stroll by the standards of northern Britain and should be enjoyed and appreciated as such.

The route is well marked with the familiar National Trail 'acorn' signposts, arrows and other waymarks, so keeping to the trail shouldn't really be a problem.

GPS

Whilst modern Wainwrights will scoff, more open-minded walkers will accept that GPS technology can be an inexpensive, well-established if non-essential navigational aid. In no time at all a GPS receiver with a clear view of the sky will establish your position and altitude in a variety of formats, including the British OS grid system (see pp209-11), to within a few metres. However, a GPS is not a replacement for a map and compass. Although modern units are robust and durable, it only takes a flat battery to render them useless. You should view the two systems as compatible and use both older and newer technologies together. A GPS will prevent you from making exaggerated errors when navigating and will reduce the time it takes to correct mistakes if you do stray off the path.

Using GPS with this book is an option. Without it you could conceivably end up ambling confidently along the wrong path (though with all the paths well waymarked and given the detail on the maps in this book it would actually be quite an achievement to get lost!). However, with GPS you can quickly establish your position and work out how to return to your last known position on the trail.

Using GPS with this book

It is not expected that you will walk along checking off the GPS waypoints found throughout the book, since the detailed maps and route descriptions are more than sufficient for finding your way most of the time. Only when you are unsure of your position or need reassurance as to which way to go might you feel the need to reach for your GPS for confirmation.

The maps in the route guide include numbered waypoints; these correlate to the list on pp209-11, which gives the latitude/longitude position in a decimal minute format as well as a description. Where the path is vague, or there are several alternatives, you will find more waypoints. Typically landmarks or other significant features are also waymarked. Waypoints are less common in towns or villages but can still be found to help you pin down the path ahead or identify a junction.

You can manually key the nearest presumed waypoint from the list into your GPS as and when the need arises. Alternatively, with less room for error when inputting the co-ordinates, download the complete list for free as a GPS-readable file (that doesn't include the text descriptions) from the Trailblazer website. You'll need the correct cable and adequate memory in your unit (typically the ability to store 500 waypoints or more). The file as well as instructions on how to interpret an OS grid reference can be found on the Trailblazer website: ⌨ www.trailblazer-guides.com (click on GPS waypoints).

It's also possible to buy state-of-the-art digital mapping to import into your GPS unit, assuming that you have sufficient memory capacity, but it's not the most reliable way of navigating and the small screen on your pocket-sized unit will invariably fail to put places into context or give you the 'big picture'. This is also a far more expensive option than buying the traditional OS paper maps which, whilst bulkier, are always preferable.

Bear in mind that the vast majority of people who tackle the Hadrian's Wall Path do so perfectly successfully without a GPS unit. Instead of rushing out to invest in one, consider putting the money towards good-quality waterproofs or footwear instead. That said, a GPS unit may assist in the odd dicey decision, and if used correctly in tandem with this book's waypoints might just see you safely to the next pub or overnight stop that much more quickly.

HOW LONG DO YOU NEED?

According to the statistics (see box opposite), people take an average of around six days to complete the walk, making it one of the shorter national trails. Of course, if you're fit there's no reason why you can't go a little faster, if that's what you want to do, and finish the walk in five days (or even less), though you will end up having a different sort of trek to most of the other people on the trail. For where theirs is a fairly relaxing holiday, yours will be more of a sport. What's more, you won't have much time to enjoy the forts and other attractions, one of the main reasons for visiting the Wall in the first place. There's nothing wrong with this approach – *chacun à son goût*, as the French probably say. However, what you mustn't do is try to push yourself too far. That road leads only to exhaustion, injury or, at the absolute least, an unpleasant time.

When deciding how long to allow for the trek, those intending to camp and carry their own luggage shouldn't underestimate just how much a heavy pack can slow them down. On p40 there are some suggested itineraries covering different walking speeds. If you have only a few days, don't try to walk it all; concentrate instead on one area such as the popular central section, or the quieter Cumbrian section from Carlisle to Bowness.

PLANNING YOUR WALK

❏ **Some statistics on the Hadrian's Wall Path**

The Countryside Agency (now part of Natural England) spent a total of £6 million establishing a trail along Hadrian's Wall. Not peanuts, of course, and initially there was much concern about the amount that was spent on a walk that was, after all, going to appeal only to a small minority of the British public: trekkers.

However, it's probably safe to say now that the trail has become one of the unqualified success stories of the region. Up to the end of the 2007 season (the latest date for which we have figures), 27,350 people had opted for the full Roman holiday and walked the entire trail from end to end since its inception in 2003 – and over 1,172,032 'day walkers' had been counted along part of the trail. Unsurprisingly, perhaps the biggest positive impact of this influx of visitors has been on the local economy. Statistics show that end-to-end walkers spend an average of £37.85 per day during their trek; given that walkers take an average of 6.3 days to complete the trail, that means almost £6.5 million has been contributed to the local economy by these end-to-end walkers. Even day walkers spend an average of £10.86, contributing an estimated £12.7 million in total. Furthermore, new businesses have set up directly as a result of the trail, such as the café set up by two locals in Walltown Quarry to quench the demands of thirsty walkers.

Nor is it just the sheer size of the numbers that is so encouraging; the statistical trends provided positive results too, with every year from 2003 (when the walk opened) to 2006 showing an increase in the number of walkers. For example, in 2003 the number of end-to-end walkers was 3720. This rose to 3817 in 2004, jumped to 6632 in 2005 and showed a further increase of 1% to 6667 in 2006. It then leapt again to 7420 in 2007. The breakdown of the figures is also interesting. Of those who trekked in 2007, 30% took six days, though 19% took their time and spent at least eight days on the trail. At the other end of the scale, 4% took three days or less to complete the walk!

So who, exactly, is visiting the Wall? Well, taking the years from 2003 to 2007, by far the greatest number of trail users were from England (77%, as opposed to 4% from Scotland and 3% from Wales). Of those English visitors, almost a quarter (23%) came, unsurprisingly, from Yorkshire and the North-East. (Though the next highest, surprisingly, was the South-East, with 10%.) Amongst foreign tourists, the Dutch (4% of the total number of visitors) surprisingly supplied the most, followed by the US (3.2%), Canada (1.7%) and Australia (1.9%).

There were some other interesting figures from this survey too. Regarding age, 24% of trail users were in the 45-54 age group, 22% were aged 35-44, 18% fell in the 25-34 category, while 10% were aged 18-24. Nor was 54 the upper-age limit: 19% were age 55-64, and an impressive 7% were aged 65 or more.

As for motivation, the chance to see the area's nature and heritage (34%), walking the dog (12%) and a sense of adventure (20%) were all cited by walkers.

Practical information for the walker

ACCOMMODATION

The trail guide (Part 5) lists a fairly comprehensive selection of places to stay along the length of the trail. You have three main options: camping, staying in hostels/bunkhouses/camping barns, or using B&Bs/guesthouses/hotels. Few people stick to just one of these options the whole way, preferring, for example, to camp most of the time but spend every third night in a hostel, or perhaps use hostels where possible but splash out on a B&B every once in a while.

Note that when booking accommodation, remember to ask if a pick-up and drop-off service is available (usually only B&Bs provide this service). Few of the B&Bs actually lie on the Wall, and at the end of a tiring day it's nice to know a lift is available to take you to your accommodation rather than having to traipse another two or three miles off the path to get to your bed for the night.

The facilities' table on pp42-3 provides a quick snapshot of what type of accommodation is available in each of the towns and villages along the way, while the tables on p40 provide some suggested itineraries. The following is a brief introduction to what to expect from each type of accommodation.

Camping

There are campsites all the way along the Hadrian's Wall Path except in Newcastle and Carlisle, and towards the trail's western end you may find yourself walking a mile or two off the path to find somewhere to pitch your tent. That said, few people choose to camp every night on the trail. You're almost bound to get at least one night where the rain falls relentlessly, soaking equipment and sapping morale, and it is then that most campers opt to spend the next night drying out in a hostel or B&B. There are, however, many advantages with camping. It's more economical, for a start, with most campsites charging somewhere around £5. There's rarely any need to book either, except possibly in the very high season, and even then you'd be very unlucky not to find somewhere.

Campsites vary; some are just the back gardens of B&Bs or pubs; others are full-blown caravan sites with a few spaces put aside for tents. Showers are usually available, occasionally for a fee though more often than not for free. Note that none of the YHA hostels on the Hadrian's Wall Path accepts campers. Note, too, that **wild camping** (ie not in a regular campsite) is not allowed.

Camping is not an easy option; the route is wearying enough without carrying your accommodation around with you. Should you decide to camp, therefore, we advise you to look into employing one of the baggage-carrying companies mentioned on p32, though this does, of course, mean that it will cost more and that you will lose a certain amount of freedom as you have to tell the company, at least a day before, of your next destination – and stick to it – so that you and your bag can be reunited every evening.

Bunkhouses/camping barns

The term 'bunkhouse' can mean many different things, though usually it's nothing more than a converted barn in a farmer's field with a couple of wooden benches to sleep on. Sleeping bags are usually necessary in these places. While not exactly the lap of luxury, a night in a bunkhouse is probably the nearest non-campers will get to sleeping outside, while at the same time providing campers with shelter from the elements should the weather look like taking a turn for the worse. Some of the better bunkhouses provide a shower and simple kitchen with running water and perhaps a kettle, and occasionally pots, pans, cutlery and crockery.

Hostels

There are a few YHA (Youth Hostel Association) hostels along the Hadrian's Wall Path and if you haven't visited one recently because the words 'youth' and 'hostel' still conjure up images of cold, crowded dorms, uncomfortable beds and lousy food all overseen by little-Hitler staff who take a sadistic pleasure in treating you like schoolchildren, we advise you to take a second look.

The YHA has, in fact, got some of the best-value accommodation on the route. Each hostel comes equipped with a whole range of facilities from drying rooms to televisions and fully equipped kitchens for guests to use. Many also have a shop selling emergency groceries, snacks and souvenirs and some offer wi-fi (£3 per hour, £5 per day) and/or internet access (£1 for 20 mins). Some offer breakfast, an evening meal and/or a packed lunch; several even have a licence to sell alcohol. They are also good places to meet fellow walkers, swap stories and compare blisters.

Weighed against these advantages is the fact that beds are still arranged in dormitories, some of them quite large, thereby increasing your chances of sharing the night with a heavy snorer. The curfew (usually 11pm) is annoying too. Nor is it really feasible to stay in hostels every night, for there are some areas where they don't exist and where they do some are at least a mile or two from the path.

If you are travelling in April/May or September, at the beginning or end of the trekking season, you may find many shut for two or three days per week, or that they are entirely taken over by school groups, leaving trekkers shut out. Contact the YHA or the relevant hostel to find out the exact opening dates. Even in high season some are not staffed during the day and trekkers have to wait until 4 or 5pm before checking in. Furthermore, it is rumoured that most YHA hostels will save your booked bed only until 6pm, though to be fair, I never came across this rule on the route and if it does exist it doesn't seem to be rigidly enforced. And besides, they will keep it until later if you phone to let them know when you're due to arrive. Finally, the cost of staying in a hostel, once breakfast has been added on, is in most instances not that much cheaper (starting at £15 for members, though more usually around £20) than staying in a B&B.

Booking a hostel Despite the name, anybody of any age can join the YHA. This can be done at any hostel or by contacting the **Youth Hostels Association**

of England and Wales (☎ 0800-019 1700 or ☎ 01629-592700, 🖥 www.yha .org.uk). The cost of a year's membership is £15.95 per year (£9.95 for anyone under 26). Having secured your membership, YHA hostels are easy to book, either online or by ringing the YHA, or each individual hostel separately. The hostels also offer a booking service and will reserve a bed at the next stop on the path for you. You don't need to be a member to book/stay at a YHA hostel but will be charged an additional £3 per night.

❑ **Should you book your accommodation in advance?**
When walking the Hadrian's Wall Path, it's essential that you have your night's accommodation booked by the time you set off in the morning, whether you're planning to stay in a hostel or a B&B. Nothing is more deflating than to arrive at your destination at day's end only to find that you've then got to walk a further five miles or so, or even take a detour off the route, because everywhere in town is booked.

That said, there's a certain amount of hysteria regarding the booking of accommodation, with many websites, B&Bs and other organisations suggesting you book at least six months in advance. Whilst it's true that the earlier you book the more chance you have of getting precisely the accommodation you require, booking so far in advance does leave you vulnerable to changing circumstances. Booking a full six months before setting foot on the trail is all very well if everything is to go to plan but if you break your leg just before you're due to set off or, God forbid, there's another outbreak of foot and mouth, all you're going to end up with is a lot of lost deposits. By not booking so far in advance, you give yourself the chance to shift your holiday plans to a later date should the unforeseen arise.

In my experience, the lack of accommodation is not as bad as some suggest, at least not outside the high season (ie the summer period coinciding with the long school holidays in the UK). Outside this period, and particularly in April/May or September, as long as you're flexible and willing to take what's offered, with maybe even a night or two in a hostel if that's all there is, you should get away with booking just a few nights in advance, or indeed just the night before. The exceptions to this rule are at weekends, when everywhere is busy, and where accommodation is very limited. Campers, however, have more flexibility and can often just turn up and find a space there and then.

In summary, therefore, my advice is this; it's always worth phoning ahead to book your accommodation. If you are staying in **B&Bs** and walking in high season this should be done months in advance if you have a preference for specific B&Bs. If, on the other hand, you're not too bothered which B&B you stay in, are trekking in April/May or September and don't mind the possibility of having to walk a mile or two off the route to get a room, you can probably get away with booking your accommodation a night or two before. If you can book at least a few nights in advance, however, so much the better, and at weekends it's essential you book as soon as you can.

If staying in **hostels**, the same applies though do be careful when travelling out of high season as many hostels close for a couple of days each week and shut altogether from around November to Easter. Once again, it's well worth phoning at least one night before and well before that if it's a weekend, to make sure the hostel isn't fully booked or shut.

Campers, whatever time of the year, should always be able to find somewhere to pitch their tent, though ringing in advance can't hurt and is often appreciated; it will at least mean you can confirm that the campsite is still open.

Bed and breakfast

Bed and Breakfasts (B&Bs) are a great British institution and many of those along the Hadrian's Wall Path are absolutely charming, with buildings often three or four hundred years old, and some even made with Wall stones! There's nothing mysterious about a B&B; as the name suggests, they provide you with a bed in a private room and a cooked breakfast (see below) – unless you specify otherwise beforehand – though they range in style enormously.

Rooms usually contain either a double bed (known as a double room), or two single beds (known as a twin room) though sometimes twin beds can be pushed together to make a double bed. Family rooms are for three or more people; sometimes this means there is a double bed with (a) separate single bed(s), or bunk beds, but also it could be a single bed over a double bed, bunk-bed style. Rooms are often en suite but in some cases the facilities are shared or private, though even with the latter the bathroom is never more than a few feet away. Most rooms have a TV and tea/coffee-making facilities.

An evening meal (usually around £12-15) is often provided at the more remote or bigger places, at least if you book in advance. If not, there's nearly always a pub or restaurant nearby or, if it's far, the B&B owner may give you a lift to and from the nearest place with food.

B&B rates B&Bs in this guide start at around £24 per person (pp) for the most basic accommodation rising to over £40-45 for the most luxurious en suite places. Most charge around £30-35pp. However, some places charge a room rate based on two sharing. Solo trekkers should take note: single rooms are not so easy to find so if you are on your own you will often end up occupying a double/twin room, for which you'll have to pay a single occupancy supplement. A typical supplement for a per person rate and discount for a room rate is around £10.

Rates are often discounted for stays of two or more nights.

Guesthouses, hotels, pubs and inns

The difference between a B&B and a guesthouse is minimal, though some of the better guesthouses are more like hotels, offering evening meals and a lounge for guests. Pubs and inns also offer bed and breakfast accommodation and prices are no more than in a regular B&B.

Hotels usually do cost more, however, and some might be a little incensed with a bunch of smelly trekkers turning up and treading mud into their carpet. Most on the Hadrian's Wall Path, however, are used to seeing trekkers and welcome them warmly. Prices in hotels start at around £25-30 per person, though occasionally you can get some special deals with the larger hotel chains that can be as low as £19. Hotel and pub rates may not include breakfast.

FOOD AND DRINK

Breakfast and lunch

Stay in a B&B and you'll be filled to the gills with a cooked **English breakfast**. This usually consists of a bowl of cereal followed by a plateful of eggs, bacon, sausages, mushrooms, tomatoes and possibly baked beans or black pudding, with toast and butter, and all washed down with coffee, tea and/or juice. Enormously satisfying the first time you try it, by the fourth or fifth morning you may start to prefer a lighter continental breakfast. If you have had enough of these cooked breakfasts and/or plan an early start, ask if you can have a packed lunch instead of breakfast. Your landlady or hostel can usually provide a **packed lunch** at an additional cost (unless it's in lieu of breakfast), though of course there's nothing to stop you preparing your own lunch (but do bring a penknife if you plan to do this), or going to a pub (see below) or café.

Remember, to plan ahead; certain stretches of the walk are virtually devoid of eating places (the stretch from Chollerford to Housesteads for example – save for a couple of vans that usually set up in summer along the way – and from there to Walltown Quarry) so read ahead about the next day's walk in Part 5 to make sure you never go hungry.

Cream teas

Whatever you do for lunch, don't forget to leave some room for a cream tea or two, a morale, energy and cholesterol booster all rolled into one delicious package: a pot of tea accompanied by scones served with cream and jam, and sometimes a cake or two. The jury is out on whether you should put the jam on first or the cream but either way do not miss the chance of at least one cream tea.

Evening meals

Pubs are as much a feature of the walk as moorland and sheep, and in some cases the pub is as much a tourist attraction as any Roman fort or ruined priory. *The Robin Hood Inn* to the west of Whittledene Reservoir, is one example, as

---

❏ **Local breweries**

When it comes to drinking, there are any number of local breweries competing to slake the thirst of trekkers with real ales, stouts and bitters. Of particular interest to trekkers, maybe, is the **Hadrian and Border** brewery, based in Newcastle. A merger of two breweries, Hadrian and Border's beers include Emperor Ale, Gladiator Bitter, Centurion Best, Legion Ale and Rampart. Also in Northumberland, and only a short hike from the trail, **High House Farm Brewery** (🖳 www.highhousefarmbrewery .co.uk) is based on a farm in the village of Matfen and boasts a visitor's centre, tearoom and, of course, a well-stocked bar from where you can sample one (or all!) of their half-dozen beers. Another brewery that will be of interest to Wall Walkers is **Big Lamp**, the North-East's oldest micro-brewery, based at the Keelman pub (see p102) just off the trail at Newburn. Brews include the delicious Summerhill Stout and the appropriately named Blackout (11%!). A third brewer from this neck of the Wall, **Mordue**, produce the divine Workie Ticket (4.5%), once upon a time the Champion Beer of Britain and still a cracking pint.

Heading into Cumbria, another brewery of interest is Cockermouth's **Jennings of Cumberland** (🖳 www.jenningsbrewery.co.uk), the most ubiquitous brewer in Cumbria. Further boosting Cumbria's reputation for fine brewing, **Geltsdale Brewery** (🖳 www.geltsdalebrewery.com) is based in part of the Old Brampton Brewery (which was originally founded in 1785), from where they produce seven real ales and a lager.

are *The Keelman* at Newburn and *The Hadrian Hotel* at Wall (both just off the trail) and the historic *Twice Brewed* near Steel Rigg.

Most pubs have become highly attuned to the desires of trekkers and offer lunch and evening meals (often with a couple of local dishes and usually some vegetarian options), some locally brewed beers, a garden to relax in on hot days and a roaring fire to huddle around on cold ones. The standard of the food varies widely, though is usually served in big portions, which is often just about all trekkers care about at the end of a long day. In many of the villages the pub is the only place to eat out. Note that pubs may close in the afternoon, especially in the winter months, so check in advance if you are hoping to visit a particular one, and also if you are planning lunch there as food serving hours can change.

That other great British culinary institution, the **fish 'n' chip shop**, can be found in Newcastle, Carlisle, and towns off the Wall such as Haltwhistle, Brampton and Hexham; as can Chinese and Indian **takeaways**, which are usually the last places to serve food in the evenings, staying open until at least 11pm.

Buying camping supplies

There is a shop of some description in most of the places along the route, though most are small (and often combined with the post office) and whether you'll be able to find precisely what you went in for is highly unlikely. If self-catering, therefore, your menu for the evening will depend upon what you found in the store that day. Part 5 goes into greater detail about what can be found where.

Drinking water

There are plenty of ways of perishing on the Hadrian's Wall Path but given how frequently it rains and how damp the north of England is, thirst probably won't be one of them. Be careful, though, for on a hot day in some of the remoter parts after a steep climb or two you'll quickly dehydrate, which is at best highly unpleasant and at worst mightily dangerous. Always carry some water with you and in hot weather drink three or four litres a day. Don't be tempted by the water in the streams; if the cow or sheep faeces in the water don't make you ill, the chemicals from the pesticides and fertilisers used on the farms almost certainly will. Using iodine or another purifying treatment will help to combat the former, though there's little you can do about the latter. It's a lot safer to fill up from taps instead.

MONEY

Outside Newcastle and Carlisle, banks (and ATMs) are few and far between on the Hadrian's Wall Path; see the town and village facilities table on pp42-3.

The **post office** thus provides a very useful service. You can withdraw money for free at a post office counter if you have a current/'basic' account with certain banks: the Post Office's helpline (☎ 08457-223344) or website (💻 www

HADRIAN FINANCIAL SERVICES

Independent   Financial   Advisers   01434 322468

.postoffice.co.uk; click on Counter services, then Counter money services, then Pay in and withdraw money under Use your bank account) provide a full list of banks offering withdrawal facilities through post office branches and a list of the branches with an ATM. You need to have your debit card and PIN number, or cheque book and debit card, with you. Check the town and village facilities table (pp42-3) for a list of places with a post office.

Another way of getting money in your hand is to use the **cashback** system: find a store that will accept a debit card and ask them to advance cash against the card. However, you almost always need to buy something.

However, with few local stores, pubs or B&Bs accepting credit or debit cards, and few places where you can get money out along the way, it is essential to carry plenty of **cash** with you, though do keep it safe and out of sight (preferably in a moneybelt). A chequebook could prove very useful as back-up, so that you don't have to keep on dipping into your cash reserves, especially as most B&Bs don't accept credit cards.

❏ **Information for foreign visitors**

● **Currency/money** The British pound (£) comes in notes of £100, £50, £20, £10 and £5, and coins of £2 and £1. The pound is divided into 100 pence (usually referred to as 'p', pronounced 'pee') which comes in silver coins of 50p, 20p, 10p and 5p and copper coins of 2p and 1p. Cash (see p48) is the most welcome form of payment though debit/credit cards are accepted in some places. Travellers' cheques can be cashed only at banks, foreign exchanges and some of the large hotels. Up-to-date exchange rates can be found at ▣ www.xe.com/ucc.

● **Business hours** Most shops and main post offices are open at least from Monday to Friday 9am-5pm and Saturday 9am-12.30pm. Many choose longer hours and some open on Sundays as well. However, some also close early one day a week, often Wednesday or Thursday. **Banks** are usually open 10am-4pm Monday to Friday. **Pub hours** are less predictable as each pub may have different opening hours. However, most pubs on the Hadrian's Wall Path continue to open daily between 11am and 11pm (some close at 10.30pm on Sunday) and **some still close in the afternoon**.

● **National (Bank) holidays** Most businesses are shut on 1 January, Good Friday (March/April), Easter Monday (March/April), the first and the last Monday in May, the last Monday in August, 25 December and 26 December.

● **School holidays** Generally as follows: a one-week break late October, two weeks around Christmas and the New Year, a week mid-February, two weeks over Easter, a week at the end of May, and from late July to early September. Private-school holidays fall at the same time, but tend to be slightly longer.

● **Travel insurance** The European Health Insurance Card (EHIC) entitles cardholders to any necessary medical treatment under the UK's National Health Service (NHS) while on a temporary visit here; treatment is given only on production of the card so take it with you. However, the EHIC is not a substitute for proper medical cover on your travel insurance for unforeseen bills and for getting you home should that be needed. Also consider cover for loss and theft of personal belongings, especially if you are camping or staying in hostels, as there will be times when you'll have to leave your luggage unattended.

● **Smoking** The ban on smoking in public places relates not only to pubs and restaurants, but also to B&Bs, hostels and hotels. These latter have the right to designate

OTHER SERVICES

An increasing number of places offer **internet access** and/or **wi-fi**. Most villages have a **grocery store**, often with a **post office** in part of it, and nearby you'll usually find a **phone box**.

There are **outdoor equipment shops** in Carlisle, Newcastle, Hexham, Haltwhistle and Brampton; **pharmacies** in those towns as well as Corbridge; and **tourist information centres** at Newcastle and Carlisle, as well as off the Wall at Corbridge, Hexham, Haltwhistle and Brampton. At Newburn and Once Brewed there are visitor centres for the Riverside Park and Northumberland National Park respectively.

WALKING COMPANIES

It is, of course, possible to turn up with your boots and backpack at Wallsend and just start walking, with little planned save for your accommodation (see

one or more bedrooms where the occupants can smoke, but the ban is in force in all enclosed areas open to the public – even if they are in a private home such as a B&B. Should you be foolhardy enough to light up in a no-smoking area, which includes pretty well any indoor public place, you could be fined £50, but it's the owners of the premises who carry the can if they fail to stop you, with a potential fine of £2500.

● **Weights and measures** The European Commission is no longer attempting to ban the pint or the mile: so, in Britain, milk can be sold in pints (1 pint = 568ml), as can beer in pubs, though most other liquid including petrol (gasoline) and diesel is sold in litres. Distances on road and path signs will also continue to be given in miles (1 mile = 1.6km) rather than kilometres, and yards (1yd = 0.9m) rather than metres. The population remains divided between those who still use inches (1 inch = 2.5cm), feet (1ft = 0.3m) and yards (3ft = 1 yard = 0.9m) and those who are happy with millimetres, centimetres and metres; you'll often be told that 'it's only a hundred yards or so' to somewhere, rather than a hundred metres or so.

Most food is sold in metric weights (g and kg) but the imperial weights of pounds (lb: 1lb = 453g) and ounces (oz: 1oz = 28g) are frequently displayed too. The weather – a frequent topic of conversation – is also an issue: while most forecasts predict temperatures in Celsius (C), many people continue to think in terms of Fahrenheit (F; see the temperature chart on p37 for conversions).

● **Telephone** From outside Britain the international country access code for Britain is ☎ 44 followed by the area code minus the first 0, and then the number you require. Within Britain, to call a landline number with the same code as the landline phone you are calling from, the code can be omitted: dial the number only. If you're using a mobile phone that is registered overseas, consider buying a local SIM card to keep costs down. Mobile phone reception is generally good on and around Hadrian's Wall Path.

● **Time** During the winter, the whole of Britain is on Greenwich Mean Time (GMT). The clocks move one hour forward on the last Sunday in March, remaining on British Summer Time (BST) until the last Sunday in October.

● **Emergency services** For police, ambulance, fire or mountain rescue dial ☎ 999 or the EU standard number ☎ 112.

box on p26). The following companies, however, are in the business of making your holiday as stress-free and enjoyable as possible.

Baggage carriers and accommodation booking

There are several **baggage-carrying companies** serving the Hadrian's Wall Path, from national organisations such as Sherpa Van Project to companies that consist of little more than one man and his van. With all these services you can book up to the last moment, usually up to around 8pm the previous evening, though it's cheaper if you book in advance. The cost is around £5-7.50 to take your bag to your next destination. Most stipulate a maximum weight per bag of around 16-20kg. Some have a minimum number of bags that they will transfer from the same address (usually two).

Nearly all these companies offer **accommodation booking** as well. Alternatively you can contact the tourist information centres as most also offer accommodation booking (see box p52).

● **Brigantes Walking Holidays** (☎ 01729-830463, 🖳 www.brigantesenglish walks.com) charges approx £8pp per day; they prefer bags to be less than 17kg.

● **Explore Britain** (☎ 01740-650900, 🖳 www.xplorebritain.com) charges £35 per day for up to six bags.

● **Hadrian's Haul** (☎ 07967-564823, 🖳 www.hadrianshaul.com), charges £5 per bag with a maximum weight limit of 16kg per bag.

● **Hadrian's Wall Ltd** (☎ 01434-344650, 🖳 www.hadrianswall.ltd.uk). Charges vary but there is a 15kg weight limit per bag.

● **Sherpa Van Project** (baggage transfer ☎ 01748-826917, accommodation booking ☎ 01609-883731; 🖳 www.sherpavan.com) charge £7.50 per bag; minimum two bags with a maximum weight per bag of 20kg. The fee Sherpa charges for accommodation booking depends on how many nights and how many people in the group but expect to pay £16-23.

● **Walkers' Baggage Transfer Co** (☎ 016977-42341 or 0871-423 8803; 🖳 www.walkersbags.co.uk) charges £5-7 per bag with an 18kg weight limit.

Self-guided holidays

Self-guided basically means that the company will organise accommodation, baggage transfer, transport to and from the walk, and various maps and advice, but leave you on your own to actually walk the path. Most companies offer walks between March/April and the end of October.

● **Absolute Escapes** (0131-447 2570, 🖳 www.absoluteescapes.com; Edinburgh) Offer five- to eight-day trips along the whole of the Wall in either direction. If you want extra nights or something different they can tailor-make holidays.

● **Brigantes Walking Holidays** (☎ 01729-830463, 🖳 www.brigantesenglish walks.com; North Yorks) Can put together a walking holiday for you (generally seven walking days but any length/direction is possible). Also operates a baggage carrying service (see p32).

(Opposite) The splendid remains of Milecastle 39 (see p152) displaying the classic playing card shape, with Crag Lough in the distance.

● **Celtic Trails** (☎ 01291-689774, 💻 www.celtic-trails.com; Chepstow) Offer a four-day 'Best of the Wall' walk from Corbridge to Brampton, and six- to ten-day complete Wall walks. They also offer two standards of accommodation; regular B&Bs as well as luxury accommodation for anyone who wants to splash out on some days, or even for the whole walk.

● **Contours Walking Holidays** (☎ 017684-80451, 💻 www.contours.co.uk; Derbyshire) Offers various walks along the entire Wall ranging from four to ten days; most walks are east to west but they can tailor-make walks. They also offer a five- to six-day 'Best of Hadrian's Wall' tour which omits the less rewarding stages east of Heddon-on-the-Wall and west of Carlisle; a four- to five-day highlights tour from Corbridge to Brampton; and a two- to three-day 'Hadrian's Wall Short Break' that takes in the most dramatic section of the Wall between the fascinating fort of Cilurnum at Chollerford and Lanercost.

● **Discovery Travel** (☎ 01904-632226, 💻 www.discoverytravel.co.uk; York) Offer standard six-, seven-, eight- and nine-night self-guided walks as well as a five-night 'Highlights of Hadrian's Wall' package from Chollerford to Lanercost. Walks are east to west but they also offer tailor-made walks in either direction.

● **Explore Britain** (☎ 01740-650900, 💻 www.xplorebritain.com; Co Durham) Various walks (in both directions but mostly west to east) of about four to five days covering mainly just the Wall's picturesque centre, plus a two-day trail exploring the Wall while based in Carlisle. Also operates a baggage carrying service (see p32).

● **Footpath Holidays** (☎ 01985-840049; 💻 www.footpath-holidays.com; Wilts) Run single-centre guesthouse-based self-guided (selected parts) walks and a guided walking tour (see p34) along the whole path. Walks (two to seven days) can be arranged in either direction with Hexham as the base.

● **Hadrian's Wall Ltd** (☎ 01434-344650, 💻 www.hadrianswall.ltd.uk; Twice Brewed) As the name suggests, this company, which is based at the central point of the Wall, specialises in Hadrian's Wall. They offer self-guided, part-guided and tailor-made treks in either direction and with a range of accommodation levels. They are also the only company to offer a camping trek (💻 www.hadrians walladventure.com); the trek operates west to east and includes five nights camping and two in a bunkhouse (with the option of upgrading to B&B accommodation if preferred). The cost includes tent hire, campsite fees and luggage transfer – the tents are set up for you by the time you arrive at the end of the day's walk. They can also provide packed lunches and equipment hire.

● **HF Holidays** (☎ 0845-470 7558; 💻 www.hfholidays.co.uk; Herts) HF offer a seven-day 'Best of Hadrian's Wall' tour beginning in Brampton and ending in Corbridge (ie west to east).

● **Let's Go Walking** (☎ 01837-880075; 💻 www.letsgowalking.com; Devon) Offers eight-night/seven-day trips and can tailor-make as required.

(Opposite) Top: King Arthur's Turret (Turret 44B, see p163) with Walltown Farm in the distance. **Bottom**: Strolling by the Wall at Willowford Farm (see p167).

PLANNING YOUR WALK

● **Macs Adventure** (☎ 0845-527 7871; 🖥 www.macsadventure.com; Glasgow) Offers four- to nine-day trips along the whole of the Wall in either direction, as well as 'Best of Hadrian's Wall' itineraries. They will also tailor-make holidays.
● **Mickledore Travel** (☎ 017687-72335; 🖥 www.mickledore.co.uk; Keswick) A number of self-guided tours ranging from a three-day short break on the most dramatic central section of the wall, between Chollerford and Gilsland, to a six- to ten-day walk (in either direction) over the entire length of the path. Luggage transfer and packed lunches are optional.
● **Open Book Visitor Guiding** (☎ 01228-670578, ☎ 07775-603397, 🖥 carol @greatguidedtours.co.uk; Cumbria) A company with over 30 years' experience; they can arrange self-guided holidays in either direction and for the whole walk or just part of it.
● **Shepherds Walks Holidays** (☎ 01830-540453; 🖥 www.shepherdswalks .co.uk; Newcastle-upon-Tyne) Offer six- to ten-day trips along the whole of the Wall in either direction as well as highlights tours. Also tailor-make holidays.
● **Sherpa Expeditions** (☎ 020-8577 2717; 🖥 www.sherpa-walking-holidays .co.uk; Middlesex) Offers an eight-day 'Inn-to-Inn' walking tour along the whole Wall from east to west but can also tailor-make holidays.
● **The Walking Holiday Company** (☎ 01600-718219; 🖥 www.thewalkinghol idaycompany.co.uk; Monmouth) Offers four- to ten-day trips along the whole of the Wall in either direction. They will tailor-make to suit requirements.

Group/guided walking tours

If you don't trust your map-reading skills or simply prefer the company of other walkers as well as an experienced guide, the following will be of interest. Packages nearly always include meals, accommodation, transport arrange- ments, minibus back-up and baggage transfer. Have a good look at each of the companies' websites before booking as each has their own speciality. Note that there is nearly always a single supplement for solo travellers.
● **Footpath Holidays** (see p33) Their seven-day guided walk (east to west) operates once a year from a base in Hexham.
● **Hadrian's Wall Ltd** (see p33) They offer a range of part-guided walks; the guide will accompany walkers for one or two days and will focus on the land- scape, history of the wall, or any aspect a group or individual is interested in; they also offer one- to two-day safari tours.
● **HF Holidays** (see p33) Offer six guided trips a year between May and October; the details are the same as for the self-guided walk.
● **Open Book Visitor Guiding** (see above) They have a team of guides and can arrange walks/tours for any size of group.
● **Ramblers Countrywide Holidays** (☎ 01707-386800; 🖥 www.ramblers countrywide.co.uk; Herts) Offers a six-day walk from Heddon-on-the-Wall to Bowness; two hotels, one near Hexham, one in Carlisle, provide the accommo- dation during your walk. The walks operate approximately once a month between April and September.
● **Shepherds Walks Holidays** (see above) Offer guided walks for the whole Wall and day walks as well as the hire of a private guide.

Budgeting

England is not a cheap place to go travelling and while the north may be one of the cheaper parts, the towns and villages on the Hadrian's Wall Path are more than used to seeing tourists and charge accordingly. You may think before you set out that you are going to try to keep your budget to a minimum by camping every night and cooking your own food but it's a rare trekker who sticks to this rule. Besides, the B&Bs and pubs on the route are amongst the path's major attractions and it would be a pity not to sample the hospitality in at least some of them.

If the only expenses of this walk were accommodation and food, budgeting for the trip would be a piece of cake. Unfortunately, in addition there are all the little extras that push up the cost of your trip: getting to and from the path, beer, cream teas, stamps and postcards, internet use, buses here and there, baggage carriers, phone calls, laundry, film, souvenirs, entrance fees (to minimise these it is worth being a member of English Heritage/National Trust)... it's surprising how much these add up. In fact statistics (see box p23) show that on average people spend £37.85 per day.

CAMPING

You can survive on less than £12 per person per day if you use the cheapest campsites, don't visit a pub, avoid all the museums and tourist attractions in the towns, cook all your own food from staple ingredients and generally have a pretty miserable time of it. Even then, unforeseen expenses will probably nudge your daily budget above this figure. Include the occasional pint, and perhaps a pub meal every now and then, and the figure will be nearer £15 a day.

BUNKHOUSES/CAMPING BARNS AND HOSTELS

The charge for staying in a bunkhouse or YHA hostel varies according to its quality and range of facilities. Bunkhouses on the Hadrian's Wall Path range widely, as shown in the price range of £9-25 per person. YHA hostel rates start at £15 (for Greenhead) and go up to £23 (for the Old Brewery Residences at Carlisle).

In some cases the price includes breakfast (eg Jesmond) but in others this is extra (usually around £5). Some hostels offer a packed lunch (around £4-5) and an evening meal (around £10, though you can use their self-catering facilities), which means that, overall, it can cost from around £30 per day, or £40 to live in a little more comfort, enjoy the odd beer and go out for the occasional meal.

B&Bs, GUESTHOUSES AND HOTELS

B&B rates start at £24pp per night but can be twice this, particularly if you are walking by yourself and are thus liable to pay single supplements. Add on the cost of lunch and dinner and you should reckon on about £50 minimum per day. Staying in a guesthouse or hotel would probably push the minimum up to £60.

Note that B&B rates are often discounted for stays of two or more nights.

When to go

SEASONS

Britain is a notoriously wet country and the north of England is an infamously damp part of it. There's a souvenir T-shirt on sale that has 'Hadrain' written on it and it's fair to say that few trekkers manage to complete the walk without suffering at least one downpour; two or three per trek are more likely, even in summer. That said, it's equally unlikely that you'll spend a week in the area and not see any sun at all, and even the most cynical of trekkers will have to admit that, during the trekking season at least, there are more sunny days than showery ones. The **trekking season**, by the way, starts at Easter and builds to a crescendo in August, before steadily tailing off in September. By September's end, few indeed are the trekkers who attempt the whole trail, although there are plenty of people on day walks, and by the end of October many places close down for the winter.

Unusually, the authorities in charge of maintaining the path request that walkers do **not attempt the trail in winter** (which they define as October to April), when the path is at its most fragile; they do not, however, rule out walking in Wall country altogether; see the box on pp68-9 for more details.

There are two further points to consider when booking your trip. Firstly, remember that most people set off on the trail at a weekend. This means that you'll find the trail quieter **during the week** and as a consequence you may find it easier to book accommodation. Secondly, towards the western end of the walk, the trail through the Solway Marshes is prone to flooding. While this won't affect when you set off (at least, not if you are starting at the eastern end of it), you do need to be aware of the time of the high tides and plan your walk through the marshes so that you are not there during high tide; the box on p192 gives advice on how to do this.

Spring

Find a dry week in springtime (around the end of March to mid-June) and you're in for a treat. The wild flowers are coming into bloom, lambs are skipping in the meadows, the grass is green and lush, and the path is not yet badly eroded. Of course, finding a dry week in spring is not easy but occasionally there's a mini-heatwave. Another advantage with walking at this time is that there will be fewer trekkers and finding accommodation is relatively easy, though do check that the hostels/B&Bs have opened. Easter is the exception; the first major holiday in the year when people flock to the Wall.

Summer

Summer, on the other hand, can be a bit *too* busy and over a weekend in August can be little short of insufferable. Still, the chances of a prolonged period of sunshine are of course higher at this time of year than any other, the days are much longer, all the facilities and public transport are operating and the heather is in bloom, turning some of the hills around the crags a fragrant purple. Our advice is this: if you're flexible and want to avoid seeing too many people on the trail, avoid the school holidays, which basically means ruling out the tail end of July, all of August and the first few days of September. Alternatively, if you crave the company of other trekkers, summer will provide you with the opportunity of meeting plenty of them, though do remember that you **must book your accommodation in advance**, especially if staying in B&Bs or similar accommodation. Despite the higher than average chance of sunshine, take clothes for any eventuality – it will probably still rain at some point.

Autumn

September is a wonderful time to trek, when many of the tourists have returned home and the path is clear. I think that the weather is usually reliably sunny too, at least at the beginning of September, though I'll admit I don't have any figures to back this claim. The B&Bs and hostels will still be open, at least until the end of the month. By then the weather will begin to get a little wilder and the nights will start to draw in. The trekking season is almost at an end.

Winter

The National Trail authorities would prefer you not to walk the trail during winter, to give the path a rest and prevent damage. It is also a little more dangerous to trek at this time, with few people around, a cold climate and a slippery trail. But while we advise against walking the actual trail, there is nothing to stop you trying one of the circular winter trails near the Wall. There's a 'Winter Days Out' leaflet with suggestions for walks you can take in Wall country that don't actually encroach on the main trail and any unexcavated archaeological treasures.

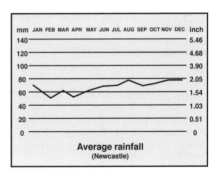

Average rainfall
(Newcastle)

RAINFALL

At some point on your walk it will rain; if it doesn't, it's fair to

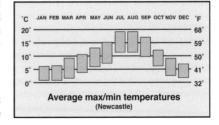

Average max/min temperatures
(Newcastle)

PLANNING YOUR WALK

say that you haven't really lived the full Hadrian's Wall experience properly. The question, therefore, is not whether you will be rained on but how often. As long as you dress accordingly and take note of the safety advice given on pp72-4, this shouldn't be a problem.

Hours of daylight
(Newcastle)

DAYLIGHT HOURS

If walking in autumn or early spring (we're assuming you're not going to walk in winter), you must take account of how far you can walk in the available light. It won't be possible to cover as many miles as you would in summer. Remember, too, that you will get a further 30-45 minutes of usable light before sunrise and after sunset depending on the weather.

In June, because the path is in the far north of England, those coming from the south may be surprised that there's enough available light for trekking until at least 10pm. Conversely, in winter you will be equally amazed how quickly the nights draw in. Bear this in mind if walking outside the summer season.

ANNUAL EVENTS

As one of the emptiest parts of England, it is perhaps not surprising that there is a bit of a dearth of traditional annual festivals. That's not to say that events don't happen, it's just that the many fairs, festivals and other happenings do not have

---

❏ **Illuminating Hadrian's Wall**
On 13 March 2010 the entire length of Hadrian's Wall from coast to coast was lit up by over a thousand volunteers carrying torches. The evening began at about 5.15pm with a performance by Berlin-based Theater Anu at Segedunum Fort in Newcastle – the start (or end) of the Hadrian's Wall Path. (Interestingly, the company had already been involved in Wall-based historical celebrations, having taken part in the 20th anniversary festivities of the downfall of the Berlin Wall). Their performance – at which angels appeared around the fort – signalled the start of the 'Line of Light', with the first torches lit at around 5.45pm. The light was then passed west along the Wall, accompanied by bands, costumed characters, and a 'Welcoming the Light' parade in Carlisle. The evening turned out to be a huge success, and was voted the top tourist event in England's north-east for that year. Unfortunately, there are currently no plans to repeat the event, despite various online campaigns for a resurrection. But a DVD on the event, *Illuminating Hadrian's Wall*, is available for just £4.99 from the dedicated website 🖳 www.illuminatinghadrianswall.com.

the weight of tradition or history behind them and as such, though they often do indeed take place annually, it's not necessarily at the same time each year.

Nevertheless, a look at the official Hadrian's Wall website does give a surprisingly large list of things going on, from lectures to Easter-egg hunts, guided tours to Roman re-enactments, bat walks to falconry displays. Indeed, it's highly likely that your trip will coincide with at least one event.

For more details and a complete list of what's on throughout the year, visit 🖥 www.hadrians-wall.org.

Itineraries

Part 5 of this book has been written from east to west, though there is of course nothing to stop you from tackling it in the opposite direction, and there are advantages in doing so – see below. To help you plan your walk there is a **planning map** (opposite the inside back cover) and a **table of village/town facilities** (pp42-3), which gives a run-down on the essential information you will need regarding accommodation possibilities and services.

You could follow one of the suggested itineraries (see p40) which are based on preferred type of accommodation and walking speeds or, if tackling the entire walk seems a bit ambitious, you can tackle it a day or two at a time. To help you, we discuss the highlights of the Hadrian's Wall Path on p41 and you can use public transport to get to the start and end of the walk. The public transport map and service details are on pp56-8, and the AD122 timetable on pp212-13. Once you have an idea of your approach turn to Part 5 for detailed information on accommodation, places to eat and other services in each village and town on the route. Also in Part 5 you will find summaries of the route to accompany the detailed trail maps.

SUGGESTED ITINERARIES

The itineraries in the boxes on p40 are based on different accommodation types, camping, hostels and B&Bs, with each one divided into three alternatives depending on your walking speed. They are only suggestions so feel free to adapt them. **Don't forget** to add your travelling time before and after the walk.

WHICH DIRECTION?

It's more common for Wall walkers ('Wallkers'?) attempting the entire trail to start from Newcastle and head west. The main reason seems to be because the official trail guide and the majority of those guidebooks that have followed in its wake were written from east to west. The justification put forward by the author of the official guide is that it seems 'more natural' to walk out of a big city into the open country, and I suppose there's some truth in that. Around 60% of Wall walkers seem to agree. Furthermore, the scenery improves the further

PLANNING YOUR WALK

STAYING IN B&Bs

Night	Relaxed Place	Approx Distance miles/km	Medium Place	Approx Distance miles/km	Fast Place	Approx Distance miles/km
0	Newcastle		Newcastle		Newcastle	
1	Newburn	11/18	Heddon	15/24	Chollerford	30/48
2	East Wallhouses	7.5/12	Chollerford	15/24	Gilsland	21/34
3	Chollerford	11.5/18.5	Once Brewed	12/19.5	Carlisle	19/30.5
4	Once Brewed	12/19.5	Walton	16/26	Bowness	14/22.5
5	Gilsland	9/14.5	Carlisle	12/19.5		
6	Newtown	9/14.5	Bowness	14/22.5		
7	Carlisle	10/16				
8	Bowness	14/22.5				

STAYING IN BUNKHOUSES/CAMPING BARNS/HOSTELS

Night	Relaxed Place	Approx Distance miles/km	Medium Place	Approx Distance miles/km	Fast Place	Approx Distance miles/km
0	Newcastle		Newcastle		Newcastle	
1	Heddon	15/24	Heddon	15/24	Heddon	15/24
2	Green Carts	16/25.5	Old Repeater Stn	19/30.5	Once Brewed	27/43.5
3	Old Repeater Stn	3/5	Greenhead	15/24	Walton	16/25.5
4	Once Brewed	8/13	Crosby	14/22.5	Carlisle *	12/19.5
5	Greenhead	7/11	Boustead Hill	14/22.5	Bowness	14/22.5
6	Walton	9/14.5	Bowness	7/11		
7	Carlisle *	12/19.5				
8	Bowness	14/22.5				

* seasonal

CAMPING

Night	Relaxed Place	Approx Distance miles/km	Medium Place	Approx Distance miles/km	Fast Place	Approx Distance miles/km
0	Newcastle		Newcastle		Newcastle	
1	Heddon *	15/24	Heddon *	15/24	(East) Wallhouses	21/34
2	Wall	14/22.5	Wall	14/22.5	Once Brewed	22/35.5
3	Old Repeater Stn	5/8	Once Brewed	14/22.5	Carlisle *	27/43.5
4	Once Brewed	9/14.5	Walton	15/24	Bowness *	14/22.5
5	Greenhead *	6/9.5	Boustead Hill	19/30.5		
6	Walton	9/14.5	Bowness *	7/11.5		
7	Carlisle *	12/19.5				
8	Boustead Hill	7/11.5				
9	Bowness *	7/11.5				

* Places marked with an asterisk have no campsite but do have a camping barn/bunkhouse/hostel though the hostel in Carlisle is seasonal west you go – up to a point – and the turrets and milecastles are also numbered from east to west (see box p112). What's more, as it's more popular to walk from east to west, those trekkers who prefer a bit of company will find more people heading in their direction.

But, that said, there are arguments that could be made for walking the other way, from Solway to Wallsend; and having trekked both ways now, I'm inclined to think this direction is slightly superior. For one thing, the prevailing winds in the UK tend to blow in from the west, and thus will be at your back if walking from west to east, which is preferable to struggling against a force nine (though to be fair, the winds aren't too severe in summer). Secondly, just as the official guide says that it's better to walk out of a city into the countryside, it could also be argued that a big city makes a suitably grand place to finish a trail – and Newcastle certainly has any number of bars, clubs and restaurants in which to celebrate the completion of a successful walk. Thirdly, I think you get a better view of the crags (on your way into Thirlwall) and can understand a little more how the Wall was laid out by travelling in this direction (and yes, of course, you can just look back and see the same view if travelling westwards – but it's a rare trekker who actually does. And finally, isn't there something poetic about finishing a walk along the Wall at a place called Wallsend?

As the majority of trekkers will, we imagine, continue to walk from east to west, that is the way this book has been written. That said, those who prefer to swim against the tide of popular opinion and walk west to east should find it easy to use this book too.

SIDE TRIPS

The Hadrian's Wall Path cuts through some of the richest trekking territory in the UK and there are plenty of opportunities for short (or long) diversions off the trail. Such trips are beyond the scope of this book but a glance at an Ordnance Survey map will give you some idea of the alternative walks available.

HADRIAN'S WALL HIGHLIGHTS

Trying to pick one particular section that is representative of the entire trail is impossible because each is very different. Undoubtedly if I had to recommend one highlight it would be from **Chollerford to Steel Rigg**, with its excellently preserved Wall, its milecastles and Wall forts. The landscape is the most dramatic here, too, as you ride the crests and bumps of the various crags. David McGlade, the National Trail Officer for Hadrian's Wall, prefers the **Walltown section** of the Wall, **Birdoswald and Segedunum forts** (the former for the views, the latter for its presentation), and the **Solway Estuary** because of its birdlife.

But just because these sections are our favourites does not mean that the others should be dismissed. The cityscape and suburbs of Newcastle, the absorbing roadside tramp from Heddon-on-the-Wall to Chollerford, the gentle rolling countryside of Cumbria, and 'The Land that Time Forgot' near Bowness are all worth experiencing.

VILLAGE AND

Place name (Places in brackets are a short walk off Hadrian's Wall path)	Distance from previous place § approx miles/km	Bank/ Cash Machine (ATM) *	Post Office	Tourist Information Centre (TIC) National Park Centre (NPC)
Newcastle/Wallsend		✔	✔	TIC
Newburn	11/18			
(Wylam)	(1/1.6)	✔	✔	
Heddon-on-the-Wall	4/6	✔	✔	
East Wallhouses	6/9.5			
Port Gate (A68)	4/6.4			
Wall	4/6.4			
Chollerford	1/1.6			
Corbridge–Hexham–Acomb alternative route				
(Corbridge)	(3/4.8 from Halton)	✔	✔	TIC
(Hexham)	(4.5/7.2)	✔	✔	TIC
(Acomb)	(1.5/2.4)		✔	
(Old Repeater Stn)	(0.5/0.8)			
(Grindon)	(2/3.2)			
Housesteads	9/14.5			
Steel Rigg	4/6.4			
(Once Brewed)	0.25/0.4			NPC/TIC
(Haltwhistle)	(2/3.2)	✔	✔	TIC
Carvoran	5.5/8.8			
(Greenhead)#	(0.3/0.5)			
Gilsland	2.5/4	✔	✔	
Birdoswald	2/3.2			
Banks	2.5/4			
Walton	2.5/4			
Newtown	2/3.2			
(Brampton)	(2/3.2)	✔	✔	TIC
(Laversdale)	(0.6/1)			
Crosby-on-Eden	5/8			
Carlisle	5/8	✔	✔	TIC
Grinsdale	3.5/5.6			
Burgh-by-Sands	3.5/5.6		✔	
(Boustead Hill)	(0.3/0.5)			
Drumburgh	2.5/4			
Glasson	1/1.6			
Port Carlisle	2.5/4			
Bowness-on-Solway	1/1.6			

TOTAL DISTANCE   84 miles/135.5km

§ Distances in **bold** are between places directly on the trail; distances in brackets are the distances off the path.

PLANNING YOUR WALK

TOWN FACILITIES

Eating Place ✔=one ✔✔=two ✔✔✔=three + (✔)= seasonal	Food Store	Campsite	Hostels YHA/ H (IndHostel)/ B (Barn or Bunkhouse)	B&B-style accommodation ✔=one ✔✔=two ✔✔✔=three+	Place name (Places in brackets are a short walk off Hadrian's Wall path)
✔✔✔	✔		YHA & B	✔✔✔	**Newcastle**
✔✔				✔	**Newburn**
✔✔✔	✔			✔✔✔	**(Wylam)**
✔✔	✔		B	✔✔	**Heddon-on-the-Wall**
✔✔✔		✔		✔	**East Wallhouses**
(✔)					**Port Gate (A68)**
✔		✔		✔	**Wall**
✔✔		✔		✔	**Chollerford**
			Corbridge–Hexham–Acomb alternative route		
✔✔✔	✔			✔✔✔	**(Corbridge)**
✔✔✔	✔			✔✔✔	**(Hexham)**
✔✔				✔	**(Acomb)**
		(✔)	H	✔	**(Old Repeater Stn)**
			H	✔✔	**(Grindon)**
				✔	**Housesteads**
			B	✔✔	**Steel Rigg**
✔		✔	YHA	✔✔	**(Once Brewed)**
✔✔✔	✔			✔✔✔	**(Haltwhistle)**
✔✔				✔	**Carvoran**
✔✔			H & B	✔✔	**# (Greenhead)**
✔✔✔	✔			✔✔✔	**Gilsland**
(✔)			YHA (seasonal)	✔	**Birdoswald**
		✔		✔	**Banks**
		✔	B	✔✔✔	**Walton**
				✔	**Newtown**
✔✔✔	✔			✔✔✔	**(Brampton)**
✔		✔			**(Laversdale)**
✔✔✔			B	✔✔	**Crosby-on-Eden**
✔✔✔	✔		YHA (seasonal)	✔✔✔	**Carlisle**
		✔			**Grinsdale**
✔		✔		✔	**Burgh-by-Sands**
		✔	B	✔✔	**(Boustead Hill)**
	✔(vending)				**Drumburgh**
✔					**Glasson**
✔		✔		✔	**Port Carlisle**
✔			B	✔✔✔	**Bowness-on-Solway**

(✔) = no official campsite though can camp nearby; ask the locals
* ✔ Cash machine (ATM) available; ✔ ATM available but charges for use
# (Greenhead) this includes Holmhead which is on the Wall

❏ **Visiting the forts – a visitor's view**

To many/most people on the Hadrian's Wall path, the various forts and museums are little more than milestones on the trail: places to tick off as they pass by rather than places to actually stop at and visit. However, some of our readers – many not even particularly interested in Roman history (or at least not before the trail) – write in to tell us how much they enjoyed the various museums on the way. The following from Jane Johnson was one such letter:

'To get an idea of the Roman remains we decided it would be good to have visited the sites before commencing the walk, establishing their location as well as those of the Roman roads. We camped for a week, basing ourselves at Haltwhistle; this enabled us to visit Chesters, Vindolanda (5hrs), Corbridge etc as well as the smaller off route places such as the bridge abutment across from Chesters. From Haltwhistle it was an easy train ride to Newcastle to visit the sites along the West Road and the Great North Museum: Hancock with its new displays.

We didn't do the actual walk until the following year but even with the gap in time we really appreciated having been to the main sites as we had some knowledge of things. Before setting off we spent two nights in Newcastle to see the rest of the sites around there. Arriving at the station in the early afternoon we hopped on the metro to South Shields to reach Arbeia, well worth visiting, before settling in to the city.

The next day we went to Segedunum and then did the short walk back to the city (not the most inspiring start to a walk!) leaving a 10-mile stretch to Heddon on the second day. This means you can visit Segedunum and walk the first five miles without baggage. What an easy start to the walk. Both Arbeia and Segedunum are great, especially having the reconstructions as they give an idea of the size of buildings. We wanted to stay in B&Bs for the actual walk and used a baggage transfer company to take our bags. Of course all this could be done in about two weeks' holiday if you have both the time and finance.'   **Jane Johnson**

While Jane's itinerary may be a bit extreme for some tastes, her email is at least further testimony that it is worth visiting at least one of the forts on the way.

TAKING DOGS ALONG THE HADRIAN'S WALL PATH

The Hadrian's Wall Path is a dog-friendly path, though it is extremely important that dog owners behave in a responsible way. Dogs should always be kept on leads while on the footpath to avoid disturbing wildlife, livestock and other walkers. It is also compulsory to keep your dog on a lead through National Trust land. Dog excrement should be cleaned up and not left to decorate the boots of others.

It is particularly important to keep your dog on a lead when crossing fields with livestock in them, especially around **lambing time**. This generally takes place from mid-March to mid-May, though can start as early as February and continue to the end of May. During this time dogs should not be taken along the path; even a dog secured on a lead can disturb a pregnant ewe. If you see a lamb or ewe that appears to be in distress contact the nearest farmer.

In August 2009, following four fatal tramplings by **cows** that summer as well as who knows how many more less serious and unreported incidents, Ramblers (see box p52) in conjunction with the National Farmers Union issued the following guidelines when passing bovine livestock:

Do
● Try not to get between cows and their calves.
● Be prepared for cattle to react to your presence, especially if you have a dog with you.
● Move quickly and quietly, and if possible walk around the herd.
● Keep your dog close and under effective control on a lead.

Don't
● Don't hang onto your dog. If you are threatened by cattle – let it go as the cattle will chase the dog.
● Don't put yourself at risk. Find another way round the cattle and rejoin the footpath as soon as possible.

MID MOORHOUSE
TEL: 01661 886675
(AFTER 5PM - 01661 886805)

● Don't panic or run! Most cattle will stop before they reach you. If they follow just walk on quietly.

Remember, when booking your **accommodation**, to check that your dog will be welcome. Some B&Bs and hotels charge extra for a dog; YHA hostels do not permit them unless they are an assistance (guide) dog.

What to take

Deciding how much to take can be difficult. Experienced walkers know that you should take only the bare essentials but at the same time you must ensure you have all the equipment necessary to make the trip safe and comfortable.

KEEP YOUR LUGGAGE LIGHT

Experienced backpackers know that there is some sort of complicated formula governing the success of a trek, in which the enjoyment of the walk is inversely proportional to the amount carried. Carrying a heavy rucksack slows you down, tires you out and gives you aches and pains in parts of the body that you never knew existed. It is imperative, therefore, that you take a good deal of time packing and that you are ruthless when you do; if it's not essential, don't take it.

HOW TO CARRY IT

If you are using one of the baggage-carrier services, you must contact them beforehand to find out what their regulations are regarding the weight and size of the luggage you wish them to carry. Even if you are using one of these serv-ices, you will still need to carry a small **daypack**, filled with those items that you will need during the day: water bottle or pouch, this book, map, sun-screen, sun hat, wet-weather gear, some food, camera, money and so on.

If you have decided to forego the services of the baggage carriers you will have to consider your **rucksack** even more carefully. Ultimately its size will depend on where you are planning to stay and how you are planning to eat. If you are camping and cooking for yourself you will probably need a 65- to 75-litre rucksack, which should be large enough to carry a small tent, sleeping bag, cooking equipment, crockery, cutlery and food. Those not carrying their home with them should find a 40- to 60-litre rucksack sufficient.

When choosing a rucksack, make sure it has a stiffened back and can be adjusted to fit your own back comfortably. Don't just try the rucksack out in the shop: take it home, fill it with things and then try it out around the house and take it out for a short walk. Only then can you be certain that it fits. Make sure the hip belt and chest strap (if there is one) are fastened tightly as this helps dis-tribute the weight more comfortably with most of it being carried on the hips. Carry a small daypack inside the rucksack, as this will be useful to carry things in when leaving the main pack at the hostel or B&B.

One reader wrote in with the eminently sensible advice of taking a **water-proof rucksack cover**. Most rucksacks these days have them 'built in' to the sack, but you can also buy them separately for less than a tenner. Lining your bag with a **bin liner** is another sensible, cut-price idea. Finally, it's also a good idea to keep everything wrapped in plastic bags inside the rucksack; I usually place all these bags inside a bin-bag which then goes inside the rucksack. That way, even if it does pour with rain, everything should remain dry.

FOOTWEAR

Boots

Only a decent pair of strong, durable trekking boots are good enough to survive the rigours of the Hadrian's Wall Path. Don't be tempted by a spell of hot weath-er into bringing something flimsier. Make sure, too, that your boots provide good ankle support, for the ground can occasionally be rough and stony and twisted ankles are commonplace. Make sure your boots are waterproof as well: these days most people opt for a synthetic waterproof lining (Gore-Tex or sim-ilar), though a good-quality leather boot with dubbin should prove just as reli-able in keeping your feet dry.

In addition, many people bring an extra pair of shoes or trainers to wear off the trail. This is not essential but if you are using one of the luggage-carrying serv-ices and you've got room in your luggage, why not? One reader said he found it more comfortable to wear lighter shoes on the Newcastle section of the walk.

Socks

If you haven't got a pair of the modern hi-tech walking socks the old system of wearing a thin liner sock under a thicker wool sock is just as good. Bring a few pairs of each.

CLOTHES

*I have sent you ... pairs of socks from Sattua, two pairs of sandals and two pairs of under-
pants ...*   Tablet 346 of the **Vindolanda Postcards** (see p155)

In a country notorious for its unpredictable climate it is imperative that you pack
enough clothes to cover every extreme of weather, from burning hot to bloomin'
freezing. Modern hi-tech outdoor clothes come with a range of fancy names and
brands but they all still follow the basic two- or three-layer principle, with an
inner base layer to transport sweat away from your skin, a mid-layer for warmth
and an outer layer to protect you from the wind and rain.

A thin lightweight **thermal top** of a synthetic material is ideal as the base
layer as it draws moisture (ie sweat) away from your body. Cool in hot weather and warm when worn under other clothes in the cold, pack at least one thermal top. Over the top in cold weather a mid-weight **polyester fleece** should suffice. Fleeces are light, more water-resistant than the alternatives (such as a
woolly jumper), remain warm even when wet and pack down small in rucksacks; they are thus ideal trekking gear.

Over the top of all this a **waterproof jacket** is essential. 'Breathable' jack-
ets cost a small fortune (though prices are falling all the time) but they do prevent the build-up of condensation.

Leg wear
Many trekkers find trekking trousers an unnecessary investment. Any light,
quick-drying trouser should suffice. Jeans are heavy and dry slowly and are thus
not recommended. A pair of waterproof trousers *is* more than useful, however,
while on really hot sunny days you'll be glad you brought your shorts. Thermal
long johns take up little room in the rucksack and could be vital if the weather
starts to close in.

Gaiters are not essential but, again, those who bring them are always glad
they did, for they provide extra protection when walking through muddy ground
and when the vegetation around the trail is dripping wet after bad weather.

Underwear
Three or four changes of underwear is fine. Any more is excessive, any less
unhygienic. Because backpacks can cause bra straps to dig painfully into the
skin, women may find a **sports bra** more comfortable.

Other clothes
You may like to consider a woolly **hat** and **gloves** – you'd be surprised how cold
it can get up on the moors even in summer – and a **sun hat**.

TOILETRIES

Once again, take the minimum. **Soap**, **towel**, a **toothbrush** and **toothpaste** are
pretty much essential (although those staying in B&Bs will find that most provide soap and towels anyway). Some **toilet paper** could also prove vital on the
trail, particularly if using public toilets (which occasionally run out).

Other items: **razor**; **deodorant**; **tampons/sanitary towels** and a high factor **sun-screen** should cover just about everything.

FIRST-AID KIT

A small first-aid kit could prove useful for those emergencies that occur along the trail. This kit should include **aspirin** or **paracetamol**; **plasters** for minor cuts; **moleskin**, **Second Skin** or some other treatment for blisters; a **bandage** or elasticated joint support for supporting a sprained ankle or a weak knee; **antiseptic wipes**; **antiseptic cream**; **safety pins**; **tweezers** and **scissors**.

GENERAL ITEMS

Essential

Everybody should have a **map**, **torch**, **water bottle or pouch**, **spare batteries**, **penknife**, **whistle** (see p72 for details of the international distress signal), some **emergency food** and a **watch** (preferably with an alarm to help you make an early start each day). Those with weak knees will find a **walking pole** or **sticks** essential. Those who've also walked in Scotland will recognise the importance of taking **insect repellent** to ward off midges, though they're not so bad here.

If you know how to use it properly you'll also find a **compass** extremely handy. Some people find a **mobile phone** invaluable too, and reception is usually pretty good. For arranging a lift from the Wall to the B&B it can also be invaluable – just don't forget the charger!

Useful items and luxuries

Suggestions here include a **book** for days off or on train and bus journeys, a camera, a pair of **sunglasses**, **binoculars** and a **CD player/Walkman/iPod**.

CAMPING GEAR

Both campers and those intending to stay in the various bunkhouses/camping barns en route will find a sleeping bag essential. A two- to three-season bag should suffice for summer. In addition, campers will also need a decent bivvy bag or tent, a sleeping mat, fuel and stove, cutlery/pans, a cup and a scrubber for washing up.

MONEY

Cash machines (ATMs) are infrequent along the Hadrian's Wall Path and banks are even rarer, with none along the trail outside Newcastle and Carlisle. Not everybody accepts **debit** or **credit cards** as payment either – though some B&Bs and many restaurants now do.

As a result, you should always carry a fair amount of **cash** with you, just to be on the safe side. A **cheque book** from a British bank is useful in those places where credit cards are not accepted.

Crime on the trail is thankfully rare but it's always a good idea to carry your money safely in a **moneybelt**.

❏ The Hadrian's Wall Path Passport

A simple piece of folded card, the Passport nevertheless could be an important measure in protecting the Wall – as well as providing walkers with a bit of fun and some proof that they actually did walk the entire trail. Open up the passport and you'll find seven blank spaces; the idea is to collect seven stamps from various places along the trail. Get the full set and you qualify for the right to purchase a commemorative badge (available at £5) and certificate from either the Segedunum Roman Fort or the King's Arms in Bowness-on-Solway. Or you can mail your completed passport and a cheque for £5 payable to Tynedale Council to Haltwhistle Tourist Information Centre, Railway Station, Station Rd, Haltwhistle, NE49 9HN.

The passport helps to protect the Wall because it is available May to October only and thus encourages walkers to view the trail as a summertime-only activity.

The **'stamping stations'** are located at:

- **Segedunum Roman Fort, Wallsend** *or* **the TOTAL petrol garage** The stamp is inside the main entrance to the museum, and thus available during museum opening hours only; alternatively, if you arrive outside these times, the garage is just 150 metres east of Segedunum.
- **Robin Hood Inn** One mile west of the Whittledene Reservoir in a box outside the front door.
- **Chesters Roman Fort** Inside the entrance to the museum during opening hours; outside these hours a stamping box is provided at the entrance to the car park.
- **Housesteads** At the Visitors' Centre/reception during opening hours.
- **Birdoswald Roman Fort** Inside the main entrance during opening hours; outside these hours a stamping box is provided by the main entrance.
- **Sands Sports Centre, Carlisle** Inside the café; entrance either via the glass door on the path, or the main entrance; available only during the centre's opening hours.
- **The Banks Promenade** *or* **the King's Arms, Bowness-on-Solway** The Promenade stamp is available at any time, while the pub is officially open daily 11am to 11pm from Easter to September, 5.30-11pm the rest of the year.

DOCUMENTS

Don't forget your **Hadrian's Wall Path Passport** (see box above). The AD122 **bus timetable** (see pp212-15) for 2011 is included in this guide but in subsequent years it may be very useful to carry a print-out; you can download it from ▣ www.hadrians-wall.org – click on the link to the timetable; you never know when it might come in handy.

If you are a member of **English Heritage** or the **National Trust**, bring your **membership cards**; membership of English Heritage in particular will save you money at the sights along the path, allowing free entrance to the Roman forts and other attractions.

MAPS

The hand-drawn maps in this book cover the trail at a scale of 1:20,000. This large scale, combined with the notes and tips written on the maps, should be more than enough to stop you losing your way. Nevertheless, some people like to have a separate map of the region; such maps can prove invaluable should you need to abandon the path and find the quickest route off the trail in an emergency. They also help in identifying local features and landmarks and devising possible side trips.

Perhaps the best map for the whole walk is the **Hadrian's Wall Path** (Walker's Route) strip map (1:40,000) published by Harvey Map Services (🖥 www.harveymaps.co.uk). The only criticism that can be levelled against it is that it only covers a narrow strip either side of the path in any detail, thus making it difficult for trekkers to identify far-off peaks and other landmarks.

The Ordnance Survey (☎ 0845-605 0505, 🖥 www.ordnancesurvey.co.uk) also produce a waterproof strip map that covers the central section of the trail (centred on Haltwhistle and Hexham) at a scale of 1:25,000 as part of their Explorer Outdoor Leisure series. In addition, you'll also need Explorer Active maps 314, 315 and 316 to cover the rest of the trail. The alternative is to buy a whole series of regular Ordnance Survey Landranger maps (1:50,000); the numbers are: 85, 86, 87 and 88. Note that older editions (pre-2003) of these maps do not have the trail marked on them.

While it may be extravagant to buy all these maps, members of Ramblers' (see box p52) can make use of their library which allows them to borrow up to ten maps for up to six weeks at just 50p per map, or £1 for waterproof maps.

In 2010 English Heritage published **The Archaeological Map of Hadrian's Wall** (£7.99). Beautiful, fascinating and insightful, the map includes sites both along and near the Wall. Probably for those with a specialist interest in the Wall's history and archaeology only, this nevertheless is, in my opinion, the most absorbing map on the Wall and its surroundings.

Several digital maps are available now; Ordnance Survey offers such a service, though the cost is over £50.

RECOMMENDED READING

There is a wealth of books on the Wall, as you'd expect, so the following is a mere overview of the better, or at least newer works. Some of the following books can be found in the tourist information centres and at the reception desks of the Roman forts en route. As well as stocking many of the titles listed below, these places also have a number of books about the towns and villages en route, usually printed by small, local publishers. Furthermore, each of the visitor centres of the major English Heritage historical attractions such as Housesteads, Chesters and Corbridge publishes their own guidebook to the site.

The journalist and author Hunter Davies, who was born at the western end of the trail, has written the historical travelogue *A Walk Along the Wall* (Frances Lincoln; originally published in 1974), the result of spending a year trekking along and studying the wall. *Hadrian's Wall*, by David Breeze and Brian Dobson, is part of the Penguin History Series and deals with the history of the Wall as well as the day-to-day activities of those who lived in its shadow, both soldiers and locals, during the Roman occupation.

On a similar subject, *Hadrian's Wall in the Days of the Romans*, by Ronald Embleton and Frank Graham (WJ Williams & Son Books Ltd), does exactly what it says on the cover; *Hadrian's Wall AD122-410* by Nic Fields (Osprey Publishing) covers much the same ground. Newer, *The Wall: Rome's Greatest Frontier* (Birlinn Ltd) by Alistair Moffatt, also deals with the building of the Wall and is perhaps the best read of the three and has a good section on the Vindolanda postcards. One of the leading Wall experts, Anthony R Birley, has produced a biography of the enigmatic man behind the Wall: *Hadrian, The Restless Emperor* (Routledge), though it must be said the text is a little dry.

Locally produced, *The Great Wall of Britain – A Walk Along Hadrian's Wall* (Hayloft) by the illustrator Anton Hodge, is a travelogue-cum-geographical/historical-tour of the Roman Wall. Hard to track down, it can be found locally or you can visit the author's website: 🖥 www.hayloft.eu. In a similar 'travelogue' vein is Bob Bibby's *On the Wall with Hadrian* (Eye Books).

English Heritage produce their own historical guide to the Wall, titled simply *Hadrian's Wall*, written by Stephen Johnson and published by BT Batsford.

Finally, for those looking to walk in the region during the winter season, *The Roman Ring* (Shepherd's Walks) by Mark Richards provides details on two trails – called the Moss Troopers' Trail and the Roman Ring – which, whilst still giving walkers plenty of opportunity to explore the Roman history of the region, visit the Wall only sporadically. With walkers advised against walking the Wall in winter to minimise damage to the path and the archaeology underneath, this book thus provides a decent alternative to the main Hadrian's Wall Path.

General guidebooks
Both Rough Guides and Lonely Planet publish guides to England; though neither, it must be said, covers the Hadrian's Wall trail in much detail.

Other guidebooks
Other guides to the trail include the official *Hadrian's Wall Path* by Anthony Burton (2010), which describes the entire route with Ordnance Survey maps

---

❏ **Fantastic historical websites**

🖥 **www.roman-britain.org** In my opinion the best website on the history and ruins of Hadrian's Wall, this is a non-commercial site seemingly written by enthusiasts whose love and knowledge of all things Roman is astounding. The site includes details of the Wall's construction, a study of the visible remains of the Wall and a whole load of stuff on Roman Britain. Just great.

🖥 **www.hadrians.com** A website dedicated to the man who ordered the construction of the Wall, including studies of his family, as well as the food, clothes, homes and work of those who lived during his reign.

🖥 **www.bbc.co.uk/history/ancient/romans** The BBC's website on the Romans, includes some useful time-lines and interesting articles by various boffins.

🖥 **www.britannia.com/history/h30.html** Described as the American gateway to the British Isles, this website is great for an overview of British history, with the address above dealing specifically with Roman Britain.

and photos but scant descriptions of the major archaeological sites. Cicerone also publish a guide, *Hadrian's Wall Path: National Trail*, by Mark Richards (2008, reprinted 2010), with descriptions for walking in both directions. Finally,

❏ SOURCES OF FURTHER INFORMATION

Trail information (online)

🖳 www.nationaltrail.co.uk/hadrianswall The essential first stop for those looking to walk the Wall, this is the official site of the Hadrian's Wall Path. Check out the slideshow, maps, sections on accommodation and publications. Best of all, register with them and they'll send you a whole load of relevant pamphlets and brochures, including the Wall Passport (see box p49).

🖳 www.hadrians-wall.org The most complete website on the Wall itself, this is the website of Hadrian's Wall Country – and thus, unlike the website above, is not specifically for walkers – with lists of tour agencies, accommodation, events, history and the latest news. They also publish a thrice-yearly Hadrian's Wall Newsletter, *Frontier*, dealing with all aspects of the Wall.

🖳 www.haltwhistle.org Website of the Haltwhistle Tourist Office.

🖳 www.cumbria-the-lake-district.co.uk Website that concentrates on the Lake District though does contain pages on Carlisle and the Hadrian's Wall Path.

🖳 www.walkinghadrianswall.co.uk The most useful website of the walking companies that arrange trips along the Wall (see pp32-4), with a list of ten tips for trekkers.

Tourist information centres (TICs)

Tourist information centres are based in towns throughout Britain and provide all manner of locally specific information and an accommodation-booking service (in many cases a 10% deposit is payable which is deducted from the final bill and sometimes a booking charge (£2-4) as well. The centres listed below are on or close to the Hadrian's Wall Path: **Newcastle** (see p77); **Corbridge** (see p128); **Hexham** (see p134); **Haltwhistle/Hadrian's Wall Information Line** (see p160; contact the information line for details on just about everything; they also operate a mail-order line for maps/guides); **Brampton** (see p179); and **Carlisle** (see p188). **Once Brewed** (see p152) is a National Park Visitor Centre but also has a tourist information centre.

Organisations for walkers

● **Backpackers' Club** (🖳 www.backpackersclub.co.uk) A club aimed at people who are involved or interested in lightweight camping through walking, cycling, skiing and canoeing. They produce a quarterly magazine, provide members with a comprehensive advisory and information service on all aspects of backpacking, organise weekend trips and also publish a farm-pitch directory. Membership is £12 a year.

● **The Long Distance Walkers' Association** (🖳 www.ldwa.org.uk) An association of people with the common interest of long-distance walking. Membership includes a journal, *Strider*, three times per year giving details of challenge events and local group walks as well as articles on the subject. Information on over 730 paths is presented in their *UK Trailwalkers' Handbook*. Individual membership is £13 a year whilst family membership for two adults and all children under 18 is £19.50 a year.

● **Ramblers** (formerly Ramblers' Association; 🖳 www.ramblers.org.uk) Looks after the interests of walkers throughout Britain. They publish a large amount of useful information including their quarterly *Walk* magazine (£3.40 to non-members), the *Walk Britain* yearbook (£5.99 to non-members), and *Walk Britain's Great Views* (£14.99), a guide to Britain's top 50 viewpoints. Membership costs £31/41 individual/joint.

the Hadrian's Wall Path Trust publish *The Essential Guide to Hadrian's Wall Path National Trail* by David McGlade, a guide to all those vital services – cash machines, parking, food, accommodation, water taps and so on – as well as notes on conservation and other essentials. Written by the Wall's very own National Trail Officer, it was last updated in 2007 and costs £3.95.

If you are a seasoned long-distance walker, or even new to the game and like what you see, check out the other titles in the Trailblazer series; see p223.

Flora and fauna field guides

Collins Bird Guide, with its beautiful illustrations of British and European birds, continues to be the favourite field guide of both ornithologists and laymen alike. Their *Trees of Britain & Europe* is also OK if you've room in your rucksack and don't know your ash from your alder. Collins also produce guides to the above and *Mushrooms*, *Butterflies*, *Insects*, *Wild Flowers* and *Birds* as part of their *Gem* series – a collection of cracking guides that are only slightly larger than a pack of playing cards and thus ideal for trekking with.

CDs and DVDs

There's a very pleasant video, *Edge of Empire*, that's produced by Striding Edge and the Ordnance Survey, in which Eric Robson takes us on a journey along the 73 miles and two millennia of the Wall. The *Lost Treasures of the Ancient World* series (Cromwell Productions) has a 48-minute documentary on the Wall; the DVD has features including a 'Test your Knowledge' section.

There is also now a DVD dedicated to the trail itself, *Hadrian's Wall Path National Trail*, narrated by Anthony Burton. Best of all, however, is *Hadrian's Wall from the Air*, a 45-minute DVD of the Wall filmed from above. A preview can be seen and copies ordered from the official National Trail website: 🖥 www .nationaltrail.co.uk/hadrianswall. They have also produced a DVD, *Illuminating Hadrian's Wall*, that celebrates the night of 13 March, 2010, when the entire length of the Wall was lit by over a thousand volunteer torch-bearers and supporters (see box p38).

Getting to and from the Hadrian's Wall Path

Carlisle and Newcastle are the main transport hubs for the trail and conveniently they all but bookend the path, with Carlisle near the western end and the Newcastle suburb of Wallsend at the eastern end. Both are well connected by public transport to the rest of the country and indeed Europe; see box p56.

NATIONAL TRANSPORT

By train

Both Newcastle and Carlisle lie on the main England–Scotland rail links. All timetable and fare information can be obtained from **National Rail Enquiries**

❏ GETTING TO BRITAIN

● **By air** Newcastle (🖥 www.newcastleairport.com) and Manchester (🖥 www.man chesterairport.co.uk) are the two major international airports serving the Hadrian's Wall Path but for most foreign visitors it is still one of the London airports that provides them with their first taste of England. Nevertheless, if you've no business in London do check out flights to Newcastle (from Europe) and Manchester (from Europe and the USA). Of the two, Newcastle Airport is the closest to the Wall. From Manchester Airport to Carlisle it's just over two hours by train.

Other airports that are fairly close include Leeds Bradford (🖥 www.leedsbrad fordairport.co.uk) and Durham & Teeside (🖥 www.durhamteesvalleyairport.com; 7 miles/11km outside Darlington).

● **From Europe by train** Eurostar (🖥 www.eurostar.com) operates the high-speed passenger service via the Channel Tunnel between Paris/Brussels and London. Conveniently, the terminal in London is St Pancras International, which is next to King's Cross, the station for departures to Newcastle. Euston, the station for trains to Carlisle, is only a five-minute walk away in the other direction on Euston Rd.

For more information about rail services from Europe contact your national rail provider, or Railteam (🖥 www.railteam.eu).

● **From Europe by coach** Eurolines (🖥 www.eurolines.com) have a huge network of long-distance coach services connecting over 500 cities throughout Europe to London. Check carefully: often, once expenses such as food for the journey are taken into consideration, it doesn't work out much cheaper than flying, particularly when compared to the prices of some of the budget airlines.

● **From Europe by ferry (with or without a car)** There are numerous ferries plying routes between ports around the UK and those in Ireland and continental Europe. However, the most convenient for Hadrian's Wall Path is DFDS Seaways (🖥 www.dfdsseaways.co.uk) with a service connecting Newcastle and Amsterdam daily. Special buses run from Newcastle Central to connect with the ferries. Also worth considering is P&O Stena Line (🖥 www.poferries.com) which operates services daily between Hull and Zeebrugge/Rotterdam.

A useful website for further information is 🖥 www.directferries.com.

● **From Europe by car** Eurotunnel (🖥 www.eurotunnel.com) operates the shuttle train service for vehicles via the Channel Tunnel between Calais and Folkestone taking just 35 minutes.

(☎ 08457-484950; 24hrs; 🖥 www.nationalrail.co.uk) or the relevant train companies. Tickets can be bought through the latter or from websites such as 🖥 www .trainline.com.

Newcastle lies on the East Coast (🖥 www.eastcoast.co.uk) line. Services connect Newcastle with London King's Cross, York and Edinburgh at least twice an hour. It takes around three hours from London to Newcastle. In addition, the Trans-Pennine Express (🖥 www.tpexpress.co.uk) operates from Manchester to Newcastle via York, Northallerton, Darlington & Middlesborough (approx 1/hr).

Carlisle is connected to London Euston, Manchester and Glasgow via the West Coast main line, with services operated by Virgin Trains (🖥 www.virgin trains.co.uk; 14/day); Euston to Carlisle takes less than four hours. Carlisle also has connections to Leeds (6-7/day) thanks to the scenic Settle to Carlisle line (🖳 www.settle-carlisle.co.uk) through Yorkshire Dales National Park.

Northern Rail (🖳 www.northernrail.org) operate several lines in the north of England including links between Carlisle and Leeds, down the coast to Barrow and across to Newcastle. Similarly, and perhaps most usefully of all, **Hadrian's Wall Country Line** connects Newcastle and Carlisle via Haltwhistle and Hexham (see box p58).

By coach

The principal coach (long-distance bus) operator in Britain is **National Express** (☎ 0871-781 8178; 8am-8pm daily; 🖳 www.nationalexpress.com). Coach travel is generally cheaper (though with the excellent advance-booking train fares and special deals offered by the train companies, that is not always the case now) but the journey time is longer than if travelling by train (both London to Newcastle and London to Carlisle take at least six hours). Service details are:

● **To Carlisle** The NX590 from London travels via Carlisle on its way to Aberdeen; NX538 Coventry to Inverness travels via Birmingham, Manchester and Carlisle; other coaches travelling via Carlisle include the NX532 Plymouth to Glasgow; NX336 Plymouth to Edinburgh; NX539 Bournemouth to Glasgow/Edinburgh. All the above stop at least once a day in Carlisle.

● **To Newcastle** The following call in at or terminate at Newcastle: NX591 between London and Edinburgh (1/day, 2/day in summer); NX425 and NX435 between London and Newcastle (each 1/day); NX534 between Hull and Glasgow (1/day); NX380 from Liverpool (2/day); NX326, 380, 383, 425 from Leeds (1/day each); NX531 from Plymouth (1/day).

In addition, a second coach company, **Megabus** (🖳 http://uk.megabus .com) serves Newcastle, with coaches travelling from London (M12, and also M20 which continues on to Edinburgh), and from Cwmbran (M35). They also run coaches to Carlisle and offer some good-value travel fares especially if you book early.

By car

There are reasonable road connections to Hadrian's Wall. Access from the western side is along the M6 from the south (junctions 42, 43 and 44) and A74 (M) from Glasgow to Carlisle. Access from the eastern side is along the A1(M) to Newcastle; take the city-centre exit and follow signs for Wallsend; or take the A19 and follow the signs for Wallsend from there. The A68 links Edinburgh and Darlington and bisects the trail around Corbridge. Finally, the A69 between Newcastle and Carlisle runs parallel to the Wall, usually around two to five miles (three to eight km) south of it, and is the main access route.

By air

Newcastle Airport (see box opposite) has frequent shuttle flights from London (Heathrow, Gatwick and Stansted), Aberdeen, Belfast, Birmingham, Bristol, Cardiff, Exeter, Southampton, Isle of Man and Jersey. The airport is 30 minutes from Central Station on the Tyneside Metro (have some change ready for the ticket machine – there are no ticket offices).

LOCAL TRANSPORT

With both a special Hadrian's Wall Country Bus service and the Newcastle to Carlisle Hadrian's Wall Country rail line (the oldest coast-to-coast service in the country), public transport along the trail is surprisingly good. At Hexham and Haltwhistle the services dovetail neatly, with the buses calling in at the train stations. For further details call the Hadrian's Wall Information Line on ☎ 01434-322002, or visit the website 💻 www.hadrians-wall.org.

Hadrian's Wall Country Bus AD122

The Hadrian's Wall Country Bus, named Spartacus and given the appropriate route number AD122, operates from late March/early April to late October/early November. Despite its name, the route taken does not faithfully follow the trail. Some of the detours (to Corbridge, Hexham, Haltwhistle, Greenhead, Lanercost Priory and Brampton) are for a good reason: to enable people to arrive at the Wall without using a car. But some places, such as St Oswalds and Walton, are *not* served by the AD122. Furthermore, Bowness-on-Solway (along with anywhere west of Carlisle) is not served by Spartacus; Stagecoach's No 93 (or the once-a-day No 71) are the only buses serving this route.

The AD122 is actually two services, one running between Newcastle and Haltwhistle/Walltown (one a day only) and the other between Hexham and Carlisle (5-6 times a day). Those looking to travel from one end of the Wall to the other are thus advised to take the train or Arriva's/Stagecoach's No 685 bus service, both of which are direct and considerably quicker. Details of these services can be found on p58.

Officially, the AD122 is not a 'hail & ride' bus (ie you have to wait at a scheduled bus stop as otherwise it won't stop for you), though unofficially I have yet to have one drive past without stopping when I've hailed it, regardless of whether I am at a 'proper' bus stop or not. The moral is, I guess, that if you're not waiting at a recognised bus stop you are reliant upon the kindness of the driver to stop for you, for they are under no obligation to do so; but the drivers,

---

❏ **Getting to the start and end of the trail**

● **Between Wallsend and Newcastle** There are numerous ways to get to Wallsend from Newcastle – you can take a bus (Stagecoach No 22, 3/hr) from Central Station, or the Metro train on the Tyne loop via Monument. For further information on public transport in Newcastle see p76. Those planning on starting at Heddon-on-the-Wall (to avoid the industrial grittiness of Wallsend) should take Arriva's No 685, Go North East's No 684 (see box p58) or the one-a-day AD122.

● **Between Bowness-on-Solway and Carlisle** The main service is operated by Stagecoach (No 93, though one of the buses on Saturday is, for some obscure reason, the No 71). Note that there is no service on Sunday. Many people, particularly those for whom Bowness is the end of the trail and are thus a bit weary, find it a whole lot more appealing to treat themselves to a cab back to Carlisle. Ask at The King's Arms (see p205) for the number of a local taxi firm, as this should be the best bet price-wise, rather than someone from Carlisle (see p190).

in my experience, are a very kind and considerate bunch. But do ensure you are at a place where they can stop safely.

However useful you find the bus, there's no doubt that it does offer a different perspective on the Wall. For example, from Gilsland to Birdoswald the bus detours a little way to the north, thereby offering a distant perspective and giving you an idea of just how imposing the original Wall, at its full height, would have been; the drive down from Carvoran offers a similar distant view of the Wall, this time from the south. The bus is equipped to take wheelchairs and can take bikes providing you book (call ☎ 01434-322002) a day in advance.

A one-day Hadrian's Wall Rover ticket (£9/4.50/18 for adults/children/family ie two adults and up to three children under 16) permits unlimited travel on the AD122 and 185 as well as Go North East Tynedale Links services between Hexham and Newcastle. Three-day (£18/9/36) and seven-day tickets (£36/18/72) are also available. Tickets can be bought from the bus driver or at local tourist information centres. Travel on Monday and up to two children travel for free with an adult on a Rover ticket. Alternatively, buy a ticket (at a staffed rail station or on the train) to Hexham from any UK railway station and for a supplement of £5.50 get unlimited travel for the day on the bus with a one-day Rover ticket.

Hadrian's Wall Country Line
A Day Ranger ticket allowing unlimited day travel on rail services between Sunderland and Ravenglass (which encompasses Newcastle to Carlisle) is available on trains or from staffed stations for £18/9 adult/child. See the box on p58 for details of services on this line.

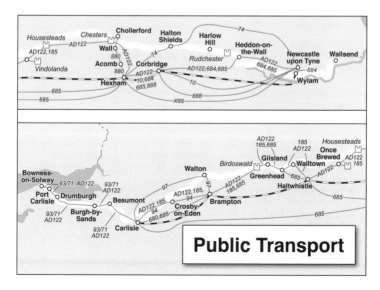

Public Transport

❏ **PUBLIC TRANSPORT SERVICES**

Bus services See box p56 for details of getting to the start and end of the trail and p76 for details of public transport services within Newcastle.

Hadrian's Wall Country Bus Service (🖳 www.hadrians-wall.org; see pp212-15 for timetables, correct at time of printing; check this website for any updates)

AD122 (Apr-Oct daily) **Newcastle to Haltwhistle/Walltown** via Heddon-on-the-Wall, Harlow Hill, Robin Hood Inn, Errington Arms, Corbridge, Corbridge Roman Town, Hexham, Acomb, Wall, Chollerford, Chesters, Housesteads, Once Brewed, Vindolanda, Twice Brewed, Milecastle Inn, Shield Hill, 1/day; **Hexham to Carlisle** via the above to Haltwhistle and then to Walltown, Greenhead, Longbyre, Gilsland, Birdoswald, Banks, Lanercost Priory, Brampton & Crosby-on-Eden, 3-4/day

Telford's Coaches (☎ 013873-75677, 🖳 www.telfordscoaches.com)
185   Haltwhistle to Carlisle via Roman Army Museum, Greenhead, Gilsland, Brampton & Crosby-on-Eden, Mon-Sat 2/day + 1/day to Brampton
680   Carlisle to Nenthead via Brampton & Alston, Mon-Sat 1/day (plus 1/day to Brampton) plus Sat 1/day (see also Wrights)

Arriva North East (🖳 www.arrivabus.co.uk)
685   Newcastle to Carlisle via Heddon, Corbridge, Hexham, Haltwhistle, Greenhead, Gilsland & Brampton, Mon-Sat 1/hr; Hexham to Carlisle, Sun 4/day
X85   Newcastle to Hexham, Mon-Fri 3/day (two in morning and one in the evening)

Go North East (🖳 www.simplygo.com)
10   Newcastle to Hexham via Corbridge, Mon-Sat 3/hr, Sun 1/hr
74   (Tynedale Links) Newcastle to Hexham via Matfen, Halton & Errington Arms, Mon-Sat 5-6/day, Sun 6/day Newcastle to Matfen only
684   (Tynedale Links) Newcastle to Hexham via Denton Burn, Lemington Road End, Wylam, Heddon-on-the-Wall & Corbridge, Mon-Sat 1/hr, Sun 2/day

Stagecoach North West/Stagecoach in Cumbria (🖳 www.stagecoachbus.com)
93/71 Carlisle to Bowness-on-Solway via Beaumont, Burgh-by-Sands, Boustead Hill, Drumburgh, Glasson & Port Carlisle, Mon-Sat 4-5/day plus 2/day Fri & Sat
94   Brampton to Carlisle via Crosby-on-Eden, Mon, Tue & Thur 2/day (1/day via Laversdale), Wed & Fri 1/day
97   Brampton to Carlisle via Walton & Laversdale, Wed & Fri 1/day
685   (jointly operated with Arriva North East, see above)

Tyne Valley Coaches (🖳 www.tynevalleycoaches.co.uk)
880   Hexham to Bellingham via Acomb, Wall (village), Humshaugh & Wark, Mon-Sat 3/day, excluding the 1/day termtime school service Hexham to Humshaugh, plus Hexham bus/rail stations to Acomb 5/day

Wright Brothers' Coaches (tel 01434-381200, 🖳 www.wrightscoaches.co.uk)
680   Carlisle to Nenthead via Brampton & Alston, Mon-Sat 2/day plus Mon-Fri termtime 1/day (see also Telford's)
888   Newcastle to Keswick via Corbridge, Hexham, Alston & Penrith, July to end Sep daily 1/day

Rail services
Hadrian's Wall Country Line (🖳 www.northernrail.org)
● Newcastle to Carlisle via Hexham and Haltwhistle, daily 1-2/hr, 6-7/day stop at Brampton, Sunday services also call at Wylam & Corbridge
● Newcastle to Hexham via Wylam & Corbridge, Mon-Sat approx 1/hr

THE ENVIRONMENT & NATURE

Flora and fauna

Northumberland and Cumbria are England's two 'wildest' counties so, as you would probably expect, much of the nation's native flora and fauna is more abundant here than elsewhere. Furthermore, given the variety of habitats that you pass through on the trail, from woodland and grassland to heathland, moor and bog, the variety of flora and fauna present is also commensurately greater.

The following is not in any way a comprehensive guide – if it were, you would not have room for anything else in your rucksack – but merely a brief run-down of the more commonly seen flora and fauna on the trail, together with some of the rarer and more spectacular species.

MAMMALS

One of the great attractions of walking any long-distance trail in Britain is the opportunity it affords of seeing a native animal in its natural environment, and the Hadrian's Wall trail is no different. That said, spotting the wildlife is another matter. Many of Britain's native species are nocturnal and those which aren't are often very shy and seldom encountered. Then of course there are those – the otter, for example, or the water vole – that are few in number anyway, and sightings are always very rare.

Nevertheless, with a bit of luck and patience, on the quieter parts of the trail you may well be rewarded with a sighting or two of something fluffy. One creature that you will definitely see along the walk is the **rabbit** (*Oryctolagus cuniculus*). Timid by nature, most of the time you'll have to make do with nothing more than a brief and distant glimpse of their white tails as they race for the nearest warren at the sound of your footfall. Because they are so numerous, however, the laws of probability dictate that you will at some stage during your walk get close enough to observe them without being spotted; trying to take a decent photo of one of them, however, is a different matter.

Incidentally, rabbits and Romans have a shared history as the Romans brought rabbits with them to use as the main ingredient in gourmet dishes. And now, 2000 years later, the descendants of those first rabbits are said to be one of the main threats to the Wall, their burrows destroying its foundations from below ground just as the boots of trekkers damage them from above. The situation is said to be so serious, some scientists are calling for a reintroduction of myxomatosis, the disease that wiped out 99% of the rabbit population in the 1950s. If you're lucky you may also come across **hares** (*Lepus europaeus*), often mistaken for rabbits but much larger, more elongated and with longer ears and back legs.

Northumberland and Cumbria play host to a number of creatures that are found in few other places in England. In particular, there's the **red squirrel** (*Sciurus vulgaris*); one time I was at the Wall there was one hanging around the trees near Birdoswald Fort. Elsewhere in the country this small, tufty-eared native has been usurped by its larger cousin from North America, the **grey squirrel** (*Sciurus carolinensis*), but in the north of England and Scotland the red squirrel maintains a precarious foothold. Fears for their survival on these shores have prompted the establishment of Red Alert, a charity aimed at protecting the species. For more information see ⌨ www.rsst.org.uk.

Two other creatures that are subject to long-term protection programmes are the otter and the water vole. Previously persecuted because it was (wrongly) believed to have an enormously detrimental effect on fish stocks – indeed, it was hunted with dogs up until 1977 – the **otter** (*Lutra lutra*) is enjoying something of a renaissance thanks to some concerted conservation efforts. At home both in saltwater and freshwater, they are a good indicator of a healthy unpolluted environment and are said to be well established on the banks of the North Tyne in Northumberland National Park.

As for the **water vole** (scientifically known as *Arvicola terrestris*, but better known as 'Ratty' from Kenneth Grahame's classic children's story *Wind in the Willows)*, this is another creature, like the red squirrel, that's fallen foul of an alien invader, in this case the **mink** (*Mustela vison)* from North America which has successfully adapted to the British countryside after escaping from local fur farms. Unfortunately, the mink not only hunts water voles but is small enough to slip inside their burrows.

Thus, with the voles afforded no protection, the mink is able to wipe out an entire riverbank's population in a matter of months. Incidentally, this is another reason why protecting the otter is important: they kill mink.

Other creatures you might see include the ubiquitous **fox** (*Vulpes vulpes*), now just as at home in the city as it is in the country. While usually considered nocturnal, it's not unusual to encounter a fox during the day too, usually lounging in the sun near its den.

Another creature of the night that you may *occasionally* see in the late afternoon is the **badger** (*Meles meles*). Relatively common throughout the British Isles, these sociable mammals with their distinctive black-and-white striped muzzles live in large underground burrows called setts, appearing around sunset to root for worms and slugs.

One creature that is strictly nocturnal, however, is the **bat**, of which there are 17 species in Britain, all protected by law. Your best chance of spotting one is at dusk while there's still enough light in the sky to make out their flitting forms as they fly along hedgerows, over rivers and streams and around street lamps in their quest for moths and insects. The commonest species in Britain is the **pipistrelle** (*Pipistrellus pipistrellus*).

In addition to the above, keep a look out for other fairly common but little seen species such as the carnivorous **stoat** (*Mustela erminea*), its diminutive cousin the **weasel** (*Mustela nivalis*), the **hedgehog** (*Erinaceus europaeus*) – these days, alas, most commonly seen as roadkill – and any number of species of **voles**, **mice** and **shrews**.

Finally, a surprisingly large number of trekkers encounter deer on their walk. Mostly this will be the **roe deer** (*Capreolus capreolus*), a small native woodland species, though it can also be seen grazing in fields. As with most creatures, your best chance of seeing one is very early in the morning, particularly in Northumberland National Park: there are said to be 6000 in Kielder Forest alone! Britain's largest native land mammal, the **red deer** (*Cervus elaphus*), is rarely seen on the walk though it does exist in small pockets in Cumbria.

REPTILES AND FISH

The **adder** (*Vipera berus*) is the only common snake in the north of England, and the only poisonous one of the three species in Britain. They pose very little risk to walkers – indeed, you should consider yourself extremely fortunate to see one, providing you're a safe distance away. They bite only when provoked, preferring to hide instead. The venom is designed to kill small mammals such as mice, voles and shrews, so deaths in humans are very rare but a bite can be extremely unpleasant and occasionally dangerous to children or the elderly. You are most likely to encounter them in spring when they come out of hibernation and during the summer when pregnant females warm themselves in the sun. They are easily identified by the striking zigzag pattern on their back. Should you be lucky enough to encounter one, enjoy it but leave it undisturbed.

Salmon (*Salmo salar*) thrive in the clean waters of Northumberland National Park.

BIRDS

The woods, moorland and hedgerows along the Hadrian's Wall trail provide homes for a wealth of different species.

While Northumberland is famed for its birdlife, in order to appreciate its richness it's often necessary to leave the trail, either by heading to one of the offshore islands or visiting the forest at Kielder. The former is one of the best birdwatching venues in Britain and the latter's not bad either, though in Kielder it's fair to say that often you can't see the birds for the trees. Nevertheless, the area is particularly rich in raptors, including **sparrowhawks** (*Accipiter nisus*), **goshawks** (*Accipiter gentilis*), **merlins** (*Falco columbarius*), **peregrines** (*Falco peregrinus*) and **kestrels** (*Falco tinnunculus*).

At the northern end of Kielder Water, Bakethin Reservoir has been declared a nature reserve and attracts **ospreys** as well as more common residents including wildfowl and gulls. The conifer forests at Kielder play host to the **crossbill** (*Loxia curvirostra*), while the deciduous, lower areas of the North Tyne Valley are popular with the **pied flycatcher** (*Ficedula hypoleuca*) and **redstart** (*Phoenicurus phoenicurus*).

Occasionally, some of these species may be glimpsed on the trail but in the main it's the usual 'garden' species that dominate: the **great tit** (*Parus major*), **coal tit** (*Parus ater*), **blue tit** (*Parus caeruleus*), **blackbird** (*Turdus merula*), **mistle thrush** (*Turdus philomelos*) and **robin** (*Erithacus rubecula*).

As for Cumbria, the AONB (Area of Outstanding Natural Beauty) along the Solway Firth at the western end of the trail is renowned as a haven for birdlife. The most famous, or at least the most voluble, inhabitant is the **barnacle goose** (*Branta leucopsis*). The goose is actually only a winter visitor, as it flees its nesting sites on the cliffs of Svalbard, Norway, to enjoy Cumbria's milder climate. Up to 30,000 of the birds arrive in November, heading back to Norway in mid-April.

LAPWING/PEEWIT
L: 320MM/12.5"

Other species you might encounter on this shoreline include **ducks**, **swans**, **ringed plovers** (*Charadrius hiaticula*), **oystercatchers** (*Haematopus ostralegus*) and **lapwings** (*Vanellus vanellus*). The latter is black and white with iridescent green upper parts and is approximately the size of a pigeon or tern. Its most distinctive characteristic, however, is the male's tumbling, diving, swooping flight pattern when disturbed, believed to be either a display to attract a female or an attempt to distract predators from its nest, which is built on the ground. Common in Solway, you can also find them on the moors in Northumberland.

One of the most common birds seen on the path is the **pheasant** (*Phasianus colchicus*). The male is distinctive thanks to his beautiful long, barred tail feathers, brown body and glossy green-black head with red flashes, while the female is a dull brown. Another way to distinguish them is by the distinctive strangulated hacking sound they make together with the loud beating of wings as they fly off. Another moorland favourite is the rare **black grouse** (*Tetrao tetrix*). Feeding on cotton grass and tree shoots, in spring they gather together in 'leks' – display grounds

BLACK GROUSE
L: 580MM/23"

THE ENVIRONMENT AND NATURE

– where the males conduct a spectacular courtship display. Its much commoner relative, the **red grouse** (*Lagopus lagopus scoticus*), is one of the few birds that stays on the moors year-round.

Less common but still seen by most trekkers is the **curlew** (*Numenius arquata*). The largest of the British wading birds, it's the emblem of Northumberland National Park and lives on the moors there throughout spring and summer, returning to the coast in autumn.

With feathers uniformly streaked grey and brown, the easiest way to identify this bird is by its thin elongated, downward curving beak.

CURLEW
L: 600MM/24"

Other birds that make their nest on open moorland and in fields include the **redshank** (*Tringa totanus*), **golden plover** (*Pluvialis apricaria*), **snipe** (*Gallinago gallinago*), **dunlin** (*Calidris alpina*) and **ring ouzel** (*Turdus torquatus*).

TREES

In the main, the Wall passes through bleak moorland bereft of any plantlife that can rise higher than the carpet of heather, though there are patches of woods and forest along the way, particularly in the Northumberland National Park and towards the western end of the trail in Cumbria.

Indeed, woodland in Cumbria is estimated to cover a surprisingly large 65,000 hectares, or 9.5% of the land in the county, though a storm at the beginning of 2005 which blew down 500,000 trees probably reduced these figures. Even more surprising, Cumbria's woodland cover has actually *increased* over the past two decades. Conifer woodland makes up the majority, though there's also a fair bit of broadleaf woodland. Popular species include willow, oak, beech and maple.

The most interesting of these is the **oak** (family name *Quercus*), which supports more kinds of insects than any other tree in Britain. Some of these insects affect the oak in interesting ways: the eggs of the gall-fly, for example, cause growths on the leaves, known, appropriately enough, as galls. Each of these growths contains a single insect.

Oak woodland is a diverse habitat and not exclusively made up of oak. Other trees that flourish here include **downy birch** (*Betula pubescens*), its relative the **silver birch** (*Betula pendula*), **holly** (*Ilex aquifolium*) and **hazel** (*Corylus avellana*) which has traditionally been used for coppicing (the periodic cutting of small trees for harvesting).

Further east, there are some examples of limestone woodland. **Ash** (*Fraxinus excelsior*) and oak dominate, along with **wych elm** (*Ulmus glabra*),

THE ENVIRONMENT AND NATURE

sycamore (*Acer pseudoplatanus*) and **yew** (*Taxus baccata*). The **hawthorn** (*Crataegus monogyna*) also grows along the path, usually in isolated pockets on pasture. These species are known as pioneer species and play a vital role in the ecosystem by improving the soil. It is these pioneers – the hawthorn and its companion the **rowan** (*Sorbus aucuparia*) – that you will see growing alone on inaccessible crags and ravines. Without interference from man, these pioneers would eventually be succeeded by longer-lived species such as the oak.

In wet, marshy areas and along rivers and streams you are more likely to find **alder** (*Alnus glutinosa*). Finally, in the Northumberland National Park there are a few examples of the **juniper** tree (*Juniperus communis*), one of only three native British species of conifer, the blue berries of which are used to flavour gin.

FLOWERS

Spring is the time to come and see the spectacular displays of colour on the Hadrian's Wall Path, when most of the flowers are in bloom. Alternatively, arrive in August and you'll see the heathers carpeting patches of the moors in a blaze of purple flowers.

Woodland and hedgerows

From March to May **bluebells** (*Hyacinthoides non-scripta*) proliferate in some of the woods along the trail, providing a wonderful spectacle. The white **wood anemone** (*Anemone nemorosa*) – wide open flowers when sunny, closed and drooping when the weather's dull – and the yellow **primrose** (*Primula vulgaris*) also flower early in spring. **Red campion** (*Silene dioica*), which flowers from late April, can be found in hedgebanks along with **rosebay willowherb** (*Epilobium augustifolium*) which also has the name fireweed due to its habit of colonising burnt areas.

In scrubland and on woodland edges you will find **bramble** (*Rubus fruticosus*), a common vigorous shrub responsible for many a ripped jacket thanks to the sharp thorns and prickles. **Blackberry** fruits ripen from late summer to autumn. Fairly common in scrubland and on woodland edges is the **dog rose** (*Rosa canina*) which has a large pink flower, the fruits of which are used to make rose-hip syrup.

Look out, too, on the water in streams or rivers for the white-flowered **water crow-foot** (*Ranunculus penicillatus pseudofluitans*) which, because it needs unpolluted, flowing water, is a good indicator of the cleanliness of the stream.

Other flowering plants to look for in wooded areas and in hedgerows include the tall **foxglove** (*Digitalis purpurea*) with its trumpet-like flowers, **forget-me-not** (*Myosotis arvensis*) with tiny, delicate blue flowers, and **cow parsley** (*Anthriscus sylvestris*), a tall member of the carrot family with a large globe of white flowers which often covers roadside verges and hedgebanks.

Heathland and scrubland

There are three species of heather. The most dominant is **ling** (*Calluna vulgaris*) with tiny flowers on delicate upright stems. The other two species are **bell**

Rosebay Willowherb
Epilobium angustifolium

Spear Thistle
Cirsium vulgare

Forget-me-not
Myosotis arvensis

Rowan (tree)
Sorbus aucuparia

Herb-Robert
Geranium robertianum

Red Campion
Silene dioica

Early Purple Orchid
Orchis mascula

Common Knapweed
Centaurea nigra

Foxglove
Digitalis purpurea

Hemp-nettle
Galeopsis speciosa

Hogweed
Heracleum sphondylium

Yarrow
Achillea millefolium

Dog Rose
Rosa canina

Common Hawthorn
Crataegus monogyna

Honeysuckle
Lonicera periclymemum

Ramsons (Wild Garlic)
Allium ursinum

Silverweed
Potentilla anserina

Bluebell
Hyacinthoides non-scripta

Gorse
Ulex europaeus

Meadow Buttercup
Ranunculis acris

Marsh Marigold (Kingcup)
Caltha palustris

Tormentil
Potentilla erecta

Birdsfoot-trefoil
Lotus corniculatus

Ox-eye Daisy
Leucanthemum vulgare

Common Ragwort
Senecio jacobaea

Primrose
Primula vulgaris

Cowslip
Primula veris

Common Dog Violet
Viola riviniana

Heartsease (Wild Pansy)
Viola tricolor

Meadow Cranesbill
Geranium pratense

Self-heal
Prunella vulgaris

Germander Speedwell
Veronica chamaedrys

Common Fumitory
Fumaria officinalis

Lousewort
Pedicularis sylvatica

Water Avens
Geum rivale

Scarlet Pimpernel
Anagallis arvensis

Bell Heather
Erica cinerea

Heather (Ling)
Calluna vulgaris

Common Vetch
Vicia sativa

heather (*Erica cinera*) with deep purple bell-shaped flowers and **cross-leaved heath** (*Erica tetralix*) with similarly shaped flowers of a lighter pink, almost white colour. Cross-leaved heath prefers wet and boggy ground. As a result, it usually grows away from bell heather which prefers well-drained soils.

Heather is an incredibly versatile plant which is put to many uses. It provides fodder for livestock, fuel for fires, an orange dye and material for bedding, thatching, basketwork and brooms. It is still sometimes used in place of hops to flavour beer and the flower heads can be brewed to make good tea; it is also used in the production of some varieties of honey. It is also incredibly hardy and thrives on the denuded hills, preventing other species from flourishing. Indeed, at times highland cattle are brought to certain areas of the moors to graze on the heather, allowing other species a chance to grow.

Not a flower but worthy of mention is the less attractive species **bracken** (*Pteridium aquilinum*), a vigorous non-native fern that has invaded many heathland areas to the detriment of native species.

Grassland

There is much overlap between the hedge/woodland-edge habitat and that of pastures and meadows. You will come across **common birdsfoot-trefoil** (*Lotus corniculatus*), **Germander speedwell** (*Veronica chamaedrys*), **tufted** and **bush vetch** (*Vicia cracca* and *V. sepium*) and **meadow vetchling** (*Lathyrus pratensis*) in both. Often the only species you will see in heavily grazed pastures are the most resilient.

Of the thistles, in late summer you should come across the **melancholy thistle** (*Cirsium helenoides*) drooping sadly on roadside verges and hay meadows. Unusually, it has no prickles on its stem.

The **yellow rattle** is aptly named, for the dry seedpods rattle in the wind, a good indication for farmers that it is time to harvest the hay.

Other widespread grassland species include **harebell** (*Campanula rotundifolia*), delicate yellow **tormentil** (*Potentilla erecta*), which often spreads onto the lower slopes of mountains along with **devil's-bit scabious** (*Succisa pratensis*). Also keep an eye out for orchids such as the **fragrant orchid** (*Gymnaadenia conopsea*) and **early purple orchid** (*Orchis mascula*).

Conservation

GOVERNMENT AGENCIES AND SCHEMES

Natural England

Natural England (🖥 www.naturalengland.org.uk) is the single body responsible for identifying, establishing and managing: National Parks, Areas of Outstanding Natural Beauty, National Nature Reserves and Sites of Special Scientific Interest.

THE ENVIRONMENT AND NATURE

The highest level of landscape protection is the designation of land as a **national park** which recognises the national importance of an area in terms of landscape, biodiversity and as a recreational resource. At the time of writing there were 15 national parks in Britain. The Hadrian's Wall Path passes through one: the 1049 sq km Northumberland National Park (🖥 www.northumberland nationalpark.org.uk), England's remotest national park, and an area that contains some of the best-preserved parts of the Wall.

The second level of protection is **Area of Outstanding Natural Beauty** (AONB), of which there are 38 in England covering some 18% of England and Wales. The only AONB on the trail is the exquisite Solway Coast (🖥 www.sol waycoastaonb.org.uk), west of Carlisle, though the trail also brushes the northern edge of the North Pennines AONB (🖥 www.northpennines.org.uk), which begins just to the south of the road running between Brampton and Hexham. Their primary objective is conservation of the natural beauty of a landscape.

Other levels of protection include: **National Nature Reserves** (NNR), of which there are 224 in England, including Greenlee Lough, north of Housesteads in Northumberland National Park, and **Sites of Special Scientific Interest** (SSSI). These range in size from little pockets protecting wild flower meadows, important nesting sites or special geological features, to vast swathes of upland, moorland and wetland. On the trail, the estuary which forms part of the AONB at Solway is an SSSI – one of over 4000 in England.

THE ENVIRONMENT AND NATURE

❏ **Campaigning and conservation organisations**

These voluntary organisations started the conservation movement in the mid-19th century and are still at the forefront of developments. Independent of government but reliant on public support, they can concentrate their resources either on acquiring land which can then be managed purely for conservation purposes, or on influencing political decision-makers by lobbying and campaigning.

● **English Heritage** (🖥 www.english-heritage.org.uk) Organisation whose central aim is to make sure that the historic environment of England is properly maintained. It is officially known as the Historic Buildings and Monuments Commission for England and is responsible for nearly all the Roman forts along the Wall that are open to the public.

● **National Trust** (NT; 🖥 www.nationaltrust.org.uk) A charity with 3.7 million members which aims to protect, through ownership, threatened coastline, countryside, historic houses, castles and gardens, and archaeological remains for everybody to enjoy. In particular the NT cares for over 700 miles of British coastline, 255,000 hectares of countryside and 350 historic buildings, monuments, parks, gardens and reserves, including George Stephenson's birthplace in Wylam, Northumberland, Housesteads, and six miles of the Wall itself!

● The umbrella organisation for the 47 wildlife trusts in the UK is **The Wildlife Trusts** (🖥 www.wildlifetrusts.org). Two relevant to the Hadrian's Wall path are **Cumbria Wildlife Trust** (🖥 www.cumbriawildlifetrust.org.uk) and **Northumberland Wildlife Trust** (🖥 www.nwt.org.uk).

● **Royal Society for the Protection of Birds** (RSPB; 🖥 www.rspb.org.uk) The largest voluntary conservation body in Europe focusing on providing a healthy environment for birds and wildlife and with 2 reserves in the UK and over a million members.

MINIMUM IMPACT & OUTDOOR SAFETY

Minimum impact walking

In April 2005 Britain was given a rude awakening by UNESCO, when it threatened to have Hadrian's Wall placed on their 'in danger' list of World Heritage sites. The warning was something of a national embarrassment, for at the time there were only 29 out of the total 600 World Heritage sites on this list and only one in the so-called 'developed world' (Cologne Cathedral in Germany).

Thankfully, the threat seems to have abated somewhat since 2005; the Wall (which is now entered as part of the 'Frontiers of the Roman Empire' which also covers the Antonine Wall) is still not on the 'in danger' list, which now includes 34 properties out of a total of 911).

UNESCO's concern arose largely because of the huge and sudden influx of walkers trekking alongside the Wall. The thousands of people who have trekked along the National Trail since it opened (23 May 2003) have left their mark on the area, eroding the land and endangering the archaeological sites that are as yet unexcavated (and the majority of the Wall and its fortifications remain unexcavated). The soil in this part of the world is particularly thin and the climate rather damp. Combine this with thousands of pairs of boots and you have the recipe for some serious erosion. Vegetation is trampled, exposing not just the soil but also, over time, archaeological deposits.

Nor is the Wall itself exempt from the depredations of walkers: in 2004, a team of 800 Dutch bankers walked *on* the Wall between Steel Rigg and Housesteads as part of a team-building exercise, sparking fury amongst conservationists and historians alike. To be fair to the bankers, they have returned since and abided much more closely to the Hadrian's Wall Code of Respect – see box pp68-9 – splitting their group up into more manageable sizes and keeping off the Wall itself!

The controversy is only exacerbated by the fact that there was so much opposition to the creation of the path in the first place, particularly amongst historians worried about protecting the Wall. Their fears were allayed only when they received assurances that the Wall and its earthworks would be protected; unfortunately, the resources just haven't been available to protect it properly.

Though some may blame the authorities for the current crisis, accusing them of inadequate preparation and provision, this doesn't mean we as trekkers can't do our bit as well. The Hadrian's Wall Code of Respect, known as **Every Footprint Counts**, helps visitors minimise their impact on the trail. But the preservation of the Wall, while of overriding importance, should not be the only concern of walkers. The whole area is affected, economically, socially and culturally, by the arrival of walkers. By following a few simple guidelines while walking the trail, you can minimise your impact on it and have a positive effect on the local communities and the environment hereabouts.

ECONOMIC IMPACT

Rural businesses and communities in Britain have been hit hard in recent years by a seemingly endless series of crises. Most people are aware of the country code; not dropping litter and closing the gate behind you are still as pertinent as ever. But in light of the economic pressures that local countryside businesses are under, there is something else you can do: buy local.

Support local businesses
Look and ask for local produce to buy and eat; not only does this cut down on the amount of pollution and congestion that the transportation of food creates

---

☐ **Caring for the Wall – the Hadrian's Wall Code of Respect**

Overriding all other concerns about caring for the natural environment is the need to protect the Wall itself, and all the forts, milecastles, turrets, earthworks and ditches that go to make up the Roman defences – whether excavated or still buried beneath the soil. With these considerations uppermost, the following code – known as **Every Footstep Counts** – has been formulated and endorsed by government agencies, English Heritage, the National Trust, local authorities, farmers, conservation and user groups concerned with the Wall.

● **Don't climb or walk on the Wall** Apart from the short stretch immediately west of Housesteads, which for some reason the relevant authorities have given permission for you to walk upon, please don't walk on the Wall or climb it for a better view, no matter how tempting.

● If walking only part of the trail, **consider following a circular route** or setting off from a place other than the usual starting points. This will limit the general wear and tear.

● **Don't walk the Wall in winter** The ground (and the unexcavated archaeological sites still buried within it) is more fragile and liable to damage then. Again, consider a nearby circular walk or visit one of the off-Wall Roman sites instead, such as Corbridge or Vindolanda. This is why the passport scheme runs only from May to October.

● Visit the Roman forts along the way, which will help to relieve the pressure suffered by the Wall itself.

● Stay and eat locally and use local services when visiting the Wall; that way the local economy will benefit from your visit.

● Keep to waymarked and signposted paths and trails only.

● Keep dogs under close control and on a leash when walking through fields with sheep; on National Trust land this is compulsory.

(the so-called 'food miles'), but also ensures that you are supporting local farmers and producers; the very people who have moulded the countryside you have come to see and who are in the best position to protect it. If you can find local food which is also organic so much the better.

It's a fact of life that money spent at local level – perhaps in a market, or at the greengrocer, or in an independent pub – has a far greater impact for good on that community than the equivalent spent in a branch of a national chain store or restaurant. While no-one would advocate that walkers should boycott the larger supermarkets, which after all do provide local employment, it's worth remembering that businesses in rural communities rely heavily on visitors for their very existence. If we want to keep these shops and post offices, we need to use them.

ENVIRONMENTAL IMPACT

A walking holiday in itself is an environmentally friendly approach to tourism. The following are some ideas on how you can go a few steps further in helping to minimise your impact on the environment while walking the Hadrian's Wall Path.

Use public transport whenever possible
Public transport along the Wall is not bad (though it can be infrequent), with most places served by at least one bus or train a day. Public transport is

---

- Never light fires, and take litter away with you.
- Use public rather than private transport whenever you can, particularly the Hadrian's Wall Country bus.
- Leave all farm gates as you find them.

In addition to the above rules, there are some other important guidelines that need to be followed to minimise the damage trekkers do to the archaeological deposits.

- Camping is allowed only on official sites. Don't 'wild camp' near the Wall.
- If the path resembles a worn line in the grass, walk alongside it to avoid exacerbating the erosion. In other words, **keep on the grass**! This is one of the most important rules – and also one of the most unusual, for on most trails you are usually told to stick to the path to prevent widening of the trail and the spreading of erosion. However, Hadrian's Wall is, of course, not your usual path and the authorities' main concern is not to preserve the state of the path but to protect the as-yet unexcavated archaeological treasures that lie beneath. This is why the path is a green sward, as it was felt that this was one of the best surfaces to protect the unexcavated treasures. But if that protective layer is eroded away, those treasures are put in danger. So avoid walking on a worn or eroded part of the trail and **walk side by side, not in single file**.
- Similarly, don't walk on any nearby ridge or hillock. Just as the trail cuts a delicate path through the Wall's numerous unexcavated mounds so you should avoid treading on any raised ground.
- If you find anything that might conceivably be of historical or archaeological interest on the trail, report your find(s) to a Wall guardian, trail officer or possibly a nearby museum. Do not, whatever you do, keep the find for yourself as a keepsake.
- Do not chip off a bit of stone or other matter from the Wall as a souvenir.

MINIMUM IMPACT & OUTDOOR SAFETY

preferable to using private cars as it benefits everyone: visitors, locals and the environment.

Never leave litter

Leaving litter shows a total disrespect for the natural world and others coming after you. As well as being unsightly, litter kills wildlife, pollutes the environment and can be dangerous to farm animals. Please carry a degradable plastic bag so you can dispose of your rubbish in a bin in the next village. It would be very helpful if you could pick up litter left by other people too.

● **Is it OK if it's biodegradable?** Not really. Apple cores, banana skins, orange peel and the like are unsightly, encourage flies, ants and wasps and ruin a picnic spot for others. Using the excuse that they are natural and biodegradable just doesn't cut any ice. When was the last time you saw a banana tree in England?

● **The lasting impact of litter** A piece of orange peel left on the ground takes six months to decompose; silver foil 18 months; a plastic bag 10 years; clothes 15 years; and an aluminium can 85 years.

Respect all wildlife

Care for all wildlife you come across along the path; it has as much right to be there as you. As tempting as it may be to pick wild flowers, leave them in place so the next people who pass can enjoy them too. Don't break branches off or damage trees in any way. If you come across wildlife, keep your distance and don't watch for too long. Your presence can cause considerable stress, particularly if the adults are with young, or in winter when the weather is harsh and food is scarce. Young animals are rarely abandoned. If you come across young birds, keep away so that their mother can return.

Outdoor toiletry

Public toilets are marked on the trail maps in this guide and you will also find facilities in pubs, cafés and campsites along the trail. A call at the end of 2004 for more toilets along the trail has been heeded with the introduction of the Hadrian's Wall Tent Project, which offers up to 50 per cent funding to farm and tourist businesses which provide toilets, campsites and other facilities. As a result, there shouldn't be any need to 'go' outdoors.

This last point is very important. Normally, when caught short outdoors and with no public facilities nearby, considerate trekkers would dig a small hole in the ground in which to bury your excrement. However, as previously mentioned many of Hadrian's Wall's treasures are as yet unexcavated. For this reason, **it is forbidden to dig anywhere near the Wall**! And this point cannot be emphasised enough.

● **Toilet paper**, **tampons and sanitary towels** These take a long time to decompose, whether buried or not, and are easily dug up by animals and may then blow into water sources or onto the path. The best method for dealing with any of these is to **pack it out**. Put the used item inside a paper bag which you then place inside a plastic bag (or two if you're worried about ruptures). Then simply empty the contents of the paper bag at the next toilet you come across and throw the bag away.

Wild camping
Wild camping is not allowed along the Wall, and with the increasing number of campsites serving the trail, there's no need to either.

ACCESS

Britain is a crowded cluster of islands with few places where you can wander as you please. Most of the land is a patchwork of fields and agriculture and the environment through which the Hadrian's Wall Path marches is no different. However, there are countless public rights of way, in addition to the main trail, that criss-cross the land.

This is fine, but what happens if you feel a little more adventurous and want to explore the moorland, woodland and hills that can also be found near the walk.

Right to roam
The Countryside & Rights of Way Act 2000 (CRoW), or 'Right (or Freedom) to Roam' as dubbed by walkers, came into effect in full on 31 October 2005 after a long campaign to allow greater public access to areas of countryside in England and Wales deemed to be uncultivated open country. This essentially means moorland, heathland, downland and upland areas. Some land is covered by restrictions (ie high-impact activities such as driving a vehicle, cycling and horse-riding are not permitted) and some land is excluded, such as gardens, parks and cultivated land. Full details are given on the Countryside visitors page of the Natural England website (💻 www.naturalengland.org.uk).

With more freedom in the countryside comes a need for more responsibility from the walker. Remember that wild open country is still the workplace of farmers and home to all sorts of wildlife. Have respect for both and avoid disturbing domestic and wild animals.

The Countryside Code
The countryside is a fragile place which every visitor should respect. The Countryside Code (see box) was revised in part because of the changes brought about by the CRoW Act (see above). While it is just common sense, do make sure you are aware of the code – and adhere to it.

> ❏ **The Countryside Code**
> ● Be safe – plan ahead and follow any signs
> ● Leave gates and property as you find them
> ● Protect plants and animals, and take your litter home
> ● Keep dogs under close control
> ● Consider other people

Other points to consider on the Hadrian's Wall Path
● **Keep to paths across farmland** Stick to the official path across arable or pasture land, though do bear in mind the Hadrian's Wall Code of Respect (see box pp68-9).
● **Use gates and stiles to cross fences**, **hedges and walls** The path is well supplied with stiles where it crosses field boundaries. On some of the side trips you may find the paths less accommodating. If you have to climb over a gate because you can't open it always do so at the hinged end.

MINIMUM IMPACT & OUTDOOR SAFETY

● **Walk side by side and on healthy grass** In other words don't walk in single file and don't walk on worn areas.

● **Help keep all water clean** Leaving litter and going to the toilet near a water source can pollute people's water supplies.

● **Take special care on country roads** Drivers often go dangerously fast on narrow winding lanes. To be safe, walk facing the oncoming traffic and carry a torch or wear highly visible clothing when it's getting dark.

● **Protect wildlife, plants and trees** Care for and respect all wildlife you come across. Don't pick plants, break tree branches or scare wild animals. If you come across young birds that appear to have been abandoned leave them alone.

● **Make no unnecessary noise** Enjoy the peace and solitude of the outdoors by staying in small groups and acting unobtrusively.

Outdoor safety

AVOIDANCE OF HAZARDS

Though the Hadrian's Wall Path passes through some pretty wild countryside, the good waymarkings, proximity of the B6318 (the so-called Military Road) and the A69 highways to the south and the lack of any major highlands, fells or mountains mean that it is unlikely you're going to get lost or come to grief on the trail. Indeed, perhaps the biggest threat to your life is provided by the roads which cut across the path, particularly on the section between Heddon-on-the-Wall and Chollerford.

That said, there are a number of hazards that beset trekkers on even the easiest trails. But with good planning and preparation these can be avoided. This information is just as important for those out on a day walk as for those walking the entire Hadrian's Wall. In addition to the points listed below, always make sure you have suitable **clothes** (see p47) to keep you warm and dry whatever the conditions and a spare change of inner clothes. Carrying plenty of **food and water** is vital too. A **compass**, **whistle**, **torch**, **map** and **first-aid kit** should be carried; see p48. The **emergency signal** is six blasts on the whistle or six flashes with a torch.

Safety on the Hadrian's Wall Path

Sadly every year people are injured walking along the trail, though usually it's nothing more than a badly twisted ankle. The most dangerous section is from Sewingshields to Walltown, where the unpredictable weather leads trekkers to their doom – though with a road never far away, there's nothing too serious to worry about. Abiding by the following rules, however, should minimise the risks:

● Avoid walking on your own if possible.

● Make sure that somebody knows your plans for every day you are on the trail. This could be a friend or relative whom you have promised to call every night or the B&B or hostel you plan to stay in at the end of each day's walk. That way, if you fail to turn up or call, they can raise the alarm.

● If the weather closes in suddenly and fog or mist descends while you are on the trail, particularly on the moors or fells, and you become uncertain of the correct trail, do not be tempted to continue. Just wait where you are and you'll find that mist often clears, at least for long enough to allow you to get your bearings. If you are still uncertain and the weather does not look like improving, return the way you came to the nearest point of civilisation and try again another time when conditions have improved.

● Always fill your water bottle or pouch at every available opportunity and ensure you have some food such as high-energy snacks.

● Always carry a torch, compass, map, whistle and wet-weather gear with you.

● Wear strong sturdy boots with good ankle support and a good grip, not trainers.

● Be extra vigilant with children.

Dealing with an accident

● Use basic first aid to treat the injury to the best of your ability.

● Work out exactly where you are. If possible leave someone with the casualty while others go to get help. If there are only two people, you have a dilemma. If you decide to get help, leave all spare clothing and food with the casualty.

● In an emergency dial ☎ 999 or ☎ 112.

The route is well signposted: you shouldn't get lost

WEATHER FORECASTS

The trail suffers from extremes of weather so it's vital that you always try to find out what the weather is going to be like before you set off for the day. Many hostels and tourist information centres will have pinned up somewhere a summary of the weather forecast. You can get an online forecast through 🖥 www .bbc.co.uk/weather/ukweather or 🖥 www.metoffice.gov.uk. Alternatively you can get a telephone forecast through **Weather Call** (☎ 09068-500418 for Northumberland, Tyne & Wear and ☎ 09068-500419 for Cumbria, 🖥 www .weathercall.co.uk); these are frequently updated and generally reliable but calls are charged at the very expensive premium rate. To save money, when prompted enter 1809 for Newcastle and 1902 for Carlisle and you will be taken to the relevant forecast. Pay close attention to it and alter your plans for the day accordingly. That said, even if the forecast is for a fine sunny day, always assume the worst and pack some wet-weather gear.

BLISTERS

It is important to break in new boots before embarking on a long trek. Make sure the boots are comfortable and try to avoid getting them wet on the inside. Air

MINIMUM IMPACT & OUTDOOR SAFETY

your feet at lunchtime, keep them clean and change your socks regularly. If you feel any hot spots, stop immediately and apply a few strips of zinc oxide tape and leave on until it is pain free or the tape starts to come off.

If you have left it too late and a blister has developed you should surround it with 'moleskin' or any other blister kit to protect it from abrasion. Popping it can lead to infection. If the skin is broken keep the area clean with antiseptic and cover with a non-adhesive dressing material held in place with tape.

HYPOTHERMIA, HYPERTHERMIA & SUNBURN

Also known as exposure, **hypothermia** occurs when the body can't generate enough heat to maintain its normal temperature, usually as a result of being wet, cold, unprotected from the wind, tired and hungry. It is usually more of a problem in upland areas such as on the moors. Hypothermia is easily avoided by wearing suitable clothing, carrying and eating enough food and drink, being aware of the weather conditions and checking the morale of your companions.

Early signs to watch for are feeling cold and tired with involuntary shivering. Find some shelter as soon as possible and warm the victim up with a hot drink and some chocolate or other high-energy food. If possible give them another warm layer of clothing and allow them to rest until feeling better.

If allowed to worsen, strange behaviour, slurring of speech and poor coordination will become apparent and the victim can quickly progress into unconsciousness, followed by coma and death. Quickly get the victim out of any wind and rain, improvising a shelter if necessary. Rapid restoration of bodily warmth is essential and best achieved by bare-skin contact: someone should get into the same sleeping bag as the patient, both having stripped to their underwear, putting any spare clothing under or over them to build up heat. Send urgently for help.

Hyperthermia occurs when the body generates too much heat, eg heat exhaustion and heatstroke. Not ailments that you would normally associate with the north of England, these are serious problems nonetheless.

Symptoms of **heat exhaustion** include thirst, fatigue, giddiness, a rapid pulse, raised body temperature, low urine output and, if not treated, delirium and finally a coma. The best cure is to drink plenty of water.

Heatstroke is more serious. A high body temperature and an absence of sweating are early indications, followed by symptoms similar to hypothermia such as a lack of coordination, convulsions and coma. Death will follow if treatment is not given instantly. Sponge the victim down, wrap them in wet towels, fan them and get help immediately.

Sunburn can happen, even up here and even on overcast days. The way to avoid it is to stay wrapped up but that's not really an option. What you must do, therefore, is to wear a hat and smother yourself in sunscreen (with a minimum factor of 15); apply it regularly throughout the day.

Don't forget your lips, nose, the back of your neck and even under your chin to protect you against rays reflected from the ground.

NEWCASTLE

City guide

Either a fittingly epic place to begin an epic walk, or the perfect venue for a post-trek knees-up, Newcastle is a grand city and, especially following its recent regeneration, a surprisingly attractive one too.

Arriving by train, the first thing you'll see as you cross the Tyne is an untidy jumble of roofs, a messy skyline that belies the uniform elegance of much of the town centre, with its stylish Classical 19th-century façades interspersed here and there with the latest in cutting-edge municipal architecture. Yet Newcastle is like that, a city that is forever defying those who dismiss it as merely a city of brown ale and the Blaydon Races, fun-runs and football. As the starting point for a major trek it's ideal: functional, convenient, with great amenities and plenty to keep you occupied round-the-clock.

The Great North Museum: Hancock, see pp86-7, is also the perfect introduction to the Wall and its history (and like just about every other museum and gallery in the city, it's free), while if you are coming to the end of your Hadrian's Wall odyssey and Newcastle is your last stop, there couldn't be a better place to celebrate than the revamped Quayside, home to numerous bars, bistros and a buzzing nightlife.

ARRIVAL

Most visitors alight at Newcastle's **Central Station** and it's hard to imagine a more appropriate place to arrive in this city. Built in 1850, the station stands in the heart of a metropolis that will forever be associated with George Stephenson (see box p106), the 'Father of the Railways' who was born in nearby Wylam, and which thrived on the back of the railways in the glory days of the late 19th century. The terminus, lying just to the north of the River Tyne, has its own metro station and three ATMs on platform two.

The **National Express coach station** stands a five-minute walk to the west on St James Boulevard.

The **ferry terminus** is 7 miles (11km) east of the city centre; the nearest metro station is Percy Main, a 20-minute walk away (or 5 minutes on Go North East's bus R19). From Percy Main it's 15-20 minutes by metro to Central Station. It's much easier, however, to catch Go North East's bus No 327 (£3 one way) which waits for disembarking passengers outside the ferry terminal before conveying them to Neville St in front of Central Station. Going the other way, the bus departs from Central Station 2½ and 1½ hours before the ferries to Amsterdam are scheduled to depart. The bus also calls in at Newgate St and the YHA hostel (see opposite) on Jesmond Rd.

The **airport** (see box p54) lies 25 minutes away from the city centre by metro and that is the best way into the city. However, if you prefer bus, Stagecoach's X78 stops on the road outside the airport and goes to Eldon Square Bus Station.

TRANSPORT

Within the city

Newcastle, or at least its centre, is a fairly compact place and the chances are you'll be walking for most of the time. The main local **bus** station (Eldon Square) is in front of the branch of John Lewis on Percy St. However, one of the most useful bus services for getting to the start of the walk, is Stagecoach's No 22 which goes to Wallsend Metro (daily 3/hr) from the Central Station. The AD122 (see pp56-7 and the timetable pp212-15) bus service also departs from and arrives at the Central Station (departing once a day).

There is also a pretty efficient **metro** (underground) service connecting most parts of the city, which runs daily from approximately 5am to midnight. A metro map can be found in most brochures and, of course, in the stations themselves. You'll probably use it to get to and from your hotel, as well as to the start of the walk at Wallsend.

Fares (£1.40-2.90/£1.90-3.80 sgl/rtn) depend on the distance travelled. Alternatively, you may wish to buy a **Day Rover pass** (£3.90, or £4.30 for before 9am Mon-Fri), which enables unlimited travel on the metro and the South Shields Ferry. Or there's the **NTL Daysaver pass** (£6.50), which allows unlimited one-day access on all metro, ferry and bus lines. Incidentally, don't be tempted to jump on the metro without a ticket, no matter how lax the ticket checking seems to be; the fine for those caught is £20 and it's a bit daft for what is, after all, a pretty inexpensive service.

The **South Shields Ferry** – useful for Arbeia, see pp88-9, a steep but shortish stroll away – costs £1.10 one-way, £2 return and runs daily every half-hour 6.15am-10.40pm.

General information about all public transport in and around Newcastle can be found on Nexus (🖥 www.nexus.org.uk), the organisation responsible for all public transport in Tyne and Wear.

Further afield

There are also lots of bus services from Newcastle to places on or near the route. Arriva's/Stagecoach's No 685 go to Carlisle, Arriva's No X85 goes to Hexham, Go North East's Nos 10, 74 & 684 also go to Hexham and Wright's No 888 goes to Keswick. Most of these services stop at a number of places en route; see pp56-8 for further information.

SERVICES

Tourist information

The **main tourist information centre** (TIC; ☎ 0191-277 8000, 🖥 www.new castlegateshead.com; Mon-Fri 9.30am-5.30pm, Sat 9am-5.30pm), at 8-9 Central Arcade on Market St, lies in the heart of the city centre. Packed to the gills with souvenirs and schedules, brochures and books, timetables and tours covering just about all Northumberland's and Tyneside's attractions (and indeed often further afield), the office provides an accommodation-booking service (see box p52) which could prove a lifesaver if you turn up with nothing pre-arranged. The TIC also offers internet access (see below) and walking tours (daily Apr-Sep/Oct; £3/2) around various parts of the city.

A second office (see map p84; contact details as above; Mon-Fri 10am-5pm, Sat 9am-5pm, Sun 9am-4pm), in the **Guildhall** on the Quayside, provides a similar service. There are also information points and kiosks throughout the city including at the bus station and the railway station.

Gateshead Heritage Centre @ St Mary's (☎ 0191-433 4699, 🖥 tourism@gateshead.gov.uk; Tue-Sun 10am-4pm; no admission charge) has displays about Gateshead and the local area. **Gateshead tourist information centre** was based at the church at the time of writing but expects to move again. However, the contact details will stay the same so check their location before going here.

Other services

You'll have no trouble finding a **bank/ATM** in the city centre: they're everywhere. There are also **post office** branches including one in WH Smith on Northumberland St and a second, Barras Bridge Post Office, 50 metres east of Haymarket metro on St Mary's Place.

The two main TICs provide free **internet access** for 15 mins. Gateshead TIC offers internet access (£2 for one year, valid also in libraries in Gateshead).

There are several **outdoor/camping/trekking** shops in town, including Tiso on Grainger St, and a Black's in the Eldon Square shopping centre. There's also Wild Trak on St Andrew St. At the junction of Clayton and Newgate streets is a branch of Jessops, the **photographic equipment** store, and directly opposite is its rival chain, Jacobs. For **chemists** there's Boots, with branches all over the city, including outside both Monument and Haymarket metro stations, and a big one in the Eldon Square shopping centre.

WHERE TO STAY

Most places do not accept one-night bookings on a Saturday night. As they say around here, that's just being canny.

Hostels

The city has two **hostels**. *Newcastle YHA Hostel* (see map p80; ☎ 0845-371 9335, 🖥 newcastle@yha.org.uk; 50 beds; open all year), 107 Jesmond Rd, is situated in the smart inner suburb of Jesmond just a few hundred metres from the metro station. The rate is from £19 for an adult. *(continued on p80)*

NEWCASTLE-UPON-TYNE

Newcastle-upon-Tyne

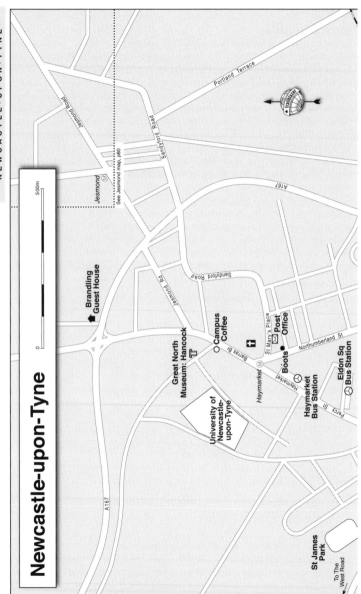

0   500m

Jesmond Road

Sandyford Road

Portland Terrace

Jesmond Ⓜ

See Jesmond map, p80

A167

Branding Guest House

Jesmond Rd

Sandyford Road

Great North Museum: Hancock

Campus Coffee

University of Newcastle-upon-Tyne

Barras Br

St Mary's Place

Post Office

Boots

Northumberland St

Haymarket Ⓜ

Haymarket

Haymarket Bus Station

Percy St

Eldon Sq Bus Station

St James Park

To The West Road

A167

(*Newcastle YHA Hostel* continued from p77) The rooms (5 x 2-bed, 2 x 4-bed, 4 x 6-bed and 1 x 8-bed) are smart and clean, and the staff are knowledgeable about the area. There's also wi-fi and **internet access** (see p25) and, of course, this being a YHA hostel, you can use their kitchen. Packed lunches (£4.50-5.50) and evening meals (from £6.95) can be booked in advance or on arrival.

The second hostel is newer, more central and seems to be more popular too. The 177-bed *Albatross* (see map p79; ☎ 0191-233 1330, 🖳 www.albatross newcastle.com; 2-, 4-, 6-, 8-, 10- and 12-bed dorms), on Grainger St, is certainly less regimented and offers slightly better value, with free toast, tea and coffee, kitchen, free wifi or internet access (£1 for 30 mins) and a satellite TV and pool table in the comfy lounge. There's a vaguely antipodean feel to this place, but it's none the worse for that. The cost of a bed depends on the size of the dorm (the bigger the dorm, the less you pay) and when you stay but expect to pay £16.50-19.95 per person; there are also a few twin rooms (£22.50-24.50pp).

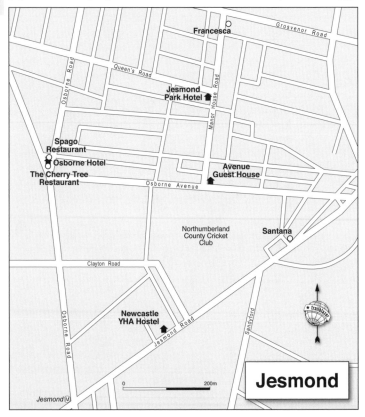

Jesmond

Accommodation in and around Jesmond

If it's a B&B you're after, the chances are you're going to end up in the Jesmond area to the north of the town centre. ***Brandling Guest House*** (see Newcastle map p78; ☎ 0191-281 3175, 🖳 www.brandlingguesthouse.co.uk; 3S/3T/3D, T or F; bath available), 4 Brandling Park, is perhaps the pick of the bunch here. Occupying a tardis of a Victorian house opposite the park itself, it's the nearest B&B to the town centre, is friendly, efficient and allows dogs. Most of the rooms are quite large and offer a mixture of en suite and shared facilities; rates are £33-39 (for a single), £58-65 (two sharing) and £72-82 (three sharing).

On Osborne Ave, on the corner of Manor House Rd, ***Avenue Guest House*** (☎ 0191-281 1396, 🖳 www.avenuenewcastle.co.uk; 4S/3T/3D/1D, T or F, all en suite) is another great choice, a long-established place with well-appointed rooms. B&B costs £39.50 for a single, £60 for two sharing, while the family room is £75-90.

Jesmond Park Hotel (☎ 0191-281 2821, 🖳 www.jesmondpark.com; 6S/3T/4D/5D, T or F; some en suite, some share facilities), 74-76 Queens Rd, is a smart place just down from Francesca pizzeria (see pp84-5). Its exterior is unimposing and though called a hotel it manages to combine the efficiency and standard of service of a big hotel with the cosiness of a simple B&B. B&B costs £32.50-42.50 for a single, £59.50-69.50 for two sharing, or £95-120 for three/four adults in a family room. Dogs are welcome subject to some conditions: they are kept off the beds and they are not left in the room on their own.

Finally, there's ***Osborne Hotel*** (☎ 0191-281 3385, 🖳 www.theosbornehotel.co.uk; 14S/3T/2D/2D, T or F, all en suite, bath available) at 13-15 Osborne Rd. A large hotel where rates are £47.50 for a single, £75 for two sharing and £95-120 for a family room. They also run Spago restaurant (see p85) next door.

Other accommodation in Newcastle

County Hotel (see map p79; ☎ 0871-376 9029, 🖳 www.thistlehotels.com; 114 rooms, all en suite, bath available), opposite the Central Station entrance on Neville St, is in a 19th-century building. As with many of Newcastle's hotels of this calibre, their tariff depends on demand and can be as low as £50 but rack rates are £167 for a single and £177-192 for a double or twin, which gives you some idea of which ballpark they're playing in. All the rooms have the usual facilities.

Vermont Hotel (see Quayside map, p84; ☎ 0191-233 1010, 🖳 www.vermont-hotel.com; 101 rooms, all en suite, bath available), up by Castle Keep (see p88), is a grand-looking place in a central yet quiet location. The rooms are equipped with all the gubbins you'd expect – satellite TV and mini-bar. The hotel offers 24-hour room service and has a couple of bars as well as a fitness centre. As with County Hotel the rates change every day; the receptionist explained that you're looking at rates from £110 up to £660 for a suite. A full English breakfast costs £16.90 and a continental breakfast is £14.80 per person. Small dogs are welcome subject to prior arrangement.

The *Copthorne Hotel* (see map p79; ☎ 0191-222 0333, 🖳 www.millennium hotels.co.uk; 156 rooms, all en suite, bath available) sits in a great location on The Close, right on the Tyne (and the Hadrian's Wall Path!) and just a couple of minutes west of the fun at the Quayside. Ugly as sin on one side, the side facing the water is better and the interior is fine, with rooms (every one of which overlooks the water) equipped with everything you'd expect from a hotel of this standard. There's also a pool, gym and more than one restaurant. Rates start at £100 for a single/double but the actual cost depends on availability and when you book.

Perhaps at the top of the pile, however, is the *Malmaison* (see map p79; ☎ 0191-245 5000, 🖳 www.malmaison.com/hotels/newcastle; 122 rooms, all en suite, bath available), a sophisticated place housed in the old Co-operative building on the Quayside overlooking the Millennium Bridge. The chic, dark reception has the décor and ambience of the pop-star Prince's boudoir and it's fair to say that this place won't be to everyone's taste. Wi-fi and cable TV are just a couple of the facilities. Weekday rack rates are £160-375, though weekend rates are far more reasonable. A continental breakfast costs £12.50 and a full English is £14.50. Dogs (£10) are welcome if arranged in advance.

For potentially the best deal in the city you could try the *Newcastle Central Travelodge* (see map p79; ☎ 0871-984 6164; 🖳 www.travelodge.co.uk; 203D or F, all en suite, bath available). Part of a nationwide chain, Newcastle's version sits right in the heart of the city just a minute from the Tyne and the path. However, it has some annoying little rules (no check-in before 3pm, for example, unless the room is available and you pay £10 extra – and they won't pick up or take in luggage from baggage carriers for their guests). But if you book at least 21 days in advance you may be able to get one of their smart, clean rooms for as little as £19 during the week, which represents very good value indeed. However, room rates are generally £55-100. Breakfast (a buffet with hot and cold food) costs £7.65pp. A maximum of two dogs can stay in a room but the minimum charge is £20.

Finally, we must mention *Hadrian Lodge Hotel* (off Map 1, p97; ☎ 0191-262 7733, 🖳 www.hadrianlodgehotel.co.uk; 9S/5T/10D/1D, T or F, all en suite, bath available), on Hadrian Rd, close to the start of the walk in Wallsend. It's a bit out of the way but the metro (Hadrian Rd stop) is just across the road and while this hotel is nothing fancy, there's wi-fi and it's reasonable value at £43 for a single, £58 two sharing a room, or £75-95 for the family room. The rate includes a continental breakfast; there is an additional charge of £5.95 for a full English.

WHERE TO EAT AND DRINK

The food in Newcastle is sometimes breathtakingly good value. Lunchtimes in particular are very inexpensive, with all manner of enticing deals offered by the restaurants and bars. In our opinion, if Newcastle is the last stop at the end of your walk, it's the best place to put on those pounds you've lost along the trail.

Cafés and bakeries   [see map pp78-9]
Bowers of Newcastle serves pasties and pies and is a good place for a quick but filling bite; their sausage stottie (bun) is just £1.99. For a break and a cup of tea

in the centre of town, **Centurion Café** (daily 9am-late), at the station, is perfectly acceptable and does some decent sandwiches, as does **Campus Coffee** (Mon-Sat 7.45am-6pm in term time, to 4pm otherwise), just by the university on Barras Bridge.

Our favourite café, however, is **Scrumpy Willow and The Singing Kettle** (☎ 0191-221 2323, 🖳 www.scrumpywillowandthesingingkettle.co.uk; Mon-Sat 10am to when people leave – last sitting 8pm, Sun 11am-4pm), at 89 Clayton St, a friendly little place where all dishes are homemade using local and organic ingredients where possible and, as you'd probably expect of such an establishment, there's a good vegetarian selection. Their full English breakfast costs £6.90, the veggie/vegan option is £5.

If it's a hot day, don't miss the chance to sample the ice cream at **Mark Toney's** (☎ 0191-232 7794; Mon-Sat 7.30am-8pm, Sun 9.30am-8pm), next to Albatross on Grainger St. They also do an all-day breakfast, home-made soups, sandwiches and quiches.

Chinatown

Less of a 'town' than a single street, **Stowell St**, Chinatown (see map pp78-9) is nevertheless chock full of restaurants, most offering some sort of special deal, and a couple of all-you-can-eat places that are ideal for that end-of-trek blowout.

Starting by the elaborate oriental gate at the northern end of Stowell St, the first place you come to is **China Town Express** (Sun-Wed noon-11.30pm, Thur-Sat noon-2am), a no-nonsense Chinese café that offers 'happy hour' meals (5-7.30pm) for £5.30, or £5.80 with a starter. Perhaps its biggest recommendation, however, comes from its customers, a large proportion of whom are Chinese – always a good sign. Come here for dinner before 6pm or you'll be queuing.

King Neptune (☎ 0191-261 6657; daily noon-1.45pm, Mon-Fri 6-10.45pm, Sat 5.30-11pm, Sun 6-10.30pm) describes itself as a seafood specialist though has a full à la carte menu. Their Diamond Banquet (£35.80pp) with lobster as a starter will leave you feeling as stuffed as that horse in the museum at Segedunum.

Further on, the large **Lau's Buffet King** (☎ 0191-261 8868; daily 11.45am-10.30pm) is in deadly rivalry with its equally cavernous neighbour over the road, **No 1 Oriental Buffet** (☎ 0191-261 5787; daily 11.45am-10.30pm). Both offer all-you-can-eat 60-dish buffets starting at £5.50, the price rising according to what time of day you eat (with the cheapest time being before 4pm, 4-6pm £6.50, and after 6pm it rises to £8.50, and £9.50 on Saturday). As with all these places, some of the dishes can be unexceptional, to say the least, but for value they're hard to beat.

For something a little more sophisticated, try the dim-sum specialists **Mango's** (☎ 0191-232 6522; Sun-Thur noon-1.30am Fri & Sat to 2am), next door to the Oriental Buffet and rated by many as the best Chinese in town.

Finally, opposite the end of the street on Bath Lane, **Fujiyama** (☎ 0191-233 0189; Mon-Sat noon-2pm & 6-11pm, Sun noon-2.30pm & 6-11pm) is a Japanese teppanyaki restaurant which seems expensive after the all-you-can-eat excesses of Stowell St. Nevertheless, the food is delicious and their salmon, at £8 for two pieces, seems fair value.

NEWCASTLE-UPON-TYNE

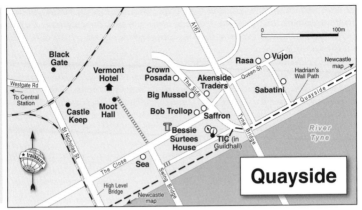

Quayside

There are several great **Indian restaurants** in the city, particularly in this area. For Indian fare with a modern twist, including that old favourite chicken tikka masala, check out *Saffron* (☎ 0191-230 5785, 💻 www.saffroncontemporary .co.uk; Sun-Thur 6pm-midnight, Fri & Sat to 3am) opposite the Guildhall. Slightly fancier, *Vujon* (☎ 0191-221 0601, 💻 www.vujon.com; Mon-Sat noon-2pm, daily 6-11.30pm), on Queen St, is a classy Indian restaurant with an unusual menu; try the pheasant tarkari (£14.90), a mild curry. Our favourite, however, is *Rasa* (☎ 0191-232 7799, 💻 www.rasanewcastle.co.uk; Mon-Sat noon-3pm & 6-11pm), though this could be because they do masala dosas – proof, in our opinion, that the Indian gods not only exist but they love us and want us to be happy. Part of a chain but still highly recommended by many trekkers, with mains starting at about £7.95.

Just to the west on The Side are more choices: *Big Mussel* (☎ 0191-232 1057, 💻 www.bigmussel.co.uk; Mon-Fri noon-2pm & 5.30-10.15pm, Sat noon-10.15pm, Sun noon-3pm & 5.30-10pm) is, as its name suggests, a seafood place specialising in mussel dishes (though vegetarian and poultry options are on the menu too); it has a variety of special offers including a two-course meal (to 7pm) for £9.95. *Sabatini* (☎ 0191-261 4415, 💻 www.sabatinis.co.uk; Mon-Sat noon-10.30pm) is a pizza/pasta joint with happy hours (noon-6.30pm) when pizzas are just £5.95 and some pasta dishes are £6.95.

Jesmond   [see map p80]

Top of the list for value comes *Francesca* (☎ 0191-281 6586; Mon-Sat noon-2.30pm & 5-9.30pm), a long-established pizzeria that's been serving the residents of this smart suburb for over 25 years. They don't take bookings and you often have to queue, such is the popularity of this great little place, though it's worth the wait; the food is cheap and plentiful, with most pasta and pizzas around £4.95-5.95; for the indecisive there's a half-pizza-half-pasta option for

£6.95-7.95. There's also a happy hour (Mon-Fri 5-6pm), with £1 off all pasta dishes. *Santana* (☎ 0191-281 7849, 🖳 www.pizzeriasantana.com; Mon-Fri noon-2.30pm & 5.30-10.30pm, Sat noon-10pm, Sun noon-9pm), five minutes east of the YHA hostel on Jesmond Rd, does a pizza-and-pasta happy 'hour' before 7pm Mon-Fri (before 5pm on Sat).

Slightly more upmarket, *Spago* (☎ 0191-281 2990, 🖳 www.spagorestaurant.co.uk; Mon-Sat noon-2pm & 5.30-10pm, Sun 1-9pm), run by Osborne Hotel next door, has a reasonable wine list and smarter décor, though still serves pizzas beginning at just £4.50.

Just the other side of the Osborne, *The Cherry Tree* (☎ 0191-239 9924, 🖳 www.thecherrytreejesmond.co.uk; Mon-Sat 9am-11.30pm, Sun 9am-9pm; food served Mon-Wed noon-2.30pm & 5-9.30pm, Thur-Sat same but to 10pm, Sun noon-9pm) serves the best of British food using delicious local and seasonal produce; it's not particularly cheap, but the food is often exquisite (fillet of turbot, wild mushrooms, surf clams, hazelnuts and citrus for £20.50, for example).

Other possibilities [see map pp78-9]

Café 21 (☎ 0191-222 0755, 🖳 www.cafetwentyone.co.uk; Mon-Sat noon-2.30pm & 5.30-10.30pm, Sun noon-3pm & 5.30-10.30pm), on Trinity Gardens, is a large, sophisticated sort of place that's great for a pre- or post-trek blowout. Though the menu changes regularly, if it's available try the enormous rump of lamb, served with fine beans, tomatoes, olives and gratin potatoes (£19.20).

A good option for pizzas is *Pinocchio* (☎ 0191-232 0708, 🖳 www.pinocchio-newcastle.co.uk; Mon-Sat noon-2.30pm & 5.30-10.30pm), with a special offer of starter and pizza for just £5.95 (Mon-Thur 12.30-2.30pm & 5.30-7.30pm, Fri & Sat noon-2.30pm.)

Other choices include a whole cluster of chain restaurants in the **Gate cinema complex**, including *TGI Friday's* (Sun-Thur noon-10.30pm, Fri & Sat to 11pm), *Ask* (Mon-Thur noon-11pm, Fri & Sat noon-11.30pm, Sun noon-10pm), *Pizza Hut* (Mon-Fri & Sun 11.30am-10.30pm, Sat 11am-11pm) and *Nando's* (Mon-Sat 11.30am-11pm, Sun noon-10.30pm).

NIGHTLIFE

For details of what's going on in Newcastle – and there's always *plenty* going on – pick up a copy of *The Crack* (🖳 www.thecrackmagazine.com) or *The Informer* (🖳 www.informermagazine.com), two free monthly listings magazines available from the tourist offices.

For most people, however, going out in Newcastle means heading to the Quayside to hit the bars and clubs there. It's beyond the scope of this book to provide a thorough review of each place, though a few places do stand out; *Sea* is housed in a lovely old warehouse by the Swing Bridge, and has its own Glitterati champagne bar and Viper Lounge.

For an older-style, traditional pub try *Bob Trollop*, which has real ales, and, across the way, *Akenside Traders* – though neither is quite as traditional as *Crown Posada*, on The Side. The *Pitcher & Piano*, part of the nationwide chain, is a typically smart affair with a great location by the Millennium Bridge, overlooking the water.

Finally, for more genteel entertainment cross the river to **The Sage** (⌨ www .thesagegateshead.org), the giant slug-shaped glass auditorium and concert venue next to the BALTIC centre (see p89). Or you can see the latest Hollywood blockbuster at the Gate Cinema in the town centre – or something more thought-provoking at one of three independent **cinemas** in town: The Side (⌨ www.amber-online.com/sections/side-cinema), on the Quayside, Tyneside Cinema (⌨ www.tynesidecinema.co.uk), on Pilgrim St, and Star & Shadow (⌨ www.starandshadow.org.uk) in Byker/Ouseburn in front of the Tanners Pub.

WHAT TO SEE AND DO

There's so much to see and do in Newcastle; the following is a brief walking tour around the city's major highlights, with a bias towards those with a Roman or Wall connection. Further details of these attractions can be obtained from the tourist office. The TIC (see p77) organises walking tours of the city or you can take one of the city's **hop-on hop-off bus tours** (☎ 0191-228 8900, ⌨ www .city-sightseeing.com; daily from week before Easter to end Nov; £8) which visit all the major sites in the metropolis. The best place to get on the bus in the first place is the railway station.

Great North Museum: Hancock

The first place any self-respecting Wall-walker should head is the rather clumsily titled Great North Museum: Hancock (☎ 0191-222 6765, ⌨ www.twmuse ums.org.uk/greatnorthmuseum; Mon-Sat 10am-5pm, Sun 2-5pm; admission is free but a donation is appreciated), opened in May 2009 following a £26 million overhaul and which now houses the collections that were once scattered across various museums in the city, including the Museum of Antiquities and the Shefton Museum.

Occupying centre stage both on the ground floor and in Wall walkers' imaginations is the interactive model of Hadrian's Wall. Characters from Roman Briton discuss various topics – construction, religion, defence of the Wall etc – at the simple press of a button, while surrounding the model are various treasures dug up from the soil near the Wall and its accompanying forts. A highlight is an ivory folding knife in the shape of a gladiator found at South Shields. There's also a reconstruction of a Mithraeum (see box pp142-3) which really gives you a flavour of what a secretive, strange and sinister religion this was. Apparently, the stone from which historians were finally able to determine that the Wall was Hadrian's construction and not that of his successor, Severus, will also be on display soon.

Perhaps the most impressive items, however, are the various pieces of jewellery. They include the gold Aemilia finger ring from Corbridge, dating back to between the 2nd and 4th centuries AD, which is believed to be one of the oldest Christian artefacts ever found on (or rather under) British soil. There's also a beautiful 3rd-century cameo of a bear on sardonyx, found in 1877, and a whole jewellery 'set' including brooch, necklace, bracelet and rings – all of which you would believe could have been made yesterday, such is their condition. The case on arms and weaponry is also enlightening, including as it does a highly decorated cheek piece from an auxiliary's cavalry helmet, again found in South Shields, and even a tiny segment of scale armour.

The wonders continue upstairs with an antiquities collection that once formed the bulk of the Shefton Museum, including some more Roman relics as well as Greek and Etruscan artefacts. Other highlights in the museum include the model of the skeleton of *Tyrannosaurus rex* at the rear of the museum on the ground floor and the giant Japanese spider crab near the entrance. Overall, a very entertaining and educational morning's outing.

❏ The Swan Hunter Shipyard

Though not as venerable as the nearby Roman ruins of Segedunum, the Swan Hunter Shipyard with its iconic, multicoloured cranes puncturing the skyline of north Tyneside, is nevertheless a vital part of the region's history. Unfortunately, it appears that history is about to come to an end. In 2007, Swan Hunter's boss Jaap Kroes declared shipbuilding to be an industry with no future, and put the yard – and its cranes – up for sale.

It was a huge body blow to both Wallsend and the city of Newcastle as a whole, an area that had suffered from more than its fair share of economic woes through the decades. Though it must be said that on this occasion the decision to close the site permanently wasn't entirely surprising, given its dramatic decline. Between 1993 and 2003 not one new ship was launched from Swan Hunter's yard, and a decision by the Ministry of Defence to hand over the work on an unfinished ship at Swan Hunter to the BAE Systems site at Govan in Glasgow in 2006 resulted in the shipyard being mothballed. Attempts to secure new contracts or change tack and become a breaking business both failed, and the managers were left with no choice but to lay off all but 10 of Swan Hunter's remaining 260 workers.

All of which seems a long way away from the time when Britain led the world in shipbuilding and the Tyne produced a staggering 25% of the world's ships. Many of the world's most famous and innovative vessels were created at Swan Hunter during the 20th century, including the Cunard liner *Mauretania*, a revolutionary steamship launched in 1906 that was, for a time, not only the world's largest ocean liner but also its fastest.

In recent years, however, the stories coming out of the Swan Hunter shipyard tended to be about job cuts and industrial disputes as the yard struggled to make its mark in the new globalised market. Jaap Kroes's decision to invest in the shipyard in 1995 brought a glimmer of hope and for a while, as several refurbishment contracts rolled in, it appeared as if the good times were back once more. But when the *Lyme Bay* was taken to Scotland to be fitted out, it was the first time a ship had left Swan Hunter unfinished, and many then saw the writing on the wall.

At the time of research the entire site lay idle and the cranes, though still standing, have all been sold off. As for the future, ship construction has officially ceased at Wallsend, with Swan Hunter now offering 'high quality engineering, design and management support to the shipbuilding and offshore industry'. Whether this actually turns around the fortunes of the yard – or is merely the last echo of a once-great industry – remains to be seen. One thing is for certain, however: the skyline of North Tyneside will look strangely empty if and when those cranes are finally dismantled.

Castle Keep/Castle Garth

Perhaps better and more precisely known as the **Castle Keep** (🖳 www.castle keep-newcastle.org.uk; Mon-Sat 10am-5pm, Sun noon-5pm, last admission 4.15pm; £4, £3 concessions), these are the most visible remains of the New Castle, the edifice that gave the city its name. Built during the reign of Henry II (1168-78), this New Castle was established on the foundations of Castle Garth, built in 1080 by William the Conqueror's eldest son Robert Curthose.

The Keep itself, and the **Black Gate**, on the northern side of the railway tracks, that was part of the same fortifications, are probably of only minimal interest to the Wall walker. However, one case in the Keep's museum section does have a few Roman artefacts, including fragments of a figure of Mercury. There are also details of the extent of the original Roman fort which was built to guard the bridge nearby. This bridge was **Pons Aelius** (*Pons* being Latin for 'bridge', Aelius being Hadrian's family name), which stretched across the Tyne in approximately the same location as the small Swing Bridge that you see today. It was from this bridge that the Roman fort took its name; a bridge that would have been about 700ft long (210m) and 18ft (5.4m) wide and the most impressive of the three main bridges the Romans built to cross the Tyne (the others were at Corbridge and Chollerford). In the 19th century, two altars were found in the water near the site of the bridge, though there's nothing left there today. Having noted the extent of the Roman fort, pop upstairs to the roof to get a better idea of its size and layout, and for good rooftop views of the city, its river and bridges.

Arbeia

(☎ 0191-456 1369, 🖳 www.twmuseums.org.uk/arbeia; Apr-Oct Mon-Sat 10am-5pm, Sun 1-5pm; Nov-Mar closed; free)

Though not strictly a Wall fort, being on the other side of the Tyne and four miles further east of the end of the Wall at Segedunum, Arbeia was, nevertheless, an important part of the whole military set-up in Britain and anybody with a taste for all-things Roman should seriously consider a visit. Though it seems a long way on the map, it's fairly straightforward to get to. Take the metro to South Shields, descend to Ocean Rd (not the bus station), turn right and walk for ten minutes past Asda, cross the roundabout and then take a left up Baring St past Vespasian (!) and Trajan (!!) streets, Claudius Court (!!!) and the Arbeia Unisex Hair Studio (!!!!). The fort lies opposite Hadrian (!!!!!) Primary School.

The name *Arbeia* means 'Place of Arabs' after the soldiers from Tigris, in what is now modern-day Iraq, who were garrisoned here in the 4th century. The history of the fort goes back further than this, however, having been built c AD163 under Emperor Marcus Aurelius to keep an eye on the sea and river. That changed in AD208 when Emperor Severus Septimus converted it into a granary and supply base for his troops campaigning in Scotland (see p17). Though Severus was killed in York just three years later and his Scottish assault ended soon after, the fort continued to supply the troops along the Wall for up to two centuries afterwards.

Because of its purpose as a storeroom, granary and unloading bay for imports arriving up the Tyne from overseas, Arbeia doesn't follow the classic playing-card layout of your average Roman fort (about which, see box p95). Nevertheless, some great finds have been dug up by archaeologists, who are still painstakingly excavating the site today. Many of these finds can be seen in the reception, including some incredible carved ringstones. The inhumation (burial) room opposite is also enlightening, showing how the Romans interred their dead.

Outside, two Roman buildings have been reconstructed. The **West Gate** provides great views over the site, though in all honesty it is probably not an exact replica of how the gate would have looked. Nevertheless, it is impressive, and contains some useful information on the history of the site.

Of more interest, however, are the barracks at the south-eastern corner that offer a telling glimpse into the rudimentary living conditions of the average soldier in South Shields at the time. Walk around the back of the barracks and you'll find the bright murals of the **Commanding Officer's House**, the exact designs of the murals taken from original Roman designs.

The South Bank: BALTIC Centre for Contemporary Art and The Sage

The regeneration of Newcastle's city centre is a thing of wonder. From a run-down and slightly sleazy area of the city, the waterfront is now the most photographed part of the metropolis; its dilapidated, crumbling constructions spruced up and given a new lease of life or replaced by some breathtaking works of modern architecture. From being the shame of the city, the waterfront is now a place to be celebrated.

Perhaps the most impressive manifestation of this regeneration is the **BALTIC Centre for Contemporary Art** (☎ 0191-478 1810, 💻 www.baltic mill.com; galleries open daily 10am-6pm, Tue from 10.30am), once a disused grain warehouse, now a world-class centre for contemporary art. It's a delight and, like most of the museums and galleries, is free, though some of the exhibitions charge and you probably won't find it easy resisting the temptation to eat in one of the cafés, including the rooftop restaurant, or to buy something from the BALTIC's gift shop. Nearby is the glass **Sage** building (see p86), an international music venue designed by architect Norman Foster that's been variously described as a glass wave, a blister or a giant slug!

The Tyne bridges

Where once there was just one bridge across the Tyne in the area we now know of as Newcastle – the Roman Pons Aelius that remained until 1248 – today there are seven bridges within reasonable distance of each other in the city centre.

The most eyecatching is also the one furthest east, the **Millennium Bridge**, which, despite the name, was formally opened in May 2002 by the Queen. One of the smallest (126m long and just 50m above water) this footbridge, also known as the **Winking Eye**, is one of the most revolutionary and even has its own cleaning mechanism: when the bridge is raised the rubbish collects in special receptacles which are then emptied.

Heading west, the next bridge is the impressive **Tyne Bridge**, opened in 1928 by George V and looking for all the world like its contemporary, the Sydney Harbour Bridge. After that we come to the comparatively small **Swing Bridge**, built on the site of the Roman Pons Aelius in 1876. As its name might suggest, it rotates through 90 degrees to allow ships to pass through.

After this there's the oldest and most impressive of Newcastle's seven crossings, the **High Level Bridge**, built by Robert Stephenson, the son of George (see box p106), and opened by Queen Victoria in 1849. The **Queen Elizabeth II Bridge**, which carries the Metro, comes next, followed by the **King Edward VII Bridge**, built in nearby Middlesbrough and another railway bridge. Finally, **Redheugh Bridge** (pronounced 'Red-yuff') was built on the site of two previous bridges and was opened in 1983 by the late Diana, Princess of Wales.

Other attractions in Newcastle

Bessie Surtees House (see map p84; 🖳 www.english-heritage.org.uk; Mon-Fri 10am-4pm, closed 24 Dec-7 Jan & Bank hols; free) sits in the heart of Quayside at 41-44 Sandhill. The name is not strictly correct, for there are in fact *two* merchants' houses here dating back to the 16th and 17th centuries, one of which is a rare example of Jacobean domestic architecture. The name comes from one of the inhabitants, who eloped with John Scott, who later became Lord Chancellor of England. There's not much to see inside, just three rooms, the main one

---

❏ The West Road – the real Wall route

Most people know that Hadrian's Wall did not follow the river, as the trail does, but originally ran through the heart of Newcastle. However, you'd struggle to find much in the way of evidence to back this up. There's a **plaque** near Central Station (head east past the George Stephenson statue and you'll find it on your right, under the Westgate Road sign on the wall of Neville Hall, before the Literary and Philosophical building), which says that the route of the Wall went under the building. And on Westgate Rd, in the small **Black Swan courtyard** by a pottery, you'll find some stone foundations unearthed in 1985 by the potter himself, David Fry, that have been interpreted as belonging to a milecastle (though it must be pointed out that it doesn't actually lie where the milecastle around here would have been). Both these 'sights' are marked on the map on pp78-9. However, apart from these two examples, and some of the stones of Castle Garth which were once part of the Wall's fabric, Hadrian's Wall is virtually invisible in Newcastle.

Virtually ... but not totally; travel up West Rd, for example, which follows the line of the Wall through the western half of the city, and you'll find a few more sights with Roman connections. These sights on West Rd are probably not going to feature heavily in any photo album of your trek because, to put it succinctly, they're not the most scintillating of Roman treasures. Nevertheless, there is something charming about finding a temple to an obscure god sitting next to 48 Broombridge Ave; and of finding the best-preserved Vallum crossing of the entire Wall at the end of an unassuming cul-de-sac, and having to knock on the door of No 26 to get the key. Furthermore, there's something delightfully incongruous about the decent chunk of Wall, complete with its own turret, that lies prone and in resigned silence next to the traffic and pollution of the A186, one of the city's main thoroughfares.

Nor, so rumour has it, are they the only ruins on this multicultural artery. Amongst the road's cafés and colleges, the tanning salons and takeaways is, so it is said, yet more evidence of those busy Romans, including, according to one report, a large Wall stone next to an air pump in a garage forecourt. We don't suggest for a moment you hike the length of the road just to see if you can spot some more for yourself – leave that to the archaeologists, Wall buffs, guidebook writers and other slightly obsessive sorts who like that sort of thing – but it is interesting to see that, no matter how much you try to cover it with more modern constructions, you just can't keep a good Roman wall down for long.

empty save for a few photos of the house in days gone by. The main attraction is, perhaps, the giant fireplace, the exquisitely carved overmantel bearing a date of 1657.

Laing Art Gallery (☎ 0191-232 7734, 💻 www.twmuseums.org.uk/laing, see map p89; Mon-Sat 10am-5pm, Sun 2-5pm; free but donations appreciated), on New Bridge St, is the city's oldest gallery, having welcomed visitors for well over a hundred years. The collection includes both contemporary works and paintings from the 18th and 19th centuries.

The **Discovery Museum** (☎ 0191-232 6789, 💻 www.twmuseums .org.uk/discovery; see map p89; Mon-Sat 10am-5pm, Sun 2-5pm; free) is the region's biggest free museum (though donation boxes are situated around the museum), housing a wealth of scientific and technological material as well as displays on social history, regimental militaria and costumes.

For this reason, however, a trip up West Rd can be recommended to anyone with a taste for the absurd as well as the antique. Your chariot for the West Rd tour should be Stagecoach North East bus No 39 or 40; buy one of the Daysaver passes (see p76) as you'll be hopping on and off several times to view the sites. The bus leaves very regularly from Eldon Sq Bus Station (make sure it's heading to Denton, not Wallsend) goes past St James Park and onto the A186 (West Rd). After ten minutes or so, and having passed the hospital, look out on your right for West Gate Community College and the TV mast after it. Jump out at the bus stop here (just before the mast) and head down Weiner Rd (which lies right by the bus stop), taking the first right onto Westholme Gdns, then the first left onto Broombridge Ave. Before the first house on the left is the **Antenociticus Temple**, complete with a platform on which a statue of the god stood, flanked by a couple of replica altars (as with most treasures, the real altars, along with the head and limbs of the statue that were found, are now in Newcastle's Great North Museum: Hancock). Antenociticus himself was probably worshipped by the Vangiones from the upper Rhineland region who lived in the nearby Benwell Fort (see below); as is usual, the soldiers built their temples away from the fort, considering the latter no place for holy sites. The current residents of Broombridge Ave do not, it is believed, still worship at this site. The next site is within easy walking distance. This is a **Vallum crossing** that would have led to the entrance to **Benwell Fort**, of which this is the only bit left above ground. The crossing can be found at the bottom end of the noose-shaped cul-de-sac known as Denhill Park; fetch the keys from No 26 for a better look. As with all the sites on this road, the Vallum crossing is owned by English Heritage, who provide a fair artist's impression of how it must have looked in its heyday.

Jumping back on the bus, about 1500m further west and just before the main intersection with the A1, is a fairly broad and impressive piece of Wall lying serenely beyond the pavement to the left of the road. Halfway along its length is a foundation that gives the whole ruin its name: **Denton Turret**. As is usual with all the forts along the Wall, the turret would have been manned by around ten men. An inscription recovered from the site suggested that it was built by the First Cohort of the Second Legion of Augusta. Presumably, the soldiers who manned the turret would have walked back to their abode at Benwell. But by good fortune there's a bus stop on the other side of the road to take you back into town.

ROUTE GUIDE & MAPS

Using this guide

The trail guide has been described from east to west and divided into six different stages. Though each of these roughly corresponds to a day's walk, do not assume that this is the only way to plan your walk. There are so many places to stay en route that you can pretty much divide up the walk wherever you want.

On p40 we have provided tables to help you plan an itinerary. To provide further help, practical information is presented on the trail maps, including walking times, places to stay, camp and eat, as well as shops where you can buy supplies, taps (for drinking water), phone boxes and public toilets. Further service details are given in the text under the entry for each settlement.

TRAIL MAPS

Scale and walking times
The trail maps are to a scale of 1:20,000 (1cm = 200m; 3¹/₈ inches = one mile). Walking times are given along the side of each map and the arrow shows the direction to which the time refers. The black triangles indicate the points between which the times have been taken. **See box opposite on walking times**.

The time-bars are a tool and are not there to judge your walking ability. There are so many variables that affect walking speed, from the weather conditions to how many beers you drank the previous evening. After the first hour or two of walking you will be able to see how your speed relates to the timings on the maps.

Up or down?
The trail is shown as a dotted line. An arrow across the trail indicates the slope; two arrows show that it is steep. Note that the arrow points towards the higher part of the trail. If, for example, you are walking from A (at 80m) to B (at 200m) and the trail between the two is short and steep, it would be shown thus: A– – – >> – – – – B. Reversed arrow heads indicate downward gradient.

Accommodation
Accommodation marked on the map is either on or within easy reach of the trail. Details of each place are given in the accompanying text. The number of rooms of each type, ie S=Single, T=Twin room,

❑ **Important note – walking times**
Unless otherwise specified, **all times in this book refer only to the time spent walking**. You will need to add 20-30% to allow for rests, photography, checking the map, drinking water etc. When planning the day's hike count on 5-7 hours' actual walking.

D=Double room, F=Family room (see p27), is given with the contact details. The rates stated are mostly given as per person (pp), often with a supplement for single occupancy, but some places quote per room based on two sharing – in this case there is often a discount for single occupancy.

Other features
Features are marked on the map when pertinent to navigation. In order to avoid cluttering the maps and making them unusable not all features have been marked each time they occur.

The trail guide:
Wallsend to Bowness-on-Solway

WALLSEND TO HEDDON-ON-THE-WALL   **[MAPS 1-8]**
Getting to the start of the walk
There are a number of ways of getting to the start of the walk. Most people choose to use public transport (see box p56) and jump out at Wallsend Metro or the adjacent coach station (which is helpfully signed in Latin – *Raedarum publicarum statio* – someone in charge of signage at the city council clearly has a sense of humour). From there you can walk north for two minutes to the Co-op for last-minute supplies, or south along the main road for a minute to Netto (another supermarket) and Segedunum.

SEGEDUNUM   **[see map p97]**
☎ *0191-236 9347;* 🖳 *www.twmuseums.org.uk/segedunum; Apr-Oct daily 10am-5pm, Nov to mid Dec & mid Jan to Mar Mon-Fri 10am-3pm; £4.35/2.60 adults/concs; children aged 16 and under are free;*
Nestling beneath the giant multicoloured cranes of the Swan Hunter shipyard (see box p87), which itself is replete with history, Segedunum is a fantastic introduction to the kind of Wall fort that will become oh-so-familiar as you progress along the trail.
    Translating as 'Strong Fort', Segedunum is the last Wall fort heading east; instead of continuing from here to the sea, the Wall took a sharp turn south at this point, heading off from the fort's south-eastern corner through the now-defunct Swan Hunter shipyard and down to the water's edge. You can see a little bit of this Wall by the side of the trail at the very start of the walk, just outside the fence that surrounds Segedunum.

At first it seems strange that the Wall doesn't actually cover the entire breadth of the country. After all, what is the point of building a wall right across an island if you're not going to finish the job, thereby allowing the locals to sneak around the end? But with Arbeia Fort (see pp88-9) guarding the river's mouth from the other side of the Tyne and this fort watching over the land to the east on this side, it's fair to say that little could cross undetected from one side, of either the Tyne or the Wall, to the other. In fact, Segedunum was actually something of an afterthought; originally, the Wall terminated at Pons Aelius (see p88) and only later did they decide to extend it a further three miles east to Segedunum.

Today, little remains of the original Roman fort, which would have held 600 men. The Saxons proved pretty efficient at carting off the masonry for their own building projects, such as Bede's monastery at Jarrow; Newcastle's Great North Museum: Hancock has proved equally efficient at appropriating much of the remainder to fill their display cases (this is, after all, the most excavated of all the Wall forts).

But what makes the fort here so appealing is not what the Romans left behind but the way the little that has survived has been presented. From the 35m-high viewing tower, which provides great views over the site, to the clear information boards and the reconstructed bath-house (open on the hour for 20 minutes only), this fort is an object lesson in how history should be told. And whilst some may complain at the slightly child-centric **galleries**, with their games and quizzes designed to keep young minds interested, many will find it stimulating and useful and the reconstructed cavalry barrack (complete with horse!) gives a fair idea of what living conditions were like on the Wall. The third-floor galleries were being refurbished at the time of research; the aim was to create a larger temporary exhibition space but also to install a new permanent display, focusing on the theme of landscape change on and around the site, to replace the Industry gallery.

Highlights of Segedunum include the aforementioned **Panorama Tower**, where you get a better idea of just how large the fort was (note that the fort originally covered the large paved area to the north of the main road too, which today is outside the official site). The **Roman baths** are good, too, though if you've seen other Roman baths you may well be disappointed by the rather plain, undecorated look of this one. There's a reason for this: Roman baths along the Wall, including this one (which would not have stood originally on this spot but outside the fort, near where the *Ship Inn* is today), would have been for the use of soldiers rather than Roman civilians and as such would have been less fancy than the average mosaic-floored *balineum* of popular imagination. Still, it's done as authentically as possible using recreated Roman cement, *opus signinum*, for the floors, and there are frescoes on the walls. Outside, there's a small Roman-style medicinal **herb garden**. One other highlight is the only **stone toilet seat** surviving from Roman Britain.

Don't forget to visit the reconstructed Wall, either, which lies outside the site on the north-west corner; accurate, as far as we know, though some have quibbled about the crenellations, which may be a mere embellishment to make it look more like a military construction. Following the recent demolition of a scaffolding yard that lay to the north of this reconstructed wall, the remains of another Roman construction has been found, though its exact purpose has yet to be determined. One place that is open to public gaze, however, is **B Pit**, an old colliery shaft discovered during the Segedunum excavations. Incidentally, while we're on the subject of collieries and coal, the coal industry – the making of Wallsend – was another thing that the Romans brought to the area, having been the first to mine it here. As such, the Romans could be said to have been the first to bring coals to Newcastle!

The route

From the entrance to Segedunum, turn right and head down Station Rd, which runs along the back of Segedunum's reception and museum. A path runs east–west above the road; this is the start of the trail. Before you begin, however, don't forget to stamp your passport at the Segedunum reception or, if they're

---

❏ **The layout of the Wall forts**

The fort at Segedunum is pretty typical of the design of all Wall forts along the trail. Often described as '**playing-card shaped**', the layout varied little from one to the next. At its centre were the **headquarters**, the *Principia*, the heart and brains of the fort. It was here that justice was dispensed, plans formulated, men paid and ceremonies, both secular and religious, performed. Sometimes, as with Segedunum, a **shrine** was housed within this building under which, in a small safe-room underneath, the money to pay the soldiers' wages would be stashed. The commanding officer's house, or *praetorium*, where he lived with his family and servants, stood next door, usually to the east of the HQ, while the **hospital** and other public buildings sat next to its west. Often you'd find the fort's **granary** here too, one of the most interesting buildings, architecturally, of the whole fort. The granary's sides were buttressed to help the walls withstand the pressure created by all that grain being housed within it, while the floor itself was raised to allow air to circulate, thus preventing the grain at the bottom of the heap from going mouldy. The granary would have had a porch, too, to stop the grain getting wet when it was being unloaded from the carts. There's a particularly good granary, complete with the porch pillars, at Corbridge.

Flanking these buildings to north and south were the barracks. **Cavalry barracks** are distinguishable from the infantry barracks by a recess or ditch hewn into the floor – dug to collect the horse's urine and prevent it from seeping into the cavalry officer's quarters next door. Segedunum has fine examples of these. Usually, three men and three horses would share one of these 'apartments' and there would be about nine apartments to each barrack. **Infantry barracks** were much simpler affairs, housing about five men to a room. At the end of each barrack were the living quarters of the *decurian*, the man in charge of the barrack. The fort at Arbeia has recreated a block of infantry barracks. Scattered amongst these buildings were others, such as the **public latrines**, of which Housesteads has a particularly fine example.

As with Segedunum, the whole fort would often lie on both sides of the Wall, with its northern end extending beyond the Wall's line into 'barbarian' territory. There would usually be more gates on the northern side than the southern side, too, to allow the soldiers to charge out quickly to meet their barbarian foes.

Other buildings associated with the fort would lie outside its walls, including religious buildings such as **temples** (witness the Mithraeum outside Brocolitia, for example), and **public baths** (the ruins at Chesters have a great example of these). A **civilian settlement**, or *vicus*, would often grow up around the Wall, too, peopled with retired soldiers from the fort, their children (who automatically became Roman citizens when their father did), wives (who *didn't*), traders and locals.

closed, the Total petrol station 200m or so further east of the fort on the main road. This **15-mile (24km; 4³⁄₄-5hrs)** first stage begins by the only remaining piece of the Wall that originally ran down from the fort to the Tyne, and which now stands just over the railings outside the fort grounds. As the easternmost part of the Wall still in existence, this is an appropriate place to begin. Through all of Newcastle, by the way, the trail is called **Hadrian's Way** for some reason and this is what you'll see on the signs. Heading west, the path you are following was originally an old railway track, an extension of the Blyth and Tyne Railway. By the side of the trail are the abutments of old bridges and the ironmongery of various parts of the railway, now finding secondary employment as resting posts.

It must be said that, though not without interest, this is not the most auspicious start to a trail. It's not the way the trail leads through the industrial heart of the city that disappoints; if you're in the right frame of mind a short walk through an entirely man-made landscape can be as diverting as any country romp. But hemmed in by warehouses and the backs of housing estates, there's little industry, or indeed anything to see. Unfortunately, one or two trekkers have also been subjected to insults and threats from local kids on both this stretch and the one that leads across Denton Dene (see Map 5, p103) and have written to say that they felt threatened in these areas. We should, I suppose, be thankful that the abuse has so far been just verbal and that these incidents, as unpleasant as they are, are still quite rare. If nothing else, at least you are getting the worst of the trail out of the way now – and it will also make you appreciate the rest of the trek more!

Crossing roads and following the signposts, eventually the path passes a school and a gas tower, drops away from the railway track and heads down to the water's edge and the **Walker Riverside Park** (an appropriate name for a park at the start of a national trail).

Beginning at peaceful **St Anthony's Point** (Map 2), the path heads westward through the smart **St Peter's Marina** and on to the very heart of the city, past such modern Tyneside icons as BALTIC and the **Millennium Bridge** (Map 3) – the first of the city's seven bridges. (Incidentally, look out for seals swimming in the Tyne. I saw one just down from St Peter's Marina, while another trekker wrote to say that he watched one swimming by the bridge at Wylam!). At the top of the hill above the Sea nightclub is the Castle Keep (see p88 and map p84), situated on the site of the Roman fort of Pons Aelius. Note how, less than two hours into the walk, you've already encountered two of the Wall's 17 Roman forts! Though the milecastles and turrets were evenly spaced out along the Wall, the forts were not, being built instead at strategic points along it – in this case, to overlook one of the two Wall bridges to cross the Tyne. This bridge would have stood where the Swing Bridge now stands. Alas, nothing remains today.

After the seventh and final Tyne bridge, Redheugh, the trail continues, hugging the river through mile after mile of business parks and industrial estates.

(Opposite) Top: The first view of Newcastle's city centre from the Hadrian's Wall Path takes in the 'Winking Eye' Millennium Bridge, the BALTIC gallery and Norman Foster's Sage building (see p89). **Middle**: Chollerford Bridge (see p122) from the Roman bridge abutment. **Bottom**: By the Wall at Black Carts (see p138).

WALLSEND

TO THE BUS &
METRO STATION

TOTAL PETROL
STATION

TO HADRIAN
LODGE HOTEL

NETTO FOODSTORE

001 → SEGEDUNUM
START/FINISH OF
THE TRAIL

BIT OF WALL
OUTSIDE
SEGEDUNUM
LEADING
DOWN TO
RIVER

SMALL RECONSTRUCTION
OF THE WALL

STATION
RD

SWAN HUNTER

FACTORIES

SHIP
INN

MULTICOLOURED
CRANES

FOLLOW THE ROUTE OF
A DISUSED RAILWAY -
BRIDGE ABUTMENTS
AND THE OLD GIRDER
DECORATE THE
TRAIL

BENCH

PLAQUES TO
HADRIANUS
AUGUSTUS

OLD RAILWAY
BRIDGE
ABUTMENT

FACTORIES

WALKER

River Tyne

MAP 1

MILEPOST

002

WINCOMBLEE
HOTEL

WINCOMBLEE
WORKSHOPS

SCRAP
METAL

SMALL TARMAC
PATH

CRANES BEYOND
THE TREES TO THE
EAST OF THE TRAIL

START/END OF THE HWP

START/END OF THE HWP

30 MINS FROM GAS TOWER (MAP 2)

30 MINS TO GAS TOWER (MAP 2)

ROUTE GUIDE AND MAPS

0   ¼ mile

0   APPROX SCALE   500m

2

(Opposite) Top: Market day at Hexham (see p135) in front of the abbey. **Bottom**: Through the dazzling fields of oilseed rape near Halton Shields.

MAP 2

COMING FROM THE EAST, CAN SEE THE SAGE BUILDING, AND ST NICHOLAS'S CHURCH FOR THE FIRST TIME ON THE TRAIL

GAS TOWER

BENCHES

003

SHORTCUT DOWN STEPS

WALKER RIVERSIDE PARK

SAINT ANTHONY'S POINT

IGNORE PATHS - STICK BY THE WATER!

River Tyne

AKZO NOBEL

BYKER

St Peter's MARINA

THE ROPERY

BOTTLEHOUSE ST

BASCULE BAR & BISTRO

CAR PARK

004

St Lawrence Rd

SPILLERS

3

MERCHANT WHARF

OFFICE (RED & YELLOW)

FRIARS GOOSE WATERSPORTS CLUB

ELEPHANT ON TYNE

¼ mile
500m
0
0
APPROX SCALE

Trailblazer

30 MINS FROM MILLENNIUM BRIDGE (MAP 3)

St Peter's MARINA

40 MINS

GAS TOWER

GAS TOWER

35 MINS

St Peter's MARINA

30 MINS TO MILLENNIUM BRIDGE (MAP 3)

MAP 3

ST LAWRENCE

2

CAR PARK

TYNE BAR

Ouseburn

EXCLUSIVE APARTMENTS

River Tyne

BALTIC

SAGE

MILLENNIUM BRIDGE (2002)

CAR PARK

005

OUSEBURN WATER SPORTS ASSOCIATION

GATESHEAD HERITAGE CENTRE @ ST MARY'S & GATESHEAD TIC

TYNE BRIDGE (A1R)

SWING BRIDGE (1876)

HIGH LEVEL BRIDGE (1849)

QUEEN ELIZABETH II BRIDGE (METRO, 1981)

KING EDWARD VIII BRIDGE (1906)

Malmaison Hotel

006

Quayside Bar

Copthorne Hotel

007

CENTRAL STATION

SEE NEWCASTLE MAP

REDHEUGH BRIDGE (1983)

4

APPROX SCALE
0   500m
0   ¼ mile

This is Armstrong country (see box below) and his crest can be seen at various points along the trail.

The dominant architectural feature of this section, however, lies across the river on the south bank. These are the **Dunston Coal Staithes** (Map 4), which were used to load coal from the collieries onto the colliers – the ships that would transport the cargo south to London and elsewhere.

❏ William Armstrong – the forgotten man of the Industrial Revolution

However high we climb in the pursuit of knowledge we shall still see heights above us, and the more we extend our view, the more conscious we shall be of the immensity which lies beyond.   **William Armstrong**

Though something of a local hero, William Armstrong's star has faded when compared to the lustre of his near contemporary, George Stephenson (see box p106). Yet the impact of both men on the history of Newcastle, Britain, and the wider world was equally enormous.

Born in 1810 in Pleasant Row, in the Shieldfield area of Newcastle, William George Armstrong's first calling was as a solicitor, a vocation in which he showed enough talent and ambition to become a partner in a legal practice in the city. Yet throughout this time Armstrong's first love was not the law of man but the immutable laws of science and, in particular, engineering. Indeed, he used to give lectures at Newcastle's Lit and Phil Society on this very subject, and it wasn't long before he was turning his hand to constructing the machines he talked about. His first major project was a hydro-electric generator, which he unveiled to the world in 1842. Switching from hydro-electrics to hydraulics, just four years later Armstrong was persuading a number of wealthy local businessmen to back his plans to develop hydraulic cranes, which would be powered with the assistance of the Whittle Dene Water Company, a firm that he himself had helped to set up a few years previously. (You'll pass Whittledene Reservoir on the trail.) The result of all this endeavour was the Newcastle Cranage company, based at Elswick, which later became known as Armstrong's Factory – as mentioned in the song *Blaydon Races*. The manufacture of cranes became the cornerstone both of his industrial empire and of the Industrial Revolution itself; Isambard Kingdom Brunel was just one of his regular customers.

Yet Armstrong wasn't finished yet; with the advent of the Crimean War Armstrong became involved in the development of arms, manufacturing an 18lb breach-loading gun that was sold all over the world. Indeed, such was the popularity of his weapons that *both* sides in the American Civil War were armed with Armstrong's artillery! He also developed an interest in bridges, constructing Newcastle's Swing Bridge and much of London's Tower Bridge.

There were, of course, considerable financial benefits to his success. By 1850 over 300 men were employed in Armstrong's Elswick factory, bringing unprecedented prosperity to the area. (The modern incarnation of his company, Vickers, formerly Vickers Armstrong, still operates in the area and lies just off the path; see Map 4.) The country at large also benefited, with Armstrong gifting his patents to the British government, an ostensibly selfless act which was nevertheless rewarded with a knighthood. His success also enabled him to own most of Jesmond Dene, as well as a magnificent mansion at Cragside. But as was typical of the man, despite the riches, he continued to invent, even though he became less involved in the company that he founded. It maybe comes as no surprise, therefore, to find that Cragside has a place in history as the first house in the world to be lit by hydro-electric power.

Negotiating a rather charmless section to cross the A695, you join yet another disused railway-turned-footpath, this one originally running between **Scotswood** (Map 5), Newburn and Wylam. Though located in the midst of a veritable spaghetti bolognaise of major traffic arteries, factory showrooms and noisy warehouses, the walk itself is pleasant enough, the worst industrial excesses hidden behind a screen of trees.

Crossing the A191 to **Denton Dene**, the trail continues to seek out the city's greener elements amidst the noisy urban sprawl, hopping from one green space to the next like a frog leaping from lilypad to lilypad. Rejoining the disused railway at the end of a cul-de-sac, Ottringham Close, the path finally takes on a more peaceful aspect, though with the suburbs of Lemington and Newburn just a few metres away, you're never far from either civilisation or traffic. Note the **Lemington Glass Cone** (Map 6) ahead and to the left of the trail, and no, your eyes aren't deceiving you: it *is* made of brick. This late 18th-century cone derives its name, of course, from its former purpose as a furnace for making glass. Almost opposite, the *café* (Mon-Fri 9am-3pm) in the Lemington Centre (☎ 0191-264 1959, 🖳 www.lemingtoncentre.co.uk) is a nice (and very cheap) little stop serving snacks and lunches.

Crossing the old toll road at **Newburn** you come to *The Boathouse* (☎ 0191-229 0326; bar Mon-Sat 11am-11pm, Sun noon-10.30pm, food served Mon-Sat 10am-6pm, main meals noon-6pm, Sun noon-4pm). Look on the wall for the flood markers; the height of the water in 1771 is particularly impressive. The old toll road also marks the unofficial limits of the city, at least as far as Wall walkers are concerned, as you finally leave the hullabaloo of Newcastle behind to enter the delightful **Tyne Riverside Country Park**. It's a lovely way to wind down at the end of the first stage, a pleasant and peaceful riparian stroll with dog-walkers, joggers, butterflies, swans and the first truly mature trees on the trail as company. There's also a **Visitor Centre**, and while its opening hours are limited (generally weekends and school holidays), it shares the building with toilets and sinks that have potable water.

Those who don't want this initial stage to end may like to consider calling in at *The Keelman* (☎ 0191-267 1689, 🖳 www.keelmanslodge.co.uk; 8D/6D, T or F, all en suite, bath available), behind the Visitor Centre. It's one of the best pubs on (or rather, just off) the route, a vast place with real ales and its own micro-brewery, **Big Lamp**. They serve food (restaurant open Sun-Fri noon-9pm, Sat to 9.30pm) and, in case the attractions of the beer already outweigh those of the walk, they charge £61.50 for two sharing (£46 single occupancy) plus £7.95 for a full English breakfast or £4.95 for a continental breakfast. Breakfast is available from 7am for both residents and non residents but it must be booked in advance.

❏ **Walk side by side and on healthy grass** Don't walk in single file or on worn areas. Protect our heritage!

BENWELL

WHITEFIELD RD SCOTSWOOD

MAP 5

¼ mile

500m

0

0

APPROX SCALE

FENCE

PAVILION/
CLUB HOUSE

A191

013

DENTON DENE

PITCHES

012

COMING FROM THE EAST,
TURN RIGHT AT BOLLARDS

011
MILEPOST

PATH FOLLOWS
DISMANTLED RAILWAY

EMBANKMENT

BRIDGE
ABUTMENT

BENCH

A693

WHITEHOUSE
ENTERPRISE
CENTRE

BRIDGE
ABUTMENTS

4

DON'T CROSS
ROAD BRIDGE -
KEEP STRAIGHT ON

CARISH
WAREHOUSE

TARMAC PATH
THROUGH
URBAN PARK

FIELD

014

OTTRINGHAM
CLOSE

SCHOOL

6

ROUTE GUIDE AND MAPS

MAP 6

60 MINS TO PATH JUNCTION & MILEPOST (MAP 5)

BRIDGE OVER THE A6085

45 MINS FROM GOLF COURSE (MAP 7)

60 MINS FROM PATH JUNCTION & MILEPOST (MAP 5)

BRIDGE OVER THE A6085

45 MINS TO GOLF COURSE (MAP 7)

LEMINGTON

LEMINGTON CENTRE & PHONE BOX
CAFÉ
BUS STOPS
POST OFFICE
LEMINGTON GLASS CONE
UNDER ROAD & FOOTBRIDGE
A6085
NEWBURN INDUSTRIAL ESTATE
BENCHES
PATH FOLLOWS COURSE OF DISMANTLED RAILWAY
OVERHEAD CABLES
NEWBURN
BENCH
DILAPIDATED STEELWORKS
TARMAC PATH
River Tyne
016
017
THE BOATHOUSE - LOOK FOR FLOOD MARKER ON THE WALL
MONUMENT TO BATTLE OF NEWBURN FORD, 1640
CAR PARK
SPORTS FIELD
NEWBURN BRIDGE - OLD TOLL ROAD
OVERHEAD CABLES
THE KEELMAN PUB
VISITOR CENTRE
BOAT LAUNCH

1/4 mile
500m
APPROX SCALE
0
0

MAP 7

45 MINS TO BRIDGE OVER A6085 (MAP 6)

45 MINS FROM BRIDGE OVER A6085 (MAP 6)

GOLF COURSE

GOLF COURSE

GOLF COURSE

GOLF COURSE

POND

TO WYLAM (15 MINS) & STEPHENSON'S COTTAGE (10 MINS)

THE FIRST (OR LAST!) HADRIAN'S WALL PATH SIGNPOST.

020

JOIN THE ROAD JUST BY THE GOLF COURSE'S CAR PARK. HEAD UPHILL FOR A FEW METRES, THEN TURN LEFT INTO THE WOODS AND CONTINUE UPHILL

OLD PATH ALONG RIVER STILL EXISTS BUT NOWADAYS TREKKERS ENCOURAGED TO TAKE THE WAGGONWAY

WYLAM WAGGONWAY – DISMANTLED RAILWAY

River Tyne

JOIN (OR LEAVE) THE WYLAM WAGGONWAY

019

018

LEAVE RIVER

RYTON ISLAND

TYNE RIVERSIDE COUNTRY PARK

CHILDREN'S PLAY AREA

BENCHES

FOOTPATH

TREE-LINED PATH

RUINED BUILDING BY THE RIVER

6

8

0   ¼ mile
0   500m
APPROX SCALE

ROUTE GUIDE AND MAPS

Otherwise, it's onwards and upwards, having forsaken the water's edge to join, briefly, the **Wylam Waggonway** (Map 7).

Thanks to the popularity of the trail, and the relative paucity of B&B options in Heddon-on-the-Wall, **Wylam**, 15-20 minutes along the Waggonway from the trail, is seeing an increasing number of trekkers looking for somewhere to stay on their first (or last) night.

ROUTE GUIDE AND MAPS

❑ **George Stephenson and the Wylam Waggonway**

Born (on 9 June 1781) and raised on the eastern fringes of Wylam, right by the old Wylam Waggonway, it was perhaps inevitable that George Stephenson – who must, as a child, have watched the progress of those early horse-drawn waggons passing his house – would somehow be drawn into the industry. Indeed, his very first job was working on the waggonway, where he was hired as a boy to keep a neighbour's herd of cows off the tram road.

Lacking formal education and unable to read or write, Stephenson joined his dad at Killingworth Colliery, though it wasn't long before his fascination for machinery, combined with a single-minded nature and fierce ambition, was leading him in new directions. In 1812 he became enginewright at the colliery and less than a year later Stephenson had persuaded his manager to let him try his hand at building a railway engine. The result was *Blucher*, a slow and clumsy beast (it was said to do no more than 4mph) which nevertheless became the first engine to avoid using cog-and-rack pinions – a breakthrough that thrust Stephenson to the very forefront of steam technology at the relatively tender age of 32.

Sixteen locomotives later and in 1819 Stephenson, his reputation for engine building now unmatched, was asked to construct an eight-mile line from Hetton to Sunderland. It was his – and the world's – first major steam railway project. It was also the task that convinced Stephenson that steam railways, if they were to have a future, needed to be constructed on as level a ground as possible; the hilly terrain that separated Hetton from Sunderland meant that his locomotive could not complete the journey without significant help from fixed hauling engines to help it negotiate the steeper parts, which slowed down the engine's progress considerably.

Further success followed; on 27 September 1825 – a date now known as the Birth of the Railways – his invention, *Locomotion*, carried 450 passengers at 15mph (24km/h) between Darlington and Stockton along his own railway line. Several years later, in 1829, an updated version of *Locomotion*, built with the help of his son Robert and called *Rocket*, won a competition to find the fastest locomotive when it travelled at an average speed of 36mph (58km/h) from Liverpool to Manchester, the line for which Stephenson had become chief engineer. It became his most celebrated achievement and firmly established his reputation as 'Father of the Railways'. With his new-found fortune Stephenson bought Tapton House, a grand Georgian manor near Chesterfield, where he kept busy opening coal mines, ironworks and limestone quarries in the nearby area. It was at Tapton that he died, on 12 August 1848, aged 67.

Today, it's possible to visit Stephenson's childhood home (☎ 01661-853457, 🖳 www.nationaltrust.org.uk/main/w-georgestephensonsbirthplace; mid-Mar to end Oct Thur-Sun 11am-5pm; £1.80; free for NT members) at Wylam, which is now owned by the National Trust. The white-stone cottage is a simple miner's affair that's been furnished to reflect the typical living arrangements of the late 18th century (when Stephenson was born), with everybody living in the one room.

WYLAM

Thankfully, there are a couple of decent accommodation options in the village, as well as good places to eat.

There's also a **pharmacy**, a **post office**, a Spar **supermarket** (daily 6am-9pm) with an **ATM**, JA Stobo vegetable shop, and the Wylam Wine Lodge and Food Store (Mon-Sat 7am-9pm, Sun 9am-8pm), the owners of which also run *Wormald House* (☎ 01661-852529, 🖳 www.wormaldhouse.co.uk; 2D/1T, all en suite, bath available), the first place you come to as you reach the village from the trail. B&B costs £30pp (£33.50 for single occupancy); packed lunches are £5. If prearranged they will pick you up at Heddon and drop you off the next morning.

Further up the hill, *Black Bull* (☎ 01661-853112, 🖳 www.blackbull-wylam.co.uk; 1S/4D/2D, T or F, all en suite; food served Tue-Sat 6-9pm, Sun noon-4.30pm) has rooms starting from £25 for the single, £40 for two sharing and £60 for a family room. Note that they don't provide breakfast (most people go to the Wine Lodge), nor do they accept debit/credit cards. They claim to have some of the cheapest food in the North-East, with special nights such as the Wednesday steak night, where steaks for two cost a very reasonable £19.50. Be warned, though, that it can get crowded when there's a big football match on.

Bistro en Glaze (☎ 01661-852185; 🖳 www.bistroenglaze.webs.com; 1D/3D, T or F, all en suite, bath available), near the top of the village is the most charming place in town. Its rooms have all the usual facilities and they charge £65-70 (£45 for single

occupancy). If booked in advance they will collect you from the path and take you back the next morning. Dogs are welcome, subject to prior arrangement. They also do the classiest food (Tue-Sat 6-10pm); their menu changes every couple of months or so.

Booking is advised if you want to eat at the *Fox and Hounds* (☎ 01661-853246; food served Tue-Sat noon-2pm & 6-9pm, Sun noon-4pm) in the evening.

Finally, at the other end of town, just across the river, the *Boathouse* (☎ 01661-853431; Mon-Sat 11am-11pm, Sun noon-10.30pm; food served daily noon-6pm) is renowned for its award-winning cask ales (it regularly wins the CAMRA Northumberland Pub of the Year).

Go North East's No 684 **bus** service calls here; see pp56-8 for further details.

It's a bit of an exhausting schlep to the top of the hill but **Heddon-on-the-Wall**, with its pubs, accommodation and, best of all, a great chunk of Hadrian's Wall on its outskirts, is a worthy reward at the end of a long but interesting first day.

HEDDON-ON-THE-WALL
[MAP 8, p109]

A fine place for a first night, Heddon-on-the-Wall lies at the culmination of a steep haul up from the River Tyne. As such, it marks the start of your Wall-walk proper (as opposed to the riverside meanderings you've enjoyed up to now) and, as if to emphasise that point, there's a **sizeable chunk of Wall** for you to savour, just a minute away from the path.

You'll notice over the next few days that the Wall turns up in the unlikeliest of places, and it's no different here: lying parallel to the busy B6528, this portion is, at over 100m, the longest section of *broad* Wall remaining. As you'll see on the next stage, the Romans soon reduced their building ambitions, for although they still had the foundations for a broad Wall, west of here they built a narrow Wall on top of them. The flat circular platform that's incorporated into the Wall is a kiln that post-dates the Roman era.

As for Heddon itself, it's not a bad little place and is rather quaint in parts. It also has a few services for trekkers, including a **tearoom-cum-delicatessen**, the highly rated *Dingle Dell Tearooms* (Mon-Fri 9am-5pm, Sat 9.30am-3.30pm), serving a range of local cheeses, meat, preserves and pickles; a **post office-cum-newsagent** (Mon-Fri 7.15am-6pm, Sat 7.15am-5pm, Sun 7.15am to noon; post office Mon-Fri 9am-5.30pm, Sat 9am-12.30pm) next door; a petrol station that doubles as a Spar **supermarket** (Mon-Sat 7am-9pm, Sun 8am-9pm) with **cashpoints** (one in the Spar and one in The Swan, both of which charge; note that these are the last ATMs/cash machines on the path until Gilsland in Cumbria, though there are several on the alternative route via Corbridge, Hexham and Acomb.

Heddon also has a couple of **pubs**. Of these, the *Three Tuns* (☎ 01661-852172, 🖳 www.thethreetunsheddon.co.uk; daily noon-11pm), on the B6528, is a great old place, perhaps more popular with locals, though it does serve simple pub grub (daily Apr-Oct noon-8pm, Nov-Mar noon-7pm). The preferred option of most trekkers is *The Swan* (☎ 01661-853161; food served daily noon-9.30pm), with some huge meals served at their contemporary carvery (£7.99 Mon-Sat, £8.99 on Sun/Bank Hols). They also do more standard pub fare as well as sandwiches. Free wi-fi is available.

Accommodation-wise, you're pretty much limited to a couple of B&Bs and an 'accommodation'. *Ramblers' Repose* (☎ 01661-852419; 1S/1D shared bathroom/1T en suite), at 8 Killiebrigs, provides a great breakfast (organic ingredients where possible) and charges £35 for the single and £65-75 for two sharing. Smarter, *Heddon Lodge* (☎ 01661-854042 or ☎ 07802-660485; 🖳 www.heddonlodge.co.uk; 2D en suite/1D with private bathroom), at 38 Heddon Banks, has some splendid accommodation surpassed only by the fantastic breakfasts, with ingredients sourced locally and organic where possible; rates are £75 (£65 for single occupancy). Well-behaved dogs (£10) are welcome subject to prior arrangement.

The latter is *Houghton North Farm* (☎ 01661-854364, 🖳 www.hadrianswallaccommodation.com; 22 beds). Though on the surface the layout of this place may resemble a hostel this really is a cut above your average hostel or bunkhouse. There are six rooms: one sleeps two (two beds); one sleeps three (single bed and bunk bed; en suite facilities); three rooms sleep four (two bunk beds); and one sleeps five (bunk above a double bed and a separate bunk bed; en suite facilities). There's also a kitchen and dining area, free internet access, TV lounge and power shower to die for, as well as high standards of comfort and cleanliness. Rates start from £25pp but this does include a buffet-style continental breakfast. Furthermore, in spring, if you ask nicely, they may let you feed their pet lambs in the morning.

There are plenty of **buses** between Heddon and either Newcastle or Hexham, including the AD122 (see timetable pp212-15), which calls in at Heddon's Towne Gate, Arriva's/Stagecoach's No 685 service and Go North East's No 684; see pp56-8 for further information.

HEDDON-ON-THE-WALL TO CHOLLERFORD [MAPS 8-16]

Introduction

Anyone glancing at the maps for this **15-mile (24km; 6³/₄-7hrs)** stage will find their heart sinking and probably conclude that this is a walk to be endured, not

HEDDON-ON-THE-WALL   25 MINS TO GOLF COURSE (MAP 7)

MAP 8

HEDDON-ON-THE-WALL

SHELL PETROL STATION, SPAR SUPERMARKET & ATM

TO THROCKLEY

THE FIRST (OR LAST) MAJOR PIECE OF WALL ON THE TRAIL

023

Three Tuns

The Swan (ATM)

LOOK FOR EXPOSED STONES IN ROAD EMBANKMENT

FARM WALL

B6318

Dingle Dell Tearooms

PO

Ramblers' Repose

Heddon Lodge

B6528

SIGN TO HOUGHTON

3 MINUTE SHORT CUT

A SHADY WALK WITH SOME BEAUTIFUL TREES

7

022

SHORT CUT TO/FROM HOUGHTON NORTH FARM

TO HOUGHTON

GATE

021

WALK IN THE WOODS TO THE LEFT OF THE TRACK

SHAPE OF MILE-CASTLE 13

A69

024

WALK ON PATH BY SIDE OF B6318 WITH A69 ROARING DOWN BELOW TO THE SOUTH

Houghton North Farm

WALKING ON BRIDLEWAY, TREES TO LEFT

B6318 MILITARY RD

9

NOTICE SOME WALL STONES EMERGING FROM THE EMBANKMENT TO THE NORTH OF YOU HERE

trailblazer

¼ mile   500m

APPROX SCALE

0   0

ROUTE GUIDE AND MAPS

HEDDON-ON-THE-WALL   35 MINS FROM GOLF COURSE (MAP 7)

enjoyed. Why? Because most of the trail on this stage is owned by Northumberland Highway Department and throughout much of its length this walk is accompanied by one of its most important charges, the thundering B6318.

Indeed, based on what the map is telling you, some of you may even decide to take the Corbridge–Hexham–Acomb deviation instead (see pp125-38), and rejoin the official trail again towards the end of the stage at Heavenfield. This deviation is even more attractive on a Monday, when a couple of eating places on this stage are closed and the only places to get food are The Robin Hood Pub and Vallum Café, which lie opposite each other near the beginning of the day. But to put it succinctly, it would be wrong to do so, because this stage is packed with interest. For one thing, though the road is a constant companion, for most of this stage you'll be trekking slightly away from it in fields alive with livestock and other, wilder creatures of the British countryside such as hares, rabbits and a superb variety of birdlife including crows, lapwings, finches, swallows and, on the waters of Whittledene Reservoir, the great-crested grebe, tufted duck and dunlin.

Furthermore, permanent presence though it may be, the road is rarely an obtrusive one. Besides, the reason the trail follows the highway in the first place is because it is built right *upon* the Wall: the B6318 is merely the modern and more mundane moniker for the **Military Road**, built on top of the Wall on General Wade's orders in the 18th century to facilitate the rapid movement of his troops across the country in order to ward off incursions by Bonnie Prince Charlie and his followers. And though the Wall itself may not make much of an appearance until after St Oswald's (see p118), this allows its accompanying defences – the Vallum and, on the Wall's (and thus the road's) northern side, the Roman ditch – a chance to bask in the spotlight for a change; and it will be these, and the expansive views beyond, that will be occupying your attention today.

So, by all means, take the Corbridge–Hexham alternative if you prefer – it's a cracking walk – but not if your only reason for doing so is because you believe the official trail to be a bit duff. It's not. And my advice to those who are hoping to take the detour would be to take it and *then* come and do the proper trail. While those noble foot soldiers who intend to follow the official Hadrian's Wall Path faithfully should gird their loins and prepare themselves for an eventful march; just watch out for the chariots!

The route

The day begins as it means to continue: on the B6318 which starts behind the Three Tuns. It's not long before the first evidence of the Wall appears: as you enter a field following a diversion to cross the A69, stones from the Roman Wall lie where they emerged from the road embankment. Those with eagle eyes may be able to make out the platform outline of Milecastle 13, though it's extremely faint and you shouldn't worry if you can't make it out; there are plenty of better examples of milecastles to come.

MAP 9

RUDCHESTER FORT (VINDOBALA) UNEXCAVATED

55 MINS FROM HARLOW HILL (MAP 10)

40 MINS TO HEDDON-ON-THE-WALL (MAP 8)

RUDCHESTER FORT

40 MINS FROM HEDDON-ON-THE-WALL (MAP 8)

60 MINS TO HARLOW HILL (MAP 10)

NOW IN ROMAN DITCH. WILD FLOWERS ABOUND HERE IN SPRING

GATE

STONE SLABS OVER MUDDY GROUND

THE VALLUM IS HERE BUT IT'S HARD TO SPOT

STEPS EITHER SIDE OF ROAD

EPPIES HILL

027

026

HIGH SEAT

TWO HOOTS

Ironsign

TREE PLANTING GOING ON HERE

B6318

BRIDGE

WILD FLOWERS IN FIELD HERE

025

TELEGRAPH POLE

¼ mile

APPROX SCALE

500m

trailblazer

> ❏ **Milecastle numbers**
> The **milecastles** built along the Wall have each been assigned their own unique figure – whether the milecastles can be seen today or not. The order runs from east to west, so the first milecastle on the Wall (which would have been near Segedunum in Newcastle) is called Milecastle 1, and so on up to Milecastle 80 at Bowness-on-Solway.
>
> In addition to this designation, some of the more famous have been given their own name, such as the Grindon Milecastle (aka Milecastle 34). The Wall's **turrets** also have their own special number, each derived from the milecastle immediately to their east, with the turret closest to that milecastle given the letter A, and the next one to the west labelled B. So, for example, the turret immediately to the west of Milecastle 38 is known as Turret 38A, the next one to the west Turret 38B.
>
> Note, by the way, that a number of these milecastles were destroyed soon after they were built, when it was decided to move the forts up to the Wall from the Stanegate (see p10), many were built on top of old milecastles or turrets. Cilurnum (Chesters) Fort, for example, was built on Turret 27A and remains of it can still be seen.

More impressive tumescences appear just a few hundred metres further on in the next field. These are the subterranean remains of **Rudchester Fort** (aka Vindobala Fort; Map 9), once heavily pillaged by local farmers and the builders of the Military Road in the 18th century but now lying undisturbed beneath the soil of Rudchester Farm. Now owned by the local county council, there are hopes that this 4^1/$_2$-acre (1.8-hectare) fort will be excavated and developed properly one day – though what exactly is left after all these depredations remains to be seen.

The next few miles provide scant evidence that you are following a Wall, though other Roman constructions are evident. *Ironsign* (☎ 01661-853802, ⌨ www.ironsignfarm.co.uk; 3T, all en suite, bath available; Mar-Oct) is a pleasant B&B which charges £65 (single occupancy £35); if booked in advance evening meals (£17.50 for three courses) and packed lunches (about £5) are available.

A little beyond Ironsign one crosses the road to walk in the **Roman ditch**, the fortification that lay to the north of the Wall. This you follow almost all the way up to **Harlow Hill** (Map 10), a tiny, lonely little settlement whose most noticeable feature is its old church, now converted into a farmyard barn. Harlow Hill is a Request stop on the AD122 bus service.

The trail continues in the ditch down to **Whittledene Reservoir**'s Great Northern Lake. With the Welton Burn feeding this reservoir and the Whittle Dene Aqueduct from Hollington Reservoir flowing into the Great Southern Lake at the southern end, this series of lakes rarely freezes over even in the depths of winter, and as such attracts birdlife year-round. Indeed, over 190 species of birds, as well as red squirrels and deer, have been spotted on or near the lakes. This gigantic series of reservoirs is more than just a nature reserve, however, for the reservoir pumps 25 million gallons of water a day to the treatment works. With picnic tables, a hide that could provide invaluable shelter from the rain, and views opening up north and south, it's a highly disciplined

MAP 10

HARLOW HILL

WIND TURBINES IN DISTANCE TO NORTH

OLD CHURCH - NOW A BARN

Belvedere Campsite

FENCE

TO ALBEMARLE BARRACKS

B6318

PETROL STATION

PIG FARM

THROUGH SMALL TREE PLANTATION

BIRD HIDE & PICNIC TABLES

WALKING ON ROAD WITH FENCE TO THE RIGHT AND A ROAD BARRIER TO THE LEFT

STONE STILE IN THE WALL

GREAT NORTHERN LAKE

GREAT SOUTHERN LAKE (WHITTLEDENE RESERVOIR)

WALKING IN ROMAN DITCH ON PAVING SLABS

B6318

PAVING SLABS

028

¼ mile

APPROX SCALE

0   500m

individual who resists taking a break here. After the reservoir, the path keeps to the north of the road until Robin Hood Inn (see below).

EAST WALLHOUSES   [MAP 11]

About a mile to the north, and signposted off the trail, is *Matfen High House Farm* (☎ 01661-886192, 🖳 www.highhousefarm brewery.co.uk), part **tearoom/restaurant** (Sun-Tue   10.30am-5pm,   Thur-Sat 10.30am-9pm), part farm and part **brewery**. You can find out exactly how beer is made on a tour (by appointment; £5pp) of the brewery, sample some at the Real Ale Bar, then buy a barrel or two of the product to take along the trail with you. Incidentally, John Clayton (see p124), the man whom, after Hadrian himself, is most associated with the Wall, was one of the previous owners of the farm. Across the yard, *Matfen High House B&B* (☎ 01661-886592,   🖳   struan@struan.enterprise-plc.com; 1D/1T en suite, 1D/1T shared bathroom) dates back to 1735 and is said to serve 'fantastic' breakfasts. Rates are £30-40pp. They don't do evening meals (but offer lifts to the Robin Hood Inn when the restaurant at Matfen High House Farm is closed) but will prepare a packed lunch (from £4.50). Dogs (£5) are welcome, subject to prior arrangement.

There is also **Wellhouse Farm** (☎ 01661-842193, 🖳 www.wellhousefarm.co .uk; £5pp) **campsite**, with 45 pitches, a toilet and shower block, a coin-operated washing machine and dryer, a mile to the south of the trail. Wellhouse Farm can be

reached by continuing along the B6318 (while the path turns right into fields by East Wallhouses) then take the first left (see Map 11).

Robin Hood Inn (☎ 01434-672273, 🖳 www.robinhoodnorthumberland.co.uk), a pub dating back to 1752, is a favourite stop for trekkers with some hearty food (served Easter-Sep daily noon-9pm, Oct to Easter Mon-Fri noon-2.30pm & 6-9.30pm, Sat & Sun noon-9.30pm) and a **passport stamping point** (see box p49). **Campers** can pitch a tent at the back for free as long as they eat in the pub. However, there aren't any facilities.

As an alternative to the pub, just a few minutes down the road is *Vallum Farm Tearoom* (☎ 01434-672652, 🖳 www.val lumfarm.co.uk; daily 10am-4.30pm), a licensed café with a great selection of cakes. As for the food, I can personally recommend the scones, and it can only be a matter of time before hymns are being written and sung in praise of their lemon drizzle cake. On a hot day their ice-cream parlour could be just the ticket, as could a jug of Pimms (£6). Incidentally, the name is well chosen, for you can see the unmistakable undulations of the Vallum in front of the farmhouse.

The AD122 **bus** service stops outside the Robin Hood Inn.

Having passed the Robin Hood Inn (note that on a Monday this is the last place serving food before you reach Chollerford), tiptoe through the free-range chickens in the next field and soon after go round the Wallhouses diversion. The trail now travels alongside miles of farmland before eventually arriving at a row of pretty cottages lining the busy road, known as **Halton Shields** (Map 12). Turning left off the road at the end of the hamlet, you come to the next major Roman remain on your walk: the large, soft, curvaceous undulations of the **Vallum** as it burrows its way through the fields south of the trail.

The Vallum quickly disappears again, lost beneath the corrugations caused by medieval ploughing and the depredations of an old quarry, though more incongruous grassy bumps beckon by the monumental gates of Halton Castle. These mounds in the field are the remains of **Halton Chesters** (also known as Onnum; Map 13), the second unexcavated Roman fort on this stage. *(continued on p118)*

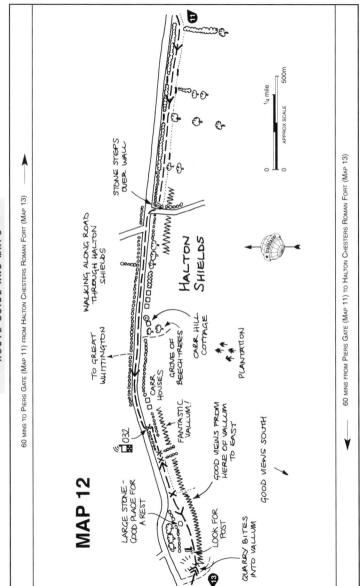

MAP 12

60 MINS TO PIERS GATE (MAP 11) FROM HALTON CHESTERS ROMAN FORT (MAP 13) →

60 MINS FROM PIERS GATE (MAP 11) TO HALTON CHESTERS ROMAN FORT (MAP 13) ←

LARGE STONE - GOOD PLACE FOR A REST

LOOK FOR POST

QUARRY BITES INTO VALLUM

GOOD VIEWS SOUTH

GOOD VIEWS FROM HERE OF VALLUM TO EAST

FANTASTIC VALLUM!

CARR HOUSES

☎ 032

TO GREAT WHITTINGTON

GROVE OF BEECH TREES

CARR HILL COTTAGE

PLANTATION

WALKING ALONG ROAD THROUGH HALTON SHIELDS

HALTON SHIELDS

STONE STEPS OVER WALL

APPROX SCALE

0   ¼ mile
0   500m

MAP 13

HALTON CHESTERS ROMAN FORT   45 MINS TO M6 TUNNEL (MAP 13A) ⟶

033

HALTON RED HOUSE

GATE

FENCE

ALTERNATIVE PATH TO CORBRIDGE

PYLON

HALTON

TO CORBRIDGE

GRAND GATES TO HALTON

'PROPER' HW

034

HALTON CASTLE

HALTON CHESTERS ROMAN FORT
(ONNUM)
UNEXCAVATED

TO CORBRIDGE

PORT GATE

035

ROMAN DERE STREET A68

WHITTINGTON FELL

Errington Arms

VALLUM TO SOUTH OF THE TRAIL BEHIND A FENCE

LADDER OVER FENCE

GREAT VIEW OVER THE VALLUM FROM THE LADDER STILE. ALSO FIRST/LAST VIEW OF NEWCASTLE

¼ mile   500m
APPROX SCALE
0   0

HALTON CHESTERS ROMAN FORT   ⟵ 50 MINS FROM M6 TUNNEL (MAP 13A)

— side margins —

35 MINS FROM ROAD FOR ACOMB (MAP 14) ⟶   HALTON CHESTERS ROMAN FORT   10 MINS ⟶   PORT GATE

35 MINS TO ROAD FOR ACOMB (MAP 14)   HALTON CHESTERS ROMAN FORT   15 MINS   PORT GATE

ROUTE GUIDE AND MAPS

12

13B

13B

14

(continued from p114) As with Vindobala, there's little to get too excited about with everything covered by a layer of turf and the undulations, other than the outline of the fort itself, difficult to distinguish from other, later, bumps.

Those wishing to take the Corbridge–Hexham–Acomb diversion (see pp125-38) or who are staying in Corbridge overnight should head south from here.

Continuing west, it's not long before the road and trail join forces for the final push up to **Port Gate** (Map 13, see p117; also spelt Portgate). A modern traffic roundabout at the junction of the A68 and the Military Road, this may not seem the most auspicious place to find evidence of Roman occupation. But the A68 to Corbridge was once the old Roman **Dere Street** that ran between the fort (and indeed further on down to York) all the way north to Scotland; and as such, the Port Gate was one of the few gateways the Romans built into the Wall. When the roundabout was built in the '60s it was deliberately moved a little way to the north so as not to disturb the unexcavated archaeological remains around here. This is also the place where the AD122 bus turns off the Wall and trail to head to Corbridge and Hexham.

Reaching the roundabout, a pause at the ***Errington Arms*** (☎ 01434-672250, 🖥 www.erringtonarms.co.uk; pub closed Sun eves and all-day Mon; food served Apr-Oct Tue-Sat noon-2.30pm & 6.30-9pm, Sun noon-4pm), named after an important local family, is scribbled into the itineraries of most trekkers and with good reason; the food here is great, with an extensive menu of dishes including plenty of sandwich options (£3.95). For evenings, try their delicious tagine (£10.95). Note the pub's opening hours are often reduced significantly in the winter. They also now have a **self-contained apartment** for let (£35pp) that sleeps six (2S/2D, bath available). They are hoping to use it as a holiday let but until the bookings pour in, walkers are welcome to stay. Go North East's No 74 **bus** service calls here; see pp56-8 for further details.

Fully refreshed, head off from behind the Errington Arms through the field, with the **Vallum** a constant and clearly defined companion to your left, before another bout of **Roman ditch** walking follows as you cross the road by the outline of **Milecastle 24** (Map 14).

Through fields and woods the trail continues to **St Oswald's Hill Head** (Map 15), with its lovely little church (see box below) set in a meadow to the north of the trail and a delightful little **tearoom**, *St Oswald's* (☎ 01434-689010;

❏ St Oswald's church

This was built to commemorate the victory of the eponymous saint over his rivals Cadwallon and Penda at the **Battle of Heavenfield**, the field in which you're now standing. In the 7th century St Oswald, who was merely a king at this stage, was the leader of the Angles following the death of Edwin (after whom Edinburgh is named) in AD633. His defeat of the combined forces of Gwynedd and Mercia, though not quite the victory of Christianity over paganism that the Venerable Bede portrays in his *History*, was nevertheless a significant victory for the Anglo-Saxons over the Celts and, as such, an important moment in English history. Incidentally, at the back of the church by the font there's a large **Roman altar**.

May-Oct Tue-Sun & bank hols 10am-4.30pm, Mar-April and Nov Fri, Sat & Sun only) just before **Heavenfield**.

Those staying in Acomb or Hexham may wish to turn left south off the trail by the large cross in the corner of Heavenfield to join the route of the Corbridge–Hexham–Acomb diversion (see pp125-38); this is also where those who took the diversion rejoin the path.

The rest of you should continue through the fields and across the road down to **Planetrees**, the first proper bit of Wall on this entire stage. Its existence is largely due to the efforts of William Hutton, who came across some workmen taking stones from the Wall to be used as raw materials for a new farmhouse. Hutton's entreaties to the local landowner responsible for the desecration, Henry Tulip, ensured that this small fragment survived; though 224 yards (204m) of the Wall which had already been pulled down by Tulip's men before Hutton arrived, did not. However, the portion that has survived is interesting: notice how, near the culvert built into the Wall to prevent water from collecting and weakening the foundations, the Wall changes from being a *broad* Wall on broad foundations, as we saw at Heddon, to a *narrow* Wall on broad foundations. A similar pattern can be seen at Brunton Turret (see below), just a little further on, and suggests that it was around here that the Romans gave up building an all-broad Wall and opted instead for a narrower version that nevertheless still made use of the original broad foundations. But before we get to Brunton Turret there's a rather dull stretch of road-walking that veers towards, and then away from, the village of Wall.

WALL   [MAP 16]

Quite a large place, it's typical of the rather perverse nature of this trail in that Wall village doesn't actually lie on the Wall. The village is perhaps of most interest to trekkers because of a decision by the local parish council to allow a night's **camping** on the village green free of charge but leaving the site as you found it. There are toilets nearby but no other facilities, nor indeed is there a shop in town. But there is a very good pub-cum-B&B at the southern end of town, about ten minutes from the trail: *The Hadrian Hotel* (☎ 01434-681232, 🖳 www

.hadrianhotel.co.uk; 2D/2T both en suite/2T shared bathroom) is an 18th-century coaching inn that offers food (summer daily noon-8.30pm, winter noon-3pm & 6-8.30pm) and has some very comfortable rooms, including a few with a four-poster bed. They also have a separate cottage (1D connecting to 1T) and a flat (1S/1D/1T). B&B costs £45-50 for single occupancy, £80/£100/£120/£140 for 2/3/4/5 people sharing. Dogs are welcome, subject to prior arrangement.

Tyne Valley's No 880 **bus** service stops here; see pp56-8.

Instead of turning left at the junction to Wall, if you keep on the path ie turn right you'll soon come upon **Brunton Turret** (officially Turret 26B), sitting in a

---

❑ **Important note – walking times**
Unless otherwise specified, **all times in this book refer only to the time spent walking**. You will need to add 20-30% to allow for rests, photography, checking the map, drinking water etc. When planning the day's hike count on 5-7 hours' actual walking.

ROUTE GUIDE AND MAPS

field to the right of the road. Said to be the finest turret extant on the Wall – up to eleven courses high in places – it was excavated, surprise surprise, by John Clayton in 1876. Note how the Wall is of different widths here, going into the turret at one width and coming out the other side at a narrower gauge. As we've already seen at Planetrees, this kind of chopping and changing with the width of the Wall continues for several miles, though nobody's really sure why. Possibly it was for economic reasons, or maybe it was because the limestone core they used west of here was stronger than the puddle clay used in the eastern section of the Wall, and thus the Romans decided a thinner Wall would suffice.

Continuing along the road, before visiting the fort or collapsing in your temporary abode at Chollerford, those with the necessary curiosity and gumption may want to check out the remains of the Roman bridge abutment on the southern side of the river facing Chesters Fort. It's about half a mile (1km) off the trail but it's a pleasant walk, and you'll be rewarded with a big fat **phallic symbol** at the end of it that would make your auntie blush; it's perhaps the best example of this Roman symbol of prosperity on the entire trail.

The symbol is carved into one of the stones on the abutment's eastern side, just above ground level. Two other piers in the water were also discovered but are visible now only when the water is low. The hub of a water wheel was also found and is now on show at Chesters. Incidentally, this was the third Roman bridge over the Tyne, the first, of course, being Pons Aelius in Newcastle and the second at Corbridge.

CHOLLERFORD [MAP 16]

There's nothing wrong with Chollerford, though to most trekkers it's a bit of a non-event: having crossed the sturdy 18th-century five-arch bridge, the trail turns immediately left and continues along the road to Chesters, all but bypassing Chollerford and its neighbour, Humshaugh.

Note that there are no cash machines here – or until Gilsland – but there are a few services of interest to trekkers. The petrol station, just over the bridge, has a small **shop** (summer Mon-Fri 8am-6pm, Sat & Sun 8am-5pm winter from 9am) selling essentials and next door is the *Riverside Tearooms* (☎ 01434-681325; Apr-Sep Mon-Fri 9am-4.30pm, Sat & Sun 10am-4.30pm, Oct-Mar to 4pm), which has **free internet access** for customers.

The owners also run the *Riverside Campsite* (contact details as for the tearoom;

Easter-Oct) in the field behind, where camping costs £6pp (including use of the shower/toilet block).

Across the other side of the roundabout is *The George* (☎ 01434-681611, 📧 www.coastandcountryhotels.com; 2S/9T/ 37D/2F, all en suite, bath available), set in its own landscaped gardens by the North Tyne and boasting its own pool and gym. Rates are about £100 for B&B (£119 DB&B) for two sharing; however, contact the hotel for details of special offers and rates for single occupancy. Dogs (£10) are welcome, subject to prior arrangement. Food is served daily (noon-2.30pm & 6-8.45pm, light snacks are available 2-5pm).

Transport-wise, the AD122 **bus** stops outside Chesters Roman fort and also in Chollerford. See pp56-8 for further infor-

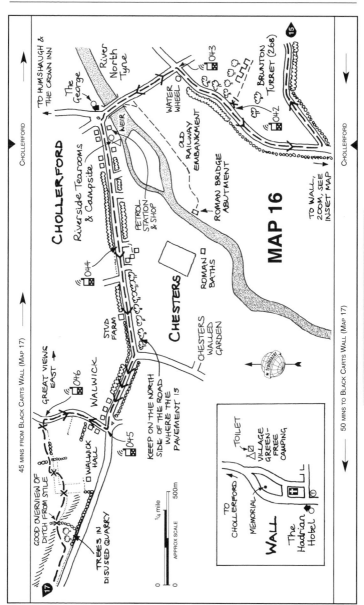

ROUTE GUIDE AND MAPS

mation and pp212-15 for the actual timetable.

If Chollerford doesn't appeal you could make your way about a mile north to the neighbouring village of **Humshaugh**,

where *The Crown Inn* (☎ 01434-681231; bar daily noon-11pm, food served Wed-Sat noon-2pm & 6-8.30pm, Sun lunch to 3pm, bank holidays lunch only) has reopened.

CHESTERS   [see map p123]

☎ 01434-681379; Apr-Sep daily 10am-6pm; Oct-Mar 10am-4pm (however, the winter days/hours may change so contact them or check on the English Heritage website before going); £5/4.50/3 adults/concessions; English Heritage members free. Note: the car park here is pay and display now.
'Jack Bob and self went to Chesters to view the remains of the Roman Fort and Bridge.' Found in the **diary of a militia officer** and dated June 1761, proving that Wall tourism is not a new phenomenon.

In its day, Chesters, or **Cilurnum** (meaning, curiously, 'Cauldron Pool') as it would have been known then, was *the* fort in which to be stationed out of all of those on the Wall. Set in a beautiful situation amongst mature trees in a bend in the river, the fort was built to guard the nearby bridge over the North Tyne, covered 5¾ acres, and was inhabited by 500 members of the Roman cavalry – who were better paid than their infantry counterparts and seemed to have enjoyed slightly preferential treatment too. The Asturian cavalry from Spain is the auxiliary force most associated with Chesters.

The fort itself was built c AD130 on land previously occupied by Turret 27A. It was excavated by that one-man preservation society, John Clayton, in the 19th century. Indeed, Chesters became the home of this Newcastle town clerk turned archaeologist and conservationist. Having inherited the estate in 1832, he continued working on this and other Wall fortifications until his death in 1890.

Today's visitors will not only be able to **stamp their passports** (see box p49) at reception (or by the gate when it's closed) but will also be able to enjoy the beautiful, traditional-style **museum** that Clayton established – full of dusty glass cases filled with some fascinating finds – as well as the ruins themselves. Top billing goes to the fort's **baths**, the highest of all the Roman ruins on the entire trail and located, as is usual, outside the fort itself, in this instance down the hill near the river.

These ruins give a really good idea of how the baths would have looked in their heyday, and how the water was channelled around and heated. Incidentally, during an early excavation of the baths in the 19th century, no less than 33 bodies, together with the remains of two horses and a dog, were discovered interred in the bathhouse. Curiously, their whereabouts are something of a mystery today, though at the time it was speculated that they dated back to the Saxon period. From the scattered remains by the baths you can also make out how the Wall itself would have travelled across the bridge, up to the fort (some Wall remains abutting the fort can be seen), right through the spot where the large country house (Clayton's old home) now stands, and beyond into the hills.

THE CORBRIDGE–HEXHAM–ACOMB ALTERNATIVE [Maps: 13 p117; 13a p126; 13b p127; 13c p132; 13d p133; 13e p137 & 15 p121]
This alternative trail (4½-4¾hrs; Halton Chesters Roman Fort to St Oswald's Hill Head via Corbridge, Hexham and Acomb) has a bit of everything. From the point of view of the scenery, the route includes magnificent stretches of woodland, a riparian stroll along the banks of the Tyne and even a few hills – thus far, for those coming from Newcastle at any rate, a rare 'treat'.

The market town of Hexham, with its ancient abbey overlooking the market place, is an unqualified delight, as is the compact town of Corbridge, home to a 17th-century bridge, a pele tower by the church that's made of Roman Wall stones and more pubs than you can shake a Roman spear at. And we haven't even mentioned the object of this diversion yet: the important Roman site (see pp130-1) just 15 minutes west of Corbridge near the banks of the Tyne.

From the Hadrian's Wall Path to Corbridge
There are any number of places where you can leave the Wall trail and head down to Corbridge, perhaps the most appropriate being the Roman Dere Street that once ran from the Firth of Forth through the Port Gate (see p118) to Corbridge and on to York. This, after all, was the main thoroughfare running north–south in Roman times. But for aesthetic reasons – not to mention the fact that it's a rather dangerous, pavement-less road in places – we suggest beginning a little way to the east of here, turning off at the grand, inviting tree-lined driveway leading to Halton Castle. This turn-off is also where the Roman Wall fort of Halton Chesters (Onnum) was once situated.

The path leads left past the castle grounds, where chickens, ducks, horses and a number of over-excitable dogs roam free, and on down the hill along country lanes. Look out for lapwings, buzzards and the ubiquitous rabbits as you go.

Eventually you pass under the A69 where a bridleway leads off right. Follow the directions on the map on p126 and, all being well, 50 minutes after leaving the main trail you arrive in front of Corbridge's old church and pretty market square.

CORBRIDGE   [See map p129]
In many ways Corbridge is a typical little English market town, smart, quaint, with a largely medieval centre and plenty of teashops and pubs to keep the floods of visitors that come every summer refreshed. At one time portrayed in the English press as Britain's snobbiest town – because of locals' objections to a fast-food van setting up in the market square – I'm sure you'll find it as friendly and approachable as everywhere else in this part of the world; and if the locals are more 'snobby' than their neighbours, well at least they've got a lot to feel superior about.

In addition to the wonderful Roman Town (see pp130-1), in the centre of Corbridge is Northumberland's finest Anglo-Saxon church, **St Andrew's**, built c AD786. In the churchyard there's a **pele tower** built using Roman stones, while a Roman gateway, which presumably originally stood at Corbridge Roman site, separates the baptistry from the rest of the church. Outside the church on the pavement is the site of the **King's Oven**, the main oven of the village in the 14th century.

ROUTE GUIDE AND MAPS

ROUTE GUIDE AND MAPS

MAP 13a

0 ___ ¼ mile
0 ___ APPROX SCALE ___ 500m

A68

DERE STREET

GRAVE HILL

110

TO AYDON CASTLE

111

112

LEAZES LANE

LEAZES COTTAGE

★ trailblazer

Carr Burn

SIGNPOST: 'TO HELEN'S LANE'. FOLLOW IT

PATH GOES UNDER A69   113

A69

BRIDLEWAY SIGN SAYS: 'TO COW LANE'

SHORTCUT TO NORGATE B&B

COW LANE

POTTERY KILN

CORCHESTER LANE

BENCH

SCHOOL

TO HIPPINGSTONES LANE

CORBRIDGE ROMAN TOWN (AKA CORSTOPITUM)

13b

50 MINS TO HALTON CHESTERS ROMAN FORT (MAP 13)

A69 TUNNEL

15 MINS FROM CORBRIDGE BRIDGE (MAP 13b)

45 MINS FROM HALTON CHESTERS ROMAN FORT (MAP 13)

A69 TUNNEL

15 MINS TO CORBRIDGE BRIDGE (MAP 13b)

13

CORBRIDGE
SEE TOWN PLAN

CORBRIDGE BRIDGE

114

CAR PARK

BUS STOP FOR HEXHAM

APPROX SCALE

0   ¼ mile

0   500m

TO CORBRIDGE ROMAN TOWN

ALTERNATIVE GORGEOUS PATH TO CORBRIDGE ROMAN TOWN

NEW EMBANKMENT BUILT FOLLOWING THE FLOODS OF 2005

MAP 13b

River Tyne

WHEN YOU REACH THE ROAD, A FEW MINUTES' WALK, TURN RIGHT TO CORSTOPITUM

LOVELY QUIET RIVER-SIDE PATH

BEAUTIFUL MATURE TREES AROUND HERE

ROMAN STONES FROM THE BRIDGE

115

DILSTON

Dilston Mill

A68

116

DILSTON PHYSIC GARDEN

117

13c

45 MINS FROM DUKE'S HOUSE (MAP 13c)   DILSTON   30 MINS   CORBRIDGE BRIDGE

55 MINS TO DUKE'S HOUSE (MAP 13c)   DILSTON   30 MINS   CORBRIDGE BRIDGE

Services

The centre of Corbridge is compact and in the main square you'll find the **post office**, **tourist information centre** (☎ 01434-632815, 🖳 corbridge .tic@northumberland.gov.uk; Easter-Oct Mon-Sat 10am-1pm & 1.30-5pm; Nov-Easter Wed, Fri & Sat 11am-4pm). A website worth looking at is 🖳 www .thisiscorbridge.co.uk.

You'll also find a **Co-op** and one of the town's busiest pubs, the Golden Lion. There's a **cashpoint** (ATM) at Barclays by the steps down to the riverside path to Corbridge Roman Town.

The library-cum-tourist office is also the only place in town with **internet** (£1 for 30 mins).

Transport

[See pp56-8] The AD122 **bus** calls in at Hill St and at Corbridge Roman Town; see pp212-15 for the timetable. Arriva's/Stagecoach's No 685, Go North East's Nos 10 and 684, and Wright's No 888 also stop here.

Train-wise, there are plenty of services to Hexham – with some continuing on to Carlisle – and to Newcastle. The railway station is about three-quarters of a mile south of the river.

Where to stay

Smartest of the accommodation options is probably *Priorfield* (☎ 01434-633179, 🖳 www.priorfieldbedandbreakfast.co.uk; 1T/1D, both en suite), on Hippingstones Lane, which you walk down if you take the direct route to Corbridge from the Wall. This Edwardian family house stands in half an acre (0.2-hectare) of garden but best of all, the double room has a whirlpool bath. B&B costs £65-75 (£58-68 single occupancy) – great value. They have free wi-fi and do packed lunches for about £5.

Nearer the Market Place, the *Wheatsheaf* (☎ 01434-632020, 🖳 www .wheatsheafhotelcorbridge.co.uk; 1S/4D/1T, all en suite, bath available) has undergone a recent refurbishment and looks much smarter. B&B in the single costs £70 and it's £99 for two sharing. Dogs are welcome subject to prior arrangement.

Across the other side of town, *The Angel* (☎ 01434-632119, 🖳 www .angelofcorbridge.co.uk; 1T/3D/2D, T or F, all en suite, bath available) is the smartest place in town, a former coaching inn dating back to 1726. Striking the right balance between stylish and cosy, it charges £105-115 (£65 single occupancy, £130 for three sharing) for B&B. Across the road and now under the same ownership, *The Angel Radcliffe* (contact The Angel for bookings; 1S/6D/2T, all en suite, bath available) charges £65-95 for a single/single occupancy, £105-140 for two sharing. Breakfast is served in the Radcliffe but other meals can be taken in The Angel (see Where to eat).

Heading a little further east, *2 The Crofts* (☎ 01434-633046, 🖳 www .2thecrofts.co.uk; 2D/1T, all en suite, bath available) charges £62-75 for two sharing (single occupancy £40-50). A further option would be *The Hayes* (☎ 01434-632010; 🖳 www.hayes-corbridge.co.uk; 1S/1D, T or F shared bathroom, 2D, T or F, both en suite, bath available), Newcastle Rd, a huge place set in seven acres charging £33.50 for the single, £33.50-36.50pp for two sharing.

ROUTE GUIDE AND MAPS

Where to eat and drink

Watling Coffee House (☎ 01434-634820; Mon-Sat 8am-5pm, Sun 9am-5pm) is one of the smartest of the many coffee shops in Corbridge. Up on the main square, the *Corbridge Larder* (☎ 01434-632948; 🖥 www.corbridgelarder .co.uk; shop Mon-Fri 9am-5pm, Sat to 5.30pm, café Mon-Fri 10am-4pm, Sat to 4.30pm) has local Doddington's ice cream. Food is also served at *The Angel* (see Where to stay; Mon-Thur noon-9pm, Fri & Sat to 9.30pm, Sun noon-5pm only).

Cheaper and better value is *Corbridge Sandwich Bar* (Mon-Sat 8am-5pm, Sun 11am-5pm in summer), by the square, with a range of tasty snacks and freshly made sandwiches, many of which cost less than £2.

For something more substantial try one of the pubs, such as the carvery at the *Wheatsheaf* (food served Mon-Fri noon-2.30pm & 5-9pm, Sat & Sun noon-9pm) or Corbridge's most pleasant and traditional pub, the *Black Bull* (☎ 01434-632261; food served Mon-Sat noon-9pm, Sun noon-8pm).

CORBRIDGE ROMAN TOWN [see map p126]

☎ *01434-632349; Apr-Sep daily 10am-5.30pm; Oct daily 10am-4pm; Nov-Mar Sat & Sun 10am-4pm (however, the winter days/hours may change so contact them or check on the English Heritage website before going); £5/4.50/3 adults/concessions/children, English Heritage members free*

It is, perhaps, a measure of how much we still need to learn about the Romans in Britain that when the first edition of this book was published this site was known as 'Corstopitum' after what everybody believed was the Roman name for the fortress that originally stood here. Doubt has recently been cast, however, as to whether this was true, with many experts now believing that the fortress, built to guard what was, at ten piers wide, Britain's largest stone bridge in Roman times, was actually called 'Coria' by the Romans. Proponents of this latter theory point to the Vindolanda postcards (see p155) to back up their assertions. On one of the tablets, commanding officer, Julius Verecundus reports that there were 337 soldiers at 'Coris', and this is just one of nine definite references to Coria/Coris on the Vindolanda tablets. But while it is generally accepted now that Coria was the most likely name for this site, it is not universally so, with a dwindling band of archaeologists still preferring the name Corstopitum (even though there is only one contemporary occurrence of this name, in a document known as the *Antonine Itinerary*). As such, and until the correct name can be ascertained, this site has now been 'rebranded' as Corbridge Roman Town.

Regardless of what the original name was, the new name that it's been given is actually more informative. For whilst its origins were undoubtedly as a Roman fortress – indeed it was, for many years, the nerve centre of Roman operations in northern England – the site was rebuilt time and again over the years, each time with modifications to suit its changing function. As such it is one of the most important sites near the Wall for archaeologists have been able to peel back each of these different stages, like layers on an onion, to discover the history of the fort; and bits of each of those layers are visible to the visitor today.

That history is a long and complex one. The first fort, built around AD85 under the Emperor Agricola, was situated about half a mile (1km) west of here and lasted only about 20 years before it was burnt down, to be replaced by a second, made of turf and built on this site, the following year. This, too, lasted fewer than 20 years before being abandoned, as Hadrian began to build his Wall and Roman troops were moved north to the new fortresses such as Halton Chesters (Onnum; see p114) that lay along its length. Corbridge was revived again, however, c AD140 under the Emperor Antoninus, when it became a supply base for the soldiers fighting his Scottish campaign. Soon after this, c AD180, its function seemed to change again and in place of its strictly military role the fort began to take on the appearance of a town. By the 3rd century it was home to a largely civilian population, though still with a military core, and remained like this until the Romans departed in the 5th century. Thus, while this site probably once had the typical 'playing-card' layout so familiar from the fortresses along the Wall – and, indeed, in many parts still does – there are also ruins from its days as a largely civilian settlement. And it is these that make this place unique.

The proof of the importance of this fortress to the Romans can be seen merely by looking at a Roman road atlas. Running from the fortress to the north

ROUTE GUIDE AND MAPS

❑ **The world's first archaeological dig?**
The history of the Roman site at Corbridge didn't abruptly come to an end when the Romans retreated to the Mediterranean. A few Saxon relics have been found to suggest that there was life here after the 5th century. Perhaps the most intriguing part of the fort's history, however, occurred in 1201 when King John undertook an excavation of the ruins in search of treasure. Though he found nothing except 'stones marked with bronze and iron and lead', his hunch was a good one: in 1911, more than 700 years later, 160 coins were found in a bronze jug, the largest hoard of Roman coins ever found in Britain. The find now resides in the British Museum. It may have been a fruitless search for John, but it earned him a prize of sorts: his excavation is seen by some as the first recorded archaeological dig in British history.

---

is **Dere Street**, the road the Romans built and would eventually use to launch their campaigns north into what is now Scotland; to the south, across the bridge, the same road continued to York; while running away to the west from here all the way to Carlisle was the **Stanegate**. As such, Corbridge was the transport hub of the region and a major supply town for forts along the Wall.

The Stanegate is still the main thoroughfare through the fort, though now it's at a higher level than the rest of the site thanks to all the resurfacing that went on during its lifetime. A stroll along here will take you past the **granaries** with their underfloor channels, built around AD180 when this site was metamorphosing from a regular fort into a supply base for troops on the Wall; the **fountain** next door which would once have been the centrepiece of the entire site; and the remains of various civilian buildings to the south of the Stanegate. I can't remember seeing such buildings *within* the boundaries of the Wall forts before – usually they were built outside the fort walls – which gives a good indication of just how much this Roman fort changed over time.

Incidentally, if you're wondering about the original fortress that lay half a mile (1km) west of here (the one that was built under the reign of Emperor Agricola and burnt down), that was discovered only in 1974 during the construction of the Corbridge bypass. You can see some of the things the archaeologists dug up there, as well as the best of their excavations here, in the museum adjacent to reception. You can also see a replica of the famous **Corbridge Lanx** (the original is in the British Museum, London), a silver salver discovered in the 1730s near the riverbank by a young girl out walking.

From the fort, the quickest way back into town is to turn right and head east along pavement-less Corchester Lane. A far more pleasant route, however, is to turn left and, after a short distance, left again. This leads alongside a tributary down to the North Tyne, from where it's a pleasant stroll to the impressive bridge that gave the town its name. Built in 1674, this bridge replaced an Anglo-Saxon one on the same spot that became derelict in the 17th century.

Corbridge to Hexham

The walk to Hexham is a dream as long as the weather holds. Beginning with a crossing of the bridge followed by a gentle waterside stroll, the route winds its way up through **Dilston**, home to the lovely *Dilston Mill B&B* (Map 13b; ☎ 01434-633493, 🖳 www.dilstonmill.com; 1D/1D, T or F). The 'double

DUKE'S HOUSE → 45 MINS TO DILSTON (MAP 13B) →

DILSTON PARK

★ trailblazer

SILVER BIRCH GROVE IGNORE STILES

PATH BETWEEN FENCES

13b

13d DUKE'S HOUSE

PLANTATIONS ON BOTH SIDES OF TRACK

PYLON

↓ PARK WOOD ½ MILE

SIGNPOST: 'DILSTON 1 MILE, A695 ½ MILE NORTH, HEXHAM RD ¾ MILE'

📱 119

SIGNPOST: DUKE'S HOUSE 1 MILE DILSTON ½ MILE

📱 118

0   ¼ mile
0   APPROX SCALE   500m

MAP 13c

← DUKE'S HOUSE ← 55 MINS FROM DILSTON (MAP 13B)

ROUTE GUIDE AND MAPS

room' is actually a Studio and has its own bathroom as well as a kitchen area where guests are provided with a self-serve breakfast. The 'family room' is a private suite with four rooms (including 1D/1T), a shower room and a sitting room; the rate depends on how many people are staying and for how long but expect to pay on average £39-44pp; a cooked breakfast is available if requested in advance. Most people go to Corbridge for an evening meal. Dilston Mill is definitely better for groups rather than solo travellers.

Continuing on up the hill, you then pass **Dilston Physic Garden** (🖳 www .dilstonphysicgarden.com; mid-Apr to mid-Oct; Wed & Sat 11am-4pm; £4/3 adults/concs), established by a neuroscientist at Newcastle University and containing over 500 plant species that can be used for health and healing.

The path continues on up the hill, with glorious views to the north across the valley towards the stately home of Beaufront (owned by the Errington family, after whom the pub at the Port Gate is named; see p118). These views are snatched away from you as you enter into pine plantations, the path leading from there to the riot of chimneys and turrets known as Duke's House (Map 13c), surrounded on all four sides by some beautiful woodland that plays host to deer, badgers and red squirrels. Plenty of paths lead down from here to Hexham which you'll reach about two hours – plus breaks – after leaving Corbridge.

HEXHAM   [See map p135]
The main market town for the district is a quaint and compact little place, the modern façades of shops and cafés concealing but not obliterating the medieval character of the town centre.

0   ¼ mile
0   APPROX SCALE   500m

★ trailblazer

A69

SMALL ROAD OFF TO LEFT (WEST) BEFORE ROUNDABOUT. TAKE IT!

River Tyne

RAILWAY STATION

TESCO

SHORT CUT FROM STATION

AD122 BUS STOP

HEXHAM SEE TOWN PLAN

EASTGATE

NATIONAL PARK HEADQUARTERS

GREAT VIEWS TOWARDS HEXHAM

VIEW TOWARDS MASSIVE EGGER CHIPBOARD FACTORY

SIGNPOST: 'DUKE'S HOUSE ¾ MILE' 121

SCHOOL

GALLOWSBANK

HORSE FIELD

HALFMILE WOOD

FELLSIDE – GOOD VIEWS OVER HEXHAM ABBEY

MAP 13d

FELLED TREES

SIGNPOST: 'HEXHAM ½ DILSTON 1½' 120

13e

35 MINS TO ST JOHN LEES (MAP 13E)

HEXHAM

25 MINS FROM DUKE'S HOUSE (MAP 13C)

25 MINS FROM ST JOHN LEES (MAP 13E)

HEXHAM

35 MINS TO DUKE'S HOUSE (MAP 13C)

13c

ROUTE GUIDE AND MAPS

Pride of place in the heart of town goes to the glorious **Hexham Abbey** (🖵 www.hexhamabbey.org.uk; daily 9.30am-5pm, services permitting). The first abbey was built here in AD672, though much of today's construction dates from the 12th century when it was refounded as an Augustinian priory.

Following the Dissolution of the Monasteries in 1537 it became the Parish Church of St Andrew, which it still is today. Take your time to explore the Abbey's impressive interior and look out for the large memorial to a 25-year-old Roman standard bearer from the 1st century AD – a stone of which you'll see several casts in various museums, including Chesters and Newcastle's Great North Museum: Hancock.

Across the square from the Abbey, the **Old Gaol** (🖵 www.tynedaleheritage.org/Resources/GaolMain.htm; Mar-Oct daily 10am-4.30pm, Feb & Nov Mon, Tue & Sat only; £3.80) is England's oldest purpose-built prison, having been built in around 1330.

Services

The **tourist information centre** (☎ 01434-652220, 🖵 hexham.tic@northumberland.gov.uk; Apr-Oct Mon-Sat 9.30am-5pm, Sun 11am-4pm, Nov-Mar Mon-Sat 9.30am-4.30pm), Hallgate, sits by the car park down the hill from the Old Gaol. They are happy to do accommodation booking (see box p52) and don't charge a fee.

For **internet access** (£1 for 30 mins) visit the library (☎ 01434-652488; Tue-Wed 9am-5pm, Fri & Mon 9am-7.30pm, Sat 9.30am-12.30pm) located in Queen's Hall, opposite the abbey grounds. For wi-fi, there's Mucho Gusto (see Where to Eat) and Wetherspoons in the centre under the Forum Cinema.

There are plenty of **banks/ATMs** in town, a **post office** (though the department store it was in is now under new ownership so it is not clear whether it will stay here), a Boots the **chemist**, a branch of the **trekking shop** Millets as well as a Tesco (see Map 13d) **supermarket** just outside town.

Transport

[See pp56-8] There are plenty of **buses** to and from Hexham and this is one of the terminals for the AD122 bus. The AD122 (see timetable pp212-15) departs from outside the TIC (and then goes to the railway station) before heading towards Walltown, with some continuing on to Carlisle. However, only one a day goes to Newcastle, though there are plenty of other services from the **bus station** on Priestpopple to Newcastle so there's no need to rely on the AD122.

Arriva's/Stagecoach's No 685 & Arriva's X85, Go North East's Nos 10, 74 & 684, Tyne Valley's No 880 and Wright's No 888 also serve here.

From the nearby **railway station** (see Map 13d, p133) there is a frequent service to both Carlisle (approx 60 mins) and to Newcastle (35-40 mins).

Where to stay

Most of the **B&Bs** lie a little way from the centre. *Queensgate House* (☎ 01434-605592, 🖵 www.queensgatehousehexham.co.uk; 2S/1T/1D/1F, most en suite, bath available), on Cockshaw, is one of the nearest, with rates starting at £25pp; they offer a packed lunch for £2.50. Dogs are welcome subject to prior arrangement.

West Close House (☎ 01434-603307; 2S shared bathroom/1D with toilet and basin, bath available), on Hextol Terrace, is a 1920s detached house with

ROUTE GUIDE AND MAPS

an award-winning garden and, wait for it ... a revolving Victorian-design summerhouse! Needless to say, we think it's the pick of the B&Bs and good value at just £32.50pp with a wholefood continental breakfast.

Around Leazes Park, to the north-west of town, is *The Beeches* (☎ 01434-6059, 🖳 www.bandbhexham.com; 2T en suite/1T private bathroom), 40 Leazes Park, where B&B costs from £60 (£35 single occupancy). On the same road and just as smart *High Reins* (☎ 01434-603590, 🖳 www.highreins.co.uk; 4S/1T/2D, all en suite with bath) charges from £34pp.

Best Western Beaumont Hotel (☎ 01434-602331, 🖳 www.bw-beaumont hotel.co.uk; 2S/12T/19D/1F, all en suite, bath available) is in a great location on Beaumont St opposite the Abbey Gardens. B&B costs from £80 for a single, £110 for two sharing. They also offer a dinner, bed and breakfast rate of £90/130 sgl/dbl or twin.

Where to eat and drink
There are more **cafés** and **tearooms** than you can shake a cinnamon stick at. These include the popular *Mucho Gusto* (☎ 01434-606200; Mon-Sat 9am-5pm, Sun 10am-4pm), with views towards the Market Square and wi-fi; the vegetarian *Hexham Tans* (☎ 01434-656284; Tue-Sat 8.30am-4pm), on St

Mary's Chare, serving a variety of tasty snacks including jacket potatoes for
£4.50 and main meals (11.30am-2.30pm) for a very reasonable £5.50, including a delicious vegetarian chilli; *Exchange Café* (☎ 01434-652475; Mon-Sat
9am-4.30pm, Sun 11am-4pm; open on performance nights till 8.30pm), a
smart place in the Queen's Hall Arts Centre; and, nearby, *Mrs Miggins' Coffee
Shop* (☎ 01434-605808; Mon 9.30am-4pm, Tue-Sat to 5pm), a more traditional tearoom; fans of *Blackadder* may be interested to know that Rowan
Atkinson grew up not too far from here and it has been suggested this tearoom
was the inspiration for the pie shop of the same name that featured in the second and third series. However, some people say it was the other way round and
that the shop took the name from the series.

For something more substantial, our favourite spot, *Danielle's Bistro* (☎
01434-601122; Tue-Fri noon-2pm, Mon-Sat 6-10pm), is on the way into town
from Corbridge; it serves mainly hearty English dishes such as a starter of
black pudding in red wine and shallot sauce. There's also an Indian restaurant,
The Valley (☎ 01434-601234, 🖥 www.valleyrestaurants.co.uk; Tue-Sun 5.30-
11pm), right next to the abbey above a shoe shop. *Best Western Beaumont
Hotel* (see Where to stay) has a bar which serves bar snacks (daily noon-9pm)
and a restaurant (daily 6.30-9.15pm, Sun noon-2pm).

Finally, there's *Bouchon* (☎ 01434-609943, 🖥 www.bouchonbistrot
.co.uk; Tue-Sat noon-2pm & 6-9.30pm), 4-6 Gilesgate, voted 'Best Local
French Restaurant in the UK' on Gordon Ramsay's *The F Word* TV series. It's
still pretty reasonable, however, with starters from £4.95 and mains, such as
fricassée of herb gnocchi with field mushrooms & pea shoots, from £11.95.

Hexham to Acomb

The thrills of walking on this diversion from the Wall don't end at Hexham,
though you'd be forgiven for thinking otherwise as you walk on a tarmac bridleway alongside, and then across, the noisy A69. But a minute later you're
back in rural splendour, with the venerable **St John Lee Church** a diverting
distraction, followed by a tramp through sheep fields and across a stream
(where a woodpecker was busy hammering away when we last came by) and
on up to the pant (fountain) at Acomb.

ACOMB [MAP 13e]

With the sad demise of the YHA hostel, Acomb has seen a sharp decline in the
number of trekkers arriving at the end of a long day, panting at the pant (fountain) at the top of the village's Main St. That's a pity as Acomb is a friendly,
attractive place, a string of stone terrace cottages inhabited by unassuming locals
whose vowels are as flat as the caps the elder generation wear on their heads.

There's little to delay those who aren't staying here, save for a small **post
office** (Mon, Tue, Thur & Fri 9.30am-12.30pm & 1.30-5.30pm, Wed 9am-
1pm, Sat 9am-12.30pm) and one of the best pubs on the route, the *The Miner's
Arms* (☎ 01434-603909; 🖥 www.theminersacomb.com; Mon-Fri 5pm to midnight, Sat & Sun 11am-midnight), a quintessential, unpretentious place where
great local beers are served every night. Continuing down the hill, *The Sun
Inn* (☎ 01434-602934, 🖥 www.thesuninn-acomb.co.uk; 2T/2D shared/en
suite facilities, bath available; serves food Mon-Fri noon-2pm & 6-8pm, Sat &
Sun noon-2.30pm). Rates are £70-75 and £45 for single occupancy. Dogs are
welcome if arranged in advance.

GREEN GATE & SIGNPOST:
'WRITTEN CRAG 1 MILE'

0   ¼ mile
0   APPROX SCALE   500m

MAP 13e

PANT
(FOUNTAIN)

ACOMB

Sun Inn

Miner's
Arms

Queen's Arms

POST
OFFICE

CHIPPY

HOUSE

MILL

ST JOHN
LEE

For **food**, at the time of research the main alternative to The Sun Inn was the **chippy** (Fri 11.30am-1.30pm & 4.30-8.30pm, Sat to 8pm), tucked away behind the Queen's Arms at the bottom of the hill, though it is only open two days a week. However, the *Queen's Arms* (tel 01434-607857; bar daily noon-11pm) reopened in February 2011; light bar snacks are available throughout the day and lunch is served on Sunday (noon-4pm).

The AD122 **bus** service stops here as does Tyne Valley's No 880 service; see pp56-8.

Acomb to the Hadrian's Wall Path

From Acomb, the path leads north from just above The Sun Inn, round the back of the houses at the top of the village. It then continues via a stream and along-side fields of grain up to the road. At the road, turn right up the hill before taking a right through a green gate. Continuing on the path through a sheep field, the path dips at the end to reunite with the B6318 (the Military Road) and the main trail, which you rejoin by the wooden cross in the south-western corner of Heavenfield (see p120 and Map 15 p121).

CHOLLERFORD TO STEEL RIGG (FOR ONCE BREWED)
[MAP 16 p123 & MAPS 17-23]

Introduction

Perhaps the most thrilling day of the entire walk, this is a **13-mile (21km; 5¼-5½hrs)** stage to be savoured. Encompassing the best-preserved fort on the Wall, the finest views, the most complete sections of the Wall, the northernmost point of the trail and some great if slightly exhausting walking, this is a day for superlatives. So bring plenty of food and water with you (there's nowhere to stock up between Chesters and Housesteads bar perhaps the café van at Brocolitia car park), plenty of memory cards for your camera, bucketloads of stamina – and enjoy!

The route

Despite the thrills to come, the day begins in a rather mundane fashion, with a bit of road walking along the by now all-too-familiar B6318 – the Military Road. Climbing up the hill, the path takes an unexpected turn away from the road and around the back of a farm, then follows the line of General Wade's highway.

Soon after crossing the first possible turn-off for Green Carts Farm (see below) you come to the day's first treat: a cracking bit of Wall known as **Black Carts** that slopes ahead up the hill, has its own **turret** (No 29A) and is even joined, along its length, by the distinctive 'V' of the **Wall ditch**. (Incidentally, to the north the grand house you can see is Chipchase Castle, a medieval tower house with Jacobean and later additions.)

Green Carts Farm (Map 17; ☎ 01434-681320, 🖳 www.greencarts.co.uk; 3T/1D, all en suite, bath available) is about half a mile from the trail. They offer: **B&B** (£60-70 or £40 single occupancy), a well-equipped **bunkhouse** (two rooms each with four beds; £22pp including a continental breakfast; dogs can stay here), a **camping barn** (sleeping 12, £12pp) with some cooking facilities, and a **campsite** (£5pp inc use of shower/toilet facilities, coin-operated laundry

MAP 17

45 MINS TO CHOLLERFORD (MAP 16)

50 MINS FROM CHOLLERFORD (MAP 16)

55 MINS FROM BROCOLITIA (MAP 18)

50 MINS TO BROCOLITIA (MAP 18)

WALK ROUND SMALL COPSE ON PAVING SLABS

DITCH A LITTLE WAY TO THE NORTH

MUCH QUICKER ROUTE TO GREEN CARTS

Green Carts Farm

TURRET 29A

BLACK CARTS

0047

B6318

MILITARY ROAD

SHAPE OF MILECASTLE 29 IN GROUND

BLACK CARTS WALL

0048 TRIG POINT

UNEXCAVATED WALL

TREES LIKE GIANT BONSAI

LIMESTONE CORNER - THE NORTHERNMOST POINT OF THE ROMAN EMPIRE!

LOOK FOR EVIDENCE OF ROMAN WORK ON STONES IN THE DITCH

¼ mile

APPROX SCALE

500m

0

facilities, electric hook up) with 30 pitches. If requested in advance breakfast (£5 for a cooked carry out breakfast), packed lunches (£5) and evening meals (from £6) are available. If staying here it's best to take the first road to the right after passing turret 29A.

Eventually the Wall disappears but that's not the end of the Roman masonry on this part. At **Limestone Corner**, where the Wall and trail take a turn to the south-west, you'll find some large boulders lying in the Wall ditch that clearly display evidence of having been worked on by workmen – and specifically Roman workmen. The rock here is whinstone, a super-hard basalt stone, and it appears the Romans soon realised that persevering in trying to hack through this rock was pointless; so they left the blocks where they were and moved on. This is one theory, anyway, and it's interesting that the ditch does stop here (though it's worth noting that the Vallum continues unbroken on the other side of the road). Perhaps of more interest, Limestone Corner is the northernmost point of the trail – thus the Wall here would have been the northernmost point of the entire Roman Empire. Continue along the trail and, just before crossing the road you come to a turn-off for *Hallbarns* (off Map 18, around a mile from the trail – look for the signpost on the trail pointing north; ☎ 01434-681419, ☎ 0778-899 8959; 🖳 www.hallbarns-simonburn.co.uk; 1D/1T/1D, T or F en suite, 1T private bathroom), a pleasant B&B with drying facilities and wi-fi. They charge £70 (£50 for single occupancy) and can provide a packed lunch and evening meal if booked in advance. Dogs are welcome but not in the house – there is a stable they can stay in.

The next piece of Roman architecture lies across the road from the turn off to Hallbarns. The **Brocolitia** fort (aka Carrawburgh, pronounced 'Carrawbruff'; Map 18) remains unexcavated. It is, however, an unusual fort, clearly built some time after the Wall, for Brocolitia actually lies over the infilled Vallum. It was around this site in 1876 that John Clayton opened up **Coventina's Well** and discovered 13,487 coins (4 gold, 184 silver and the rest bronze) which would have been tossed into the water for good luck – just as we throw money into wishing wells today. Three hundred of these coins commemorated the pacification of northern Britain following disturbances in AD155; Britannia, who looks so regal and serene on the back of today's 50p piece, appears slumped and forlorn on these Roman coins.

In addition to the money, Clayton also found carved stones, altars, jars, pearls, brooches and incense burners – the religious stuff having been deliberately placed here for safekeeping following the Theodosian Edict which banned pagan temples in AD391 (see box pp142-3). Much of this can be seen at Chesters Museum (see p124). Coventina, by the way, was a local goddess associated with water; as you may have already seen at the temple to Antenociticus in Newcastle (see box p91), the Roman Empire was largely tolerant of other religions and

---

❏ **Walk side by side and on healthy grass** Don't walk in single file or on worn areas. Protect our heritage!

beliefs and even assimilated certain local gods into their pantheon, in much the same way that Hinduism has done with both Christianity and Buddhism.

Though Brocolitia is once more underground, the nearby **Mithras Temple** (see box below) is open to both the skies and the public, though the altars are

ROUTE GUIDE AND MAPS

❑ MITHRAISM

Considering the distant era in which Mithraism enjoyed its greatest popularity, the secrecy with which it was practised and the attempts that various people employed down the centuries to suppress it, it's amazing that, on the surface at least, we seem to know so much about this clandestine religion.

This becomes even more remarkable when we consider that much of the written information we do have for the faith comes not from its adherents – the secrecy surrounding the faith was both strict and all-encompassing – but from its detractors, such as the early Church fathers; people whom, it must be said, are probably not the most reliable of sources. But thankfully, though the followers themselves were silent about their faith, their iconography, by comparison, speaks volumes; and this iconography can be found in every temple throughout the Roman Empire, including those discovered at Hadrian's Wall.

The origins of the faith are uncertain, with one school of thought believing it to be Persian, dating back as far as 1400BC, while another suggests it was a near-contemporary of Christianity. Plutarch mentions it in 67BC, while the earliest physical remains date from the 1st century AD. Whatever its genesis, we do know that the Mithraic faith quickly gathered a huge following. One of the reasons for this popularity is undoubtedly its adoption as the unofficial faith of Roman soldiers. Though originally appealing to slaves and freedmen, the Mithraic emphasis on truth, honour, bravery and discipline would have appealed to the Roman army who would undoubtedly have proselytised the faith wherever they were stationed.

Mithraism enjoyed its heyday in the 2nd century AD; by the 5th century it had all but disappeared. The first blow came with the *sole* accession of Theodosius to the empirical throne in AD392 (prior to this he had ruled with two other 'emperors'). The last emperor of a united Roman Empire (following his demise the split between the empire's western and eastern halves, which first appeared at the beginning of the 4th century AD, became permanent), Theodosius was also the first emperor to make Christianity the official religion and went out of his way to promote his chosen faith, issuing edicts and encouraging Christian subjects to attack pagan buildings. One edict in particular, issued in AD391 before he became sole ruler, banned the worship of pagan gods, and many Mithraic temples were destroyed at this time.

The Mithraic organisation

The faith was a complicated one. Its followers were organised into a strict **hierarchy** of seven grades, or levels. An initiate new to the faith would have been known as a *Corax*, or 'Raven', the first and lowest level in the Mithraic hierarchy. At the other end of the spectrum was the rank of '*Pater*', or 'Father', the seventh and highest level. Their clothes, such as the colour of their tunic or the mask they wore at Mithraic rituals, indicated to which rank they belonged.

Rising through the ranks was no easy matter. Near to many Mithraic temples, including Carrawburgh, an 'ordeal' pit has been found, with a bench very close to what would have been a large fire. It is assumed that followers would have undergone some sort of physical trial by fire, cold or fasting in order to climb to the next level.

mere copies of the originals now housed in Newcastle's Great North Museum: Hancock. The temple was discovered by John Gillam in 1949 when a particularly dry summer 'shrank' the surrounding peat to reveal the stones. If you want to know more about the entire site, including the location of Coventina's Well

The Mithraic beliefs: one theory

As a reward for rising through the ranks, the faithful were given revelations into the secrets and mysteries of the faith. According to their beliefs, the god Mithras was born either from the living rock or from a tree. An early life filled with pain and hardship culminated in the **defeat and slaughter of the primeval bull**. This killing allowed the life force of the bull to be released for the benefit of humanity: plants and herbs came from the bull's body, while wine came from the bull's blood and all livestock came from the slayed bull's semen. This victory over the primeval bull, known as the **tauroctony**, would have been depicted in every Mithraeum, or Mithraic temple, and each time the same few characters appear in the picture, namely a dog, scorpion, snake and raven, as well as Mithras's torchbearers, Cautes and Cautopates.

As for the Mithraeum itself, this would originally have been quite a dark and gloomy place. Indeed, the temple was usually constructed underground in order to simulate the cave in which Mithras was supposed to have killed the primeval bull. Entering via a door in the south-west corner, a worshipper would have first found himself in a small antechamber with a bench and what would have been a large fire, originally the ordeal pit. Beyond a wickerwork screen at the end lay the nave, with benches arranged along the side to allow the faithful to recline when partaking of ritual meals. Four small altars lay at the end of these benches. It is estimated that the average temple would have been able to hold between 30 and 50 men.

Mithraic beliefs: an alternative theory

For 70 years or so, this interpretation of Mithraism was held to be the definitive one. There was, however, one small problem. The whole reason it was believed that Mithraism came from the east is because the name 'Mithras' is the Latin form of the Iranian god Mithra; that, and the fact that the Roman authors themselves believed it to have come from Persia. But if Mithraism did have its origins in Persia and the Indian subcontinent, why have there never been any discoveries of Mithraism in Iran or any parallels in the folklore and mythologies of that region?

Thus, recently, a new interpretation has been suggested. This postulates that the depiction of Mithras slaying the bull, with the dog, raven, snake and scorpion as onlookers, and the torchbearers, Cautes and Cautopates, in attendance, is in fact a symbolic depiction of the cosmos, with the *dramatis personae* symbols of the zodiac. For example, the dog is in fact a representation of the constellation Canis Minor, and Cautes and Cautopates are the sun and moon respectively.

In this theory, therefore, the reason these temples were 'built' underground is because this subterranean chamber represents the night sky. This new theory may sound far-fetched at first but gathers credence when we look at the remains of Mithraea on the Wall. In particular, at Housesteads, there is one depiction of Mithras emerging from what has been called a Cosmic Egg – a depiction of the cosmos in an oval frame. Could it be that this singular sculpture, found in a remote fort in a far-flung corner of Rome's conquered territories, holds the key to our understanding of this empire-wide faith?

(to the west of the main site and still producing water), as well as enjoy a lovely cup of coffee, pay a visit to Ant, the man with the tiny little *van* who usually operates out of the car park serving hot drinks to weary trekkers. I have probably received more emails and letters recommending this man and his beverages over the past twelve months than I have about any B&B, restaurant etc on the route. His drinks are lovely, his knowledge of Brocolitia profound – and his presence at this site is a very welcome one.

The AD122 **bus** service calls here though the stop is not listed in the timetable; see pp56-8 for further information.

Returning to the **Roman ditch** on the northern side of the road, the trail continues into **Northumberland National Park**. *Carraw B&B* (☎ 01434-689857, 🖳 www.carraw.co.uk; 1D/1D or T/2D, T or F, all en suite, bath available) is a great little B&B just a minute's walk off the trail on the main road. Rates are £80-90 (£60-80 for single occupancy). Given the B&B's isolated position it is worth having an evening meal here (book at least 24 hours in advance); the meal is served at 7pm and costs £25 for three courses. One advantage is that they are licensed to sell alcohol. They can also provide a packed lunch for £6.

Continuing on the trail alongside the ditch, where the B6318 drifts to the left, there's a ladder stile in the wall. Though tempting, those staying in **Grindon** should continue on the trail past Milecastle 33 (Map 19) and then climb onto the road at the next ladder stile, where there's a brief reunion with the Military Road. Turn right and, on the junction with the road down to Grindon you'll come to the wonderful **B&B** that is the *Old Repeater Station* (Map 19; ☎ 01434-688668, 🖳 www.hadrians-wall-bedandbreakfast.co.uk; 2D/1T, both en suite, two bunk-bed rooms). A wonderful converted stone-and-slate building that makes extensive use of eco-technology (including boreholes, biowaste systems, solar panels and the like), this one-man operation is run by the affable, laconic Les, a man who in this author's experience is never less than generous with his teapot. B&B in the double/twin is £30pp and £22.50pp in the bunk-bed 'rooms', one of which has two beds and the other four. Special deals are possible for those staying for more than two nights. Call in advance if you want an evening meal (they are licensed) or accommodation out of the main season. **Internet access** (charity donation welcome) is available all day (including to non-residents); he's also the person to ask about **camping** possibilities in the area. (A repeater station, by the way, was a building located roughly halfway between telephone exchanges and was where the signals on telephone cables were amplified to compensate for the loss of electricity which made speech fainter and led to a loss of clarity.) The Old Repeater Station here is great.

Further down the road, *Grindon Cartshed B&B* (☎ 01434-684273, 🖳 www.grindon-cartshed.co.uk; 1T/1T or D/1D, all en suite) is another great choice. An old cart shed that's been converted using the latest in enlightened environmental technology, the accommodation here doesn't scrimp on some smart and welcome features such as a drying room. The highlight, however, is undoubtedly the views from the light and airy breakfast room looking down toward the Stanegate. B&B starts at £37.50pp (single occupancy £49). They can

65 MINS TO BROCOLITIA (MAP 18)

25 MINS FROM TRIG POINT (MAP 20)

COESIKE TURRET

CROSS DITCH HERE USING STEPS

IGNORE THIS STILE

CAN TRULY SEE THE DEFENSIVE VALUE OF THE ROMAN DITCH HERE

18

TWO PATHS - USE THE LESS ERODED ONE

MILECASTLE 33 052

RUINED BUILDING

RESERVOIR

VALLUM (NOT VISIBLE FROM PATH)

ONLY TAKE THIS LADDER STILE IF YOU ARE HEADING FOR GRINDON AS IT GIVES ACCESS TO THE ROAD

TREES ENCLOSED BY WALL - SITE OF MILECASTLE 34 (GRINDON MILECASTLE)

COESIKE TURRET 33B

DITCH STOPS AS CRAG STARTS

SHORT CUT TO OLD REPEATER STATION

TREES BEYOND WALL

Old Repeater Station & INTERNET ACCESS

MAP 19

GRINDON TURRET 34A 053

STONE STILE

20

Grindon Cartshed B&B

TO GRINDON & HADRIAN LODGE HOTEL

COESIKE TURRET

0   ¼ mile
0   500m
APPROX SCALE

70 MINS FROM BROCOLITIA (MAP 18)

30 MINS TO TRIG POINT (MAP 20)

*Trailblazer

ROUTE GUIDE AND MAPS

provide an evening meal (three courses for £19) and packed lunch (£6) if booked in advance.

Just over a mile (1.6km) further on, down on North Rd, ***Hadrian Lodge Hotel*** (☎ 01434-684867, 🖳 www.hadrianlodge.co.uk; 5D/3T/2D, T or F, all en suite, bath available in one room) is a comfy and rather smart place with its own bar. Prices start at £64 (£44 for single occupancy). They also have a **bunkroom** (four beds; use of a shower and toilet) which costs £25pp including a continental breakfast. Meals and packed lunches are available by arrangement. Dogs (£5) are welcome but can only stay in some rooms so book in advance.

Those not staying in Grindon should continue along the line of the Wall where you will find that the trail leaves the road for good to aim for the comprehensive remains of **Turret 33B**, known as the **Coesike Turret**. It then heads up towards the small copse surrounded by a wall that marks the site of **Milecastle 34 (Grindon Milecastle)**.

The next turret, **Grindon Turret** or, more prosaically, Turret 34A, hides behind the next wall. Both it and Coesike Turret – indeed, maybe all the turrets on the Wall – were probably abandoned less than a century after they were built, before the end of the 2nd century AD as the Wall forts were established. But unlike the others, after the Romans had gone both these turrets had *shielings* (herdsmen's huts) built into their remains, from which we get the name Sewingshields. Incidentally, notice how the ditch abruptly ends shortly after the Grindon Milecastle. Never an army to leave jobs unfinished, the reason for the ditch's abrupt termination is pretty obvious once you take a look at the area's topography, for it is here that the crags start; crags that form a natural barrier, thus make the digging of a defensive ditch entirely unnecessary.

More Roman delights await beyond Sewing Shields Farm (Map 20) at the crest of the hill. This is a fine **stretch of Wall** and begins at the end of the woods that shelter the farm. To the south of the trail the land slopes away gently down to the Military Road but to the north a 200ft drop awaits those who cross the Wall. These are the **Sewingshields Crags**, a wild and rugged land that, perhaps unsurprisingly, has become the setting of a number of myths and legends, many concerning those stalwarts of British folktales, King Arthur and his knights. Sewingshields Castle, which used to stand at the foot of the crags, was also used by Walter Scott as the setting for his story *Harold the Dauntless*.

Whatever the truth or otherwise of the stories surrounding Sewingshields, there's no doubt that the Romans clearly saw no need to construct a defensive ditch to the north of the Wall here. Coming to **Milecastle 35**, you see that, with such a large drop to the north, there's no northern gate here either, presumably for the same reason. Note, too, that the Vallum is now quite a way south of the Wall, where the ground is less stony.

For many people, this is the start of the most splendid part of the trail, with great views, wonderful walking and a really fine, extensive piece of Wall. Though the Wall proper stops at the top of the hill, just past the **trig point**, it is replaced by something more modern and only slightly less attractive which leads all the way to Housesteads Fort, the Wall's finest.

35 MINS FROM HOUSESTEADS (MAP 21) ──▶   TRIG POINT   ◀── 25 MINS TO COESIKE TURRET (MAP 19)

0   500m
0   ¼ mile
APPROX SCALE

FULL WALL WITH SAXON
CRYPT/BURIAL CHAMBER
ABUTTING IT

SEWING
SHIELDS
FARM

INTO
WOODS

BARN
HOUSE

SEWINGSHIELDS CRAGS

CAT'S GATE -
A DIP IN THE
GROUND

SEWINGSHIELDS TURRET 35A

SPORADIC BITS
OF WALL

BIT OF
WALL

TRIG
POINT   35 055

MILECASTLE
35   054

MAP 20

MILITARY ROAD B6318

INCREDIBLE
VIEWS
WESTWARDS

IGNORE
STILE HERE

KING'S
HILL

NOT HADRIAN'S WALL
(BUT HADRIAN'S WALL STONE)

BROMLEE LOUGH

KENNEL
CRAGS

'BUSY GAP' - SO CALLED BECAUSE IT'S
A LONG, RELATIVELY FLAT STRETCH
WHICH WOULD HAVE SEEN A LOT OF
NORTH-SOUTH TRAFFIC

trailblazer

Those not wishing to visit Housesteads should enter the grounds then turn right through **Knag Burn Gate** (Map 21). This was another Roman gateway through the Wall, similar in that respect to the Port Gate which many of you will have passed on yesterday's stage. This gate, however, was introduced into the Wall only in the 4th century AD, presumably to allow the considerable number of locals who lived around the fort to move between the northern and southern sides of the Wall with greater ease. The trail continues north of the Wall, until the far side of Housesteads is reached.

Those who *do* wish to visit the fort, however, should continue to the south of the Wall to the ticket office, near the fort's south-west corner. Note that this office is a **passport stamping station**. They also sell hot drinks, snacks and sandwiches but have no seating (save for a couple of plastic chairs in the museum that the kindly staff will allow you to make use of). Those desiring a more 'café' experience (ie a seating area and proper toilets as opposed to the temporary chemical toilet at the ticket office) will have to saunter down to the car park, down the hill.

HOUSESTEADS   [see map opposite]
☎ *01434-344363; Easter-Sep daily 10am-6pm; Oct-Easter 10am-4pm (however, the winter days/hours may change so contact them or check on the English Heritage website before going); £5/4.50/3 adults/concs/children, free for English Heritage and National Trust members*
'The grandest station in the whole line – in some stations the antiquary feeds upon shells, but here upon kernels'.   **William Hutton**, 1802 (see pp19-20)
This quote pretty much sums up Housesteads. For if you visit only one fort on the Wall, make it this one. In this author's opinion, Housesteads is the one place where you can really get a feel for how a Roman fort would have looked. Where the ruins of most other sites are rather fragmentary and barely break the surface of the earth, here the walls in places run to six courses or more – up to ten feet (almost 3m) high – with only the roof apparently missing to complete the structure. For this, as usual, considerable thanks must go to John Clayton, who bought the site in 1838 to protect and excavate it.

By positioning yourself up near the Wall at the top of the hill near the North Gate, you get a great overview of the fort as well as some incomparable views north and south, which is presumably why the Romans built it here in the first place. Known to them as **Vercovicium**, Housesteads was constructed around AD122, making it one of the first to be built along the Wall, and housed around 800 men on its five acres. The First Cohort of Tungrians from Belgium is the auxiliary unit most associated with Housesteads, having been based here in the 3rd and 4th centuries AD.

While the fort has the usual playing-card shape, its layout is not entirely typical. For one thing, you'll notice as you approach the fort from the trail that the *whole* of Housesteads lies south of the Wall, unlike Chesters, Segedunum and other sites which protrude north beyond the line of the Wall. Furthermore, Housesteads is elongated west–east (with the **Military Way** forming its central axis), where the longest axis of other forts runs north–south. The central core of the fort is familiar, with the **headquarters** at the centre and the Commander's House or **praetorium** next door. However, on this occasion, the

latter lies to the south of the HQ, not to the east as is more typical, probably because the whole fort lies on a ridge and slope. As is usual, the **granaries** and the **hospital** lie nearby, with the near-complete ruins of the **latrines** in the south-eastern corner of the fort. Finally, to the south, in the extensive civilian settlement outside the fort walls stands the **Murder House**, so-called because the skeleton of a man with a knife stuck between his ribs was discovered during excavations.

Incidentally, for those who have had enough for the day *Beggar Bog Farm B&B* (☎ 01434-344652, 🖳 www.bandb-on-hadrianswall.co.uk; 1D/1T, both en suite) lies a few hundred yards east of the turn-off to the fort on the Military Road. A traditional stone-built farmhouse, Beggar Bog is a smart and friendly place with great breakfasts surpassed only by the view from its elevated position up towards Housesteads and along the Military Road. B&B costs £75 (£45 for single occupancy). Evening meals (£20) and packed lunches (£6) are available if requested in advance.

The AD122 (see timetable pp212-15) and Telford's No 185 **buses** call in at the car park here; see pp56-8 for further information.

The final section of this stage is no less breathtaking. Indeed, this is the finest section of Wall, known as the 'Clayton Wall' after the archaeologist John Clayton who bought and rebuilt this section. You can tell a bit of Clayton Wall as opposed to regular, unreconstructed Roman Wall because Clayton's method of rebuilding differed from the original Roman style, with no mortar and a turf top. This includes the section of Wall immediately after Housesteads that leads through the wooded Housesteads Plantation. This section is also, officially at least, the one stretch of Wall that you are allowed to walk upon. (The National Trust owns the Wall for three miles west of Housesteads; it owns the fort too, though the day-to-day maintenance of it remains in the hands of English Heritage.) However, the authorities would rather you walked along the path parallel to the Wall and we strongly recommend you take this path, though by all means do occasionally walk up to the Wall to savour the views stretching away to the north. This is Northumberland's version of the Lake District, with **Bromlee Lough** (Map 20) immediately to the north, **Greenlee Lough** to its west and **Crag Lough** (Map 22) further along the trail.

Whatever path you choose, **do not walk on the Wall beyond the wooden barrier** placed at the end of the woods. Continuing your climb, you pass **Milecastle 37**, one of the best preserved and perhaps the most important on the Wall. Excavated by Clayton in 1853, note the start of an archway over the north gate, from which the experts were able to extrapolate the height of the arch and from this the height of the milecastle. (Why a north gate was deemed necessary here but not at Milecastle 35 – see p146 – is unclear, for they both have steep drops to the north.) You can also see holes in the floor by the southern entrance – postholes for the wooden door. This whole ridge that you are walking across is called the **Whin Sill**, while the section you are on now is known locally as **Cuddy's Crags**, after St Cuthbert.

Continuing along the top of the crags, eventually the path drops down to **Hotbank Farm** (Map 22). Owned by the National Trust and built by the site of **Milecastle 38** (which currently the trail circumvents to avoid further damage to the site; it was this stretch of Wall that suffered so much from the group of

90 MINS FROM STEEL RIGG CAR PARK (MAP 23) TO HOUSESTEADS (MAP 21) ⟶

THIS PATH IS LABELLED AS A TEMPORARY VOLUNTARY DIVERSION THOUGH THE PAVING SLABS WOULD SUGGEST IT'S MORE THAN JUST TEMPORARY

SITE OF MILECASTLE 38

HOTBANK FARM

21

058

HIGHSHIELD CRAGS

WALL HERE HIDDEN BY TURF

CRAG LOUGH

MILKING GAP

MILECASTLE 39 (CASTLE NICK)

MILITARY WAY

IGNORE THIS LADDER STILE TO SOUTH OVER FENCE

ORIGINAL WALL

23

CLAYTON WALL

SYCAMORE GAP

NOTE YOU CROSS TO THE OTHER SIDE OF THE WALL HERE - LOOK FOR A SWASTIKA ON NORTHERN SIDE OF WALL

OFFICERS QUARTERS ABOVE MILECASTLE 39

B6318

MILITARY ROAD

MAP 22

trailblazer

0   ¼ mile
0   APPROX SCALE   500m

STANEGATE

MILESTONE

CAR PARK

VINDOLANDA FORT

TO ONCE BREWED

23

90 MINS TO STEEL RIGG CAR PARK (MAP 23) FROM HOUSESTEADS (MAP 21)

ROUTE GUIDE AND MAPS

Dutch bankers who walked on it, see p67), it was near here that part of an inscribed stone was found that stated the second legion built this milecastle under the governorship of Aulus Platorius Nepos. As Aulus was governor during Hadrian's time, it provided archaeologists with almost irrefutable proof that this was Hadrian's Wall and not, as had previously been believed, Severus's (see box p9).

Beyond the farm the trail now dodges through a gate to head along the north side of the line of the Wall, then goes through a pleasant wood with Crag Lough glittering in the sunlight below. The path now follows a familiar pattern, rising and falling with the undulations of the land. This includes a drop to **Sycamore Gap**, named after the solitary tree growing in the dip.

The sycamore is something of a local celebrity, having appeared in the film *Robin Hood* alongside Kevin Costner (where, despite the distinct disadvantage of being a tree, it still managed to appear less wooden than its co-star). I've been told there's a Roman carving of a swastika, another symbol of prosperity and good fortune, near the tree on the Wall's northern face, though I have to confess I've never found it.

Following the gap, there's a climb up past the remains of some **officers' quarters**, unique on the Wall, and **Milecastle 39** to **Peel Crags**, before the path falls again to Peel Gap and the very steep **Cat Stairs** via the remains of a turret. Curiously, this is an extra turret, ie a third turret in the mile between milecastles 39 and 40 where normally there would only be two. Presumably it was built to watch over Peel Gap, which is all but invisible from the two turrets on either side. The first road for almost six miles (9.6km) runs through the gap and the award-winning **Steel Rigg car park** lies hidden away behind trees at the top of the hill; indeed, follow the Hadrian's Wall Path and you'll barely notice it's there.

If you haven't already joined the road down to Once Brewed (there's a short-cut onto the road round the back of Peel Bothy – see Map 23), you can do so from here.

ONCE BREWED   [MAP 23]

There's not much to Once Brewed other than a decent pub, one of the YHA's oldest hostels, a campsite, an excellent visitor centre, a curious name and a legend. The last two are linked: according to the story, General Wade, he of Military Road fame and bane of Bonnie Prince Charlie, once stayed at an inn here and, unhappy with the quality of the beer, ordered it to be brewed again. Hence the name – or at least that's how one story has it.

The Northumberland National Park **visitor centre** (☎ 01434-344396; Apr-Oct daily 9.30am-5pm, Nov-Mar Sat/Sun only 10am-3pm) is a very helpful little place as well as being a tourist information centre.

They also have toilets, some refreshments, some picnic tables – and even wi-fi.

Once Brewed YHA Hostel (☎ 0845-371 9753, 🖳 oncebrewed@yha.org.uk; daily Feb-Nov; 77 beds), the first building you come to when dropping down from Steel Rigg, was opened in 1934. A popular stop with Pennine Way trekkers as well as Wall walkers, it provides every convenience including meals, cooking facilities and some very powerful showers. Rates are from £17 per adult; most rooms have four beds but there is one 5-bed, four 6-bed and one 8-bed room. An evening meal (from £6.95) can be booked in advance or on arrival. Note that one major disadvantage

ROUTE GUIDE AND MAPS

45 MINS FROM CAW GAP (Map 24)

STEEL RIGG CAR PARK

STEEL RIGG CAR PARK

45 MINS TO CAW GAP (Map 24)

To VINDOLANDA

YHA Hostel

VISITOR CENTRE, TOILETS, REFRESHMENTS & WI-FI

BUS STOP

Twice Brewed Inn

Vallum Lodge

TALL TREES

Winshields Farm CAMPSITE & BUNKHOUSE

MILITARY ROAD

B6318

LOOK FOR THE VALLUM DOWN THE SLOPE TO THE SOUTH

MAP 23

ONCE BREWED

PEEL BOTHY

SHORTCUT TO ONCE BREWED

059

TO SAUGHY RIGG & GIBBS HILL FARMS

ROMAN DITCH & WOOD OVER WALL

WINSHIELD CRAGS

060

GREEN SLACK, 345M – THE HIGHEST POINT ON THE PATH

061

WELL-MADE WALL – RESEMBLES HADRIAN'S WALL AND USES ROMAN STONES

BEAUTIFUL TREE OVERHANGING WALL

C.P.

STEEL RIGG

PEEL CRAGS

FUN SMALL BIT OF WALL

CAT STAIRS

TURRET (UNNUMBERED)

APPROX SCALE

500m

0   ¼ mile

0

ROUTE GUIDE AND MAPS

with this place is that it doesn't allow guests to check in before 4pm – not brilliant if you arrive at 2pm rain-lashed and windswept from your walk. Thankfully the visitor centre provides tea and shelter until they open.

A couple of hundred metres up the road, *Twice Brewed Inn* (☎ 01434-344534, 🖥 www.twicebrewedinn.co.uk; 2S/6D & 6T, some en suite others share facilities, bath available), while not *quite* so accommodating as to rebrew your beer, still aims to please and provides many a happy trekker with a meal and a bed for the night. Boasting a wide range of rooms, prices start at £34 for a single and £56-84 for two sharing. Food is served (daily summer noon-8.30pm, to 9pm Fri & Sat, winter noon-8pm, to 8.30pm Fri & Sat) and they have guest beers on tap (including one named after it); they also have **internet access** (£1 for 30 mins) and wi-fi. As a result, many are the trekkers who write in to recommend this place, with one even describing it as 'perfect'. The food is very tasty too including a delicious beef and gravy baguette (£4.25).

Other B&B accommodation in the area includes *Vallum Lodge* (☎ 01434-344248, 🖥 www.vallum-lodge.co.uk; 3T/2D/1F, all en suite, bath available; mid Mar-Oct) charging £80 (£69 for single occupancy). Packed lunches (£6) are available.

Half a mile (1km) or so further west, *Winshields Farm Campsite* (☎ 01434-344243, 🖥 www.winshields.co.uk; Apr-Oct) lies on the road; they charge £7pp to camp (60 pitches), and also have a **bunkhouse** (£10pp; sleeps 12). Booking is recommended for the bunkhouse as it is sometimes used by groups. There are shower/toilet facilities and a small shop (though the only cooking facilities are a microwave); if requested in advance a cooked breakfast (Apr-Oct only) can be provided as well as packed lunches. There's a path from the trail directly to the campsite, so there's no need to walk via Once Brewed.

The **AD122 bus** calls in at the National Park Visitor Centre, heads down to Vindolanda then returns to the Centre ten minutes later before continuing to Carlisle or Hexham. In addition, Telford's No 185 calls in here; see pp56-8 for details.

If in need of a **taxi**, call Sprouls Taxis (☎ 01434-321064 or ☎ 07712-321064) or Turnbulls (☎ 01434-320105).

Other accommodation near Steel Rigg

There are a couple of options to the north of the Wall in the heart of Northumberland National Park. *Saughy Rigg Farm* (☎ 01434-344120, 🖥 www.saughyrigg.co.uk; 2S/4D/3D or T/2F, all en suite, bath on request) is a farm dating from 1760 lying half a mile to the north of the Wall. **B&B** costs £75-85 (£50 single occupancy). Their evening meals (main courses from £12) are renowned for their freshness and are home-made or sourced locally; they can also provide a packed lunch (£5). They have a bar with draught beer. Dogs (£5) are welcome if booked in advance.

They have also built several lockable 'pods' – cosy wooden 'huts' that, as they correctly point out, offer an 'outdoor camping experience without the cold, draughts and wet associated with canvas camping'. The huts are carpeted and come with mattresses and cost £40 (sleep four if they know each other very well!), or £50 for six people at a squeeze. Pod guests can use a bathroom with shower in the house. Bedding (£2) can be rented and breakfast (£6) can be provided. Booking is recommended for the pods, especially in the main season.

Further north still, *Gibbs Hill Farm* (☎ 01434-344030, 🖥 www.gibbshillfarm.co .uk; 2T/2D, all en suite, bath available; Mar to end Nov) has a lovely guest lounge with its own open fire. Once again the hearty food is locally sourced and includes free-range eggs. B&B costs £37.50pp (£45 for single occupancy). The farm has also opened a **bunkhouse** (open all year) converted from an old hay barn, with three rooms of six beds each (so families can rent one of the rooms if required). Facilities include a well-equipped kitchen, lockable storage area, showers/toilets, and coin-operated laundry and drying facilities. Rates are £15pp, including bed and bed-

ROUTE GUIDE AND MAPS

ding; breakfast (£6.50) is available if booked in advance. Unfortunately, it's about 1¹/₂ miles north of the Wall: from the Steel Rigg Car Park head north through the Wall for a mile, then right along the sign-posted road to Gibbs Hill.

VINDOLANDA   [see map p151]

☎ 01434-344277; 💻 www.vindolanda.com; daily Apr-Sep 10am-6pm, mid-Feb to Mar & Oct to mid-Nov 10am-5pm; however, in bad weather these may change so contact them for details. Entry to Vindolanda costs £6.25/5.20/3.75/18 adults/concs/child/family; a joint-saver ticket with entrance to Carvoran Roman Museum costs £9.50/£8/£5.25/£27; the Roman Army Museum (see p163) costs £5/£4.25/£2.75/£14. There is a 10% discount for English Heritage members.

According to a panel of experts at the British Museum, the artefacts found at the fort at Vindolanda are collectively the single most important historic site on these shores, beating such treasures as the Anglo-Saxon hoard at the Sutton Hoo burial, the Roman Mildenhall Treasure and the Lewis Chessmen.

Upon first arriving at Vindolanda, you may well wonder what all the fuss is about. Sure the 1¹/₂-mile (2km) walk or bus ride (see p156) from Once Brewed is nice enough, with a Roman milepost along the road and some decent views of Sycamore Gap. But once through the gates there's none of the spectacular, near-complete ruins that one finds at Housesteads.

Here at Vindolanda the remains rise only just above foundation level. What's more, the only impressive structures on the site are the modern mock-ups of Hadrian's Wall, one in timber and turf and one in stone, that overlook the ongoing archaeological work from the south. (And isn't it ironic that the best reconstructions of the Wall lie at one of the few existing forts that never even lay on the Wall!)

Nevertheless, as those experts at the British Museum tell us, this is *the* most important site along the whole of the Wall. Indeed, it's *the* most important site in Roman Britain, and when the excavation is finally finished – a job that, according to some estimates, could take at least another hundred years – it could even turn out to be the most important Roman site in *the entire world*. And the reason why can be seen in the **museum** at the rear of the site. For thanks to a fortunate combination of silt and water in the soil at Vindolanda, an incredible array of artefacts has been uncovered here, preserved in the earth, providing us with a hitherto unrivalled glimpse into the everyday life of the Roman Empire. Most famously, this is where, in 1973, Robin Birley discovered the so-called **Roman postcards** (aka Vindolanda postcards) – paper-thin, postcard-sized wooden writing tablets used by the Romans for everything from official reports to birthday invitations, school homework to love letters. Though the 1900 or so tablets that have so far been discovered are now in the care of the British Museum, the museum in Vindolanda details some of the best including a letter from a concerned mother promising to send her son more underwear to protect him from the bitter British winter and the icy northern wind that blows up the toga at certain times of the year. Then we have a mis-quote from Virgil's *Aeneid* written in a schoolchild's hand, after which some-body else – presumably the teacher – has written 'seg', short for *segnis* or 'sloppy work'. There's also the tablet with the famous reference to the

ROUTE GUIDE AND MAPS

'Britunculli', or 'wretched Britons'. Humdrum, mundane and everyday, these tablets nevertheless add so much colour to our understanding of life in the Roman Empire.

Even better, the latest news we have from Vindolanda is that nine of the postcards are to be returned to Vindolanda – and will be on public display by the time you read this, as will recent finds such as a baby's boot and a horse's face mask; there's still plenty to amaze. Take the beautifully intricate leather sandals, for example, discarded casually by the inhabitants into a ditch when broken but immaculately preserved to this day. There are also keys, cutlery, pottery, weapons and, my personal favourite, a fragment of glass with a gladiatorial scene painted upon it, in colours that are still as vibrant today as they must have been nearly 2000 years ago. Magically, after I said in the first edition of this guide how wonderful it would be to find more of that vase, in May 2007 archaeologists did just that while digging in a ditch some 60m away from where the original piece was found! This second piece, larger than the original fragment and interlocking perfectly with it, shows two more gladiators, a third figure who could be a referee, and a fourth who seems to be awarding a prize.

Overall, the museum at Vindolanda is a fascinating, absorbing, mind-boggling collection that will ruin your planned schedule for the day. But it also, in this author's opinion, brings home just what life on the Wall during the Roman era was like more than any other attraction on the walk. Don't miss it, or it will haunt you for the rest of your walk.

The **AD122 bus** calls in here en route to Hexham, and also to Walltown for its sister museum, and Carlisle; see pp56-8 for further information and pp212-15 for the timetable.

STEEL RIGG TO BANKS   [MAPS 23-30]

Introduction

While this **12½-mile (20km; 6-6¼hrs)** stage may not be as spectacular as the previous one, it is perhaps the most interesting. It's also something of a red-letter day, for it is on this stage that we climb to the highest point of the entire trail. It is on this day, too, that we cross from Northumberland into Cumbria and the scenery changes from the windswept moors and crags that provided yesterday's backdrop to the more gentle, rolling, cultivated landscape of England's far north-west. We also cross the watershed on this day, so that by the end of it any river we encounter from now on flows west to the Irish Sea, not east to the North Sea as has been the case up to now.

The limestone runs out on this stage, too, at Banks where the Red Rock Fault splits the country. Moreover, to the west of Gilsland, at Willowford Bridge, the Wall was originally made of turf (possibly because of the lack of limestone) and rebuilt in stone only later. Also at Willowford, the broad foundations that have held up the Wall so far are reduced; from now on it is narrow wall on *narrow* foundations. Finally, and also at the River Irthing, the remains of the third Roman bridge on our walk can be seen, which would once have carried both the Wall and the Military Way. Quite a stage indeed! Nor have we even mentioned all the turrets, forts and milecastles – and even, uniquely, a Roman watchtower – that are encountered along the way.

One word of warning, however, before you set off: though this stage ends in Banks, there is just one B&B there. As such, be prepared to stay before Banks – for example at Greenhead (B&B-style accommodation, Hostel; see p166), Gilsland (B&Bs; see pp167-8) or Birdoswald (YHA hostel; see p170); or to attempt a longer walk and march on to Walton (three B&Bs and a camping barn and campsite; see p175 & p178). Off the trail there are some more B&Bs at Haltwhistle which provide further options and are described on pp160-2.

The route

The day's first treat lies just a 10-minute walk from the Steel Rigg car park. This is **Green Slack** (Map 23) on the Winshields Crags, at 345m the highest point on the trail, with a decent section of Roman Wall leading up to it. Whilst the rest of the stage is only slightly less exhausting than the relentless up-and-down rollercoaster ride of yesterday, it is at least some comfort that, for the rest of the trip, there'll be more downhill than uphill!

ROUTE GUIDE AND MAPS

45 MINS FROM GREAT CHESTERS FORT (MAP 25) ⟶   CAW GAP ⟶

TO SAUGHY RIGG FARM
(BUT NEARER FROM STEEL RIGG CAR PARK; SEE MAP 21)

MAP 24

THORNY DOORS - A GATE IN THE WALL

TURRET 41A

CAW GAP

MILECASTLE 42

CAWFIELD CRAGS

23

HOLE GAP 063

BOGLE HOLE

BLOODY GAP

25

062

NOT THIS WAY! GOOD WALL BUT NO THROUGH ROUTE

DISUSED CAWFIELDS QUARRY

BUS STOP

MILITARY ROAD

TO HALTWHISTLE

Milecastle Inn

0   1/4 mile
0   APPROX SCALE   500m

← 45 MINS TO GREAT CHESTERS FORT (MAP 25)   CAW GAP ←

By the way, if you feel like taking a breather while you're up here, according to scientists there's no better place in England to take it: the lichen that grows on the Winshields Crags requires extremely pure air and, apart from Dartmoor, this is the only place in the entire country where the air is clean enough for this lichen to thrive!

The trail varies little for the next two miles (3km) or so as you ride the crest of the crags, following the undulations through wild territory uninhabited since Roman times. The names printed on the maps – Bogle Hole, Caw Gap, Bloody Gap, Thorny Doors – only serve to add to the sense that you're in a land of folklore and myth.

After **Caw Gap** (Map 24) the Wall continues unbroken for over half a mile (1km). Look out for the swastika etched by the Romans into one of the Wall stones – another symbol of prosperity – on the way to **Milecastle 42**, which originally had an entrance in the north Wall until the builders saw the steep drop beneath, realised such a door was unnecessary and it was blocked up. The trail then rounds the flooded, disused quarry at **Cawfields**.

If in need of a hot meal turn left when you meet the road. The menu at *Milecastle Inn* (☎ 01434-321372; 🖳 www.milecastle-inn.co.uk; food served Good Friday to end Oct daily noon-8.45pm; noon-2.30pm & 6-8.30pm the rest of the year) includes standard pub fare as well as home-made pies such as wild boar and duckling pie (£10). The AD122 **bus** service calls here: see pp56-8 for further information and pp212-15 for the timetable.

Next to the quarry is a car park (Map 25) and accompanying toilet block. There are a few picnic tables here but no other reason to loiter.

Those heading to Haltwhistle should not cross over the bridge, but instead head on the path to the south of the Burn. Alternatively, you can wait until you hit Great Chesters fort, just a short walk further on, and take the path down to Haltwhistle from there. For either option, see Map 25 and the route below.

Walking to and from Haltwhistle   [Map 25]

The path down to Haltwhistle, particularly if taking the trail that shadows the Haltwhistle Burn, is both easy and lovely. Furthermore, you actually hike in woods under the shade of trees for much of the path – a stark contrast to the more exposed, wind-blasted walking along much of the Wall.

To get to the Burn trail, leave the Hadrian's Wall path at the road bridge by Cawfields Quarry, taking the path that runs south of the Burn. The path heads towards a small bridge in the middle of a field *but doesn't take it*! Instead, you bend leftwards and continue to follow, roughly, the course of the Burn until it hits the B6318. Rejoining the trail a little way west along the road, the path passes a weir, heads through a gate in a stone wall, then follows the path as it heads into the woods that shroud the Burn. The trail continues sedately down before finally ending up at the Old brickworks on the outskirts of Haltwhistle.

For the return journey, rather than taking the same path back you can follow Willia Rd all the way to its termination at a gate, which you should go through and head towards Lees Hall. Crossing the B6318 once more, you head north down the slope past Markham House, then up towards Great Chesters Fort, which you arrive at behind the old Roman altar.

65 MINS FROM WALLTOWN QUARRY CAFÉ (MAP 27) → GREAT CHESTERS FORT 45 MINS TO CAW GAP (MAP 24) →

NOTE THE ROMAN DITCH OVER THE WALL HERE

Burnhead B&B

GREAT CHESTERS FORT

26

GREAT CHESTERS FORT (AESICA)

LOOK FOR DEDICATION STONE IN WALL

BENCHES

064

24

CP

130

LOOK FOR ALTAR HERE

PUBLIC TOILETS

MAP 25

BRIDGE (BUT PATH DOES NOT GO OVER IT)

TO HALTWHISTLE (ON ROAD)

MARKHAM

135

B6318

132

131

← TO GREENHEAD

OLD CHIMNEY

LEES HALL

BRIDGE ACROSS BURN

Haltwhistle Burn

★ trailblazer

134

CANFIELD QUARRY/ GREAT CHESTERS TO HALTWHISTLE 35-45 MINS VIA HALTWHISTLE BURN

OLD BRICKWORKS

133

0   ¼ mile

0   APPROX SCALE   500m

WILLIA RD

SEE HALTWHISTLE TOWN PLAN

60 MINS TO/FROM HALTWHISTLE VIA LEES HALL

ROUTE GUIDE AND MAPS

← 60 MINS TO WALLTOWN QUARRY CAFÉ (MAP 27) GREAT CHESTERS FORT ← 45 MINS FROM CAW GAP (MAP 24)

HALTWHISTLE

Though not on the trail itself, Haltwhistle is an important place for trekkers.

Good bus and train connections (Haltwhistle is on the Newcastle–Carlisle line), a variety of accommodation, plenty of shops, restaurants and tearooms and a location almost exactly halfway along the Wall (one of the hotels on the main street is even called The Centre of Britain) ensures that many a Wall walker calls in for the night.

It's also a very historic town, with bastle (see p208) houses lined up along Main St and an even earlier Pele Tower now forming part of the Centre of Britain Hotel. These buildings were, of course, built as defensive fortifications during the long-running skirmishes between the English and the Scots, a time when much of the border region was considered bandit country. Such was the fear and enmity between both sides that a plaque in the market square recounts the sad tale of a young local girl who had attempted to run away and marry a Scot. Her reward for this act of 'treason' was to be the last person executed in the Market Sq – along with her beau – in 1597.

Today Haltwhistle is a genteel sort of place with a pretty main street and a plethora of tearooms and eateries, many of which display notices saying that 'Walkers are welcome here' – a nice touch.

Services

The **tourist information centre** (☎ 01434-322002; Easter to Oct Mon-Sat 10am-4.30pm, they will close for half an hour for lunch) is right next to the railway station and perhaps the office most dedicated to the Hadrian's Wall Path; indeed, this is where you send your completed passports (see p49) at the end of your walk in order to receive your certificate and badge. They also do accommodation booking (see box p52). However, sadly from 2011 they will not open in the winter months.

Internet access is available at the library and the nearby Haltwhistle Partnership (☎ 01434-321242, 💻 www.haltwhistle.org; Mon-Fri 10am-12.30pm & 1.30-4pm, subject to staff availability).

There are two banks (Barclays and HSBC) with **cashpoints (ATMs)** on Main St. Virtually opposite the latter is the **post office** (Mon-Fri 9am-5.30pm, Sat 9am-12.30pm), which also has an ATM, while a little further up there stands, almost uniquely on this walk, a self-service **launderette** (daily 8am-6.30pm; £3 for 8kg, 20p for 5 mins in the dryer); a little further down from the post office, on the opposite side, there's a Boots the **chemist** (Mon-Fri 9am-6pm, Sat to 1pm).

For **provisions**, there's a Co-op (daily 7am-10pm) on the main street and a Sainsbury's (Mon-Sat 8am-9pm, Sun 10am-4pm) just to the north of Main St behind the shops; Sainsbury's has an ATM and there is a path to it between Lucky Palace and Oceans. There's also a **camping/trekking shop**, Wild Outdoors (Mon-Fri 9am-5pm), on Westgate.

Transport

[See pp56-8] The AD122 **bus** (see timetable pp212-15) for Hexham stops in Market Place having called in at the railway station three minutes earlier; buses for Carlisle stop first at the Market Place and then at the station. Arriva's/Stagecoach's No 685 also calls here.

There are **trains** approximately every hour to Newcastle (journey time 50-60 mins) and Carlisle (just over 30 mins).

Where to stay

Ashcroft (☎ 01434-320213, 💻 www.ashcroftguesthouse.co.uk; 1S/2T/2D/1F suite, and an apartment sleeping up to six people, all en suite, bath available), a former vicarage on Lanty's Lonnen, just off the Westgate, is a lovely place with some award-winning terraced gardens. The rooms are full of features including wi-fi and cost from £40pp for two sharing (add £5 for a room with four-poster bed), £50-90 for the single/single occupancy.

(Opposite) Top: Walltown Crags looking from the west. **Bottom**: The granary at Housesteads Fort (see p148).

Haltwhistle

Where to stay
2 Hall Meadows B&B
8 Centre of Britain Hotel
10 Manor House Hotel
11 Ashcroft
12 Grey Bull

Where to eat and drink
1 Old Fort Tearoom
2 Beano's
3 The Pillar Box Café
4 Haltwhistle Tandoori
5 Black Bull Inn
6 Lucky Palace
7 Ocean Fish & Chips
8 Centre of Britain Hotel
9 Golden Wok
10 Manor House Hotel

Manor House Hotel (☎ 01434-322588, 🖳 www.themanorhousehaltwhistle.co.uk; 1D/2T/3D or T, all en suite, bath available) may be in the centre of Britain but from the decorations on the wall – signed photos of Alan Shearer, framed Newcastle United shirt and other football memorabilia – you can tell it looks to the immediate east for its influences. A friendly and reasonably priced place, like most around here, with B&B for £30-36pp (single occupancy £39).

Just across the road – but a few steps up in terms of quality – *Centre of Britain Hotel* (☎ 01434-322422, 🖳 www.centre-of-britain.org.uk; 5T/7D, all en suite, bath available) is the pick of the hotels on Main St; B&B costs £35-55pp, single occupancy £59-79. Dogs (£10) can stay in some rooms subject to prior arrangement.

Further east on Main St, *Grey Bull* (☎ 01434-321991, 🖳 www.greybullhotel.co.uk; 4D/1T/1D, T or F, all en suite) charges £70 for B&B (£50 for single occupancy); they have wi-fi.

Finally, *Hall Meadows* (☎ 01434-321021; 1T/1D en suite, 1D private bathroom) is a very attractive late 19th-century building covered with creepers that looks slightly out of place on Main St. Prices start at £32pp (£50 single occupancy). Packed lunches provided if arranged in advance.

(Opposite) Top: The unique arched gateway of Milecastle 37 (see p150). **Middle left**: The well-designed and well-preserved communal latrines at Housesteads Fort (see p148). **Middle right**: A mock-up of the turf-and-timber Wall at Vindolanda (see p155). **Bottom**: The extensive ruins of the Roman baths (see p124) at Chesters Fort.

Where to eat and drink

Those calling in for lunch have plenty of choices including *Pillar Box Café* (☎ 01434-321780; Mon-Sat 9.30am-4pm, to 1.30pm on Wed) by the Haltwhistle Partnership office where an all-day breakfast is £5; *Beano's* (☎ 01434-321321; Mon, Tue, Thur & Fri 8am-2.30pm, Sat & Wed to 2pm) a very good-value take-away sandwich shop where a basic bacon butty is only £2.10, jacket spuds are £2.55-3.25 and paninis £2.50-2.85; or next door; *Fort Tearoom* (☎ 01434-322037; summer daily 9am-5pm, to 4pm in winter).

For an evening meal there are several takeaway-only places: *Ocean Fish & Chips* (Mon-Sat 11.30am-1.30pm & 5-9pm), *Haltwhistle Tandoori* (☎ 01434-321388; daily 5-10pm) and two Chinese places: *Lucky Palace* (☎ 01434-322330; Tue-Sun 5-11pm) and *Golden Wok* (☎ 01434-322657; Wed-Mon 5-11pm). To eat out there is *Manor House Hotel* (see Where to stay; food served summer daily noon-2.30pm & 6-9pm, winter Mon-Thur noon-2.30pm & 7-8.30pm, Fri & Sat noon-2.30pm & 6.30-8.30pm, Sun noon-2.30pm only), *Centre of Britain* (see Where to stay; daily 6.30-9pm, advance booking recommended for non-residents) and, best of the lot, the *Black Bull Inn* (☎ 01434-320463; food served daily noon-2.30pm & 6-9pm).

To continue on the Hadrian's Wall path and reach Great Chesters fort, cross the bridge and climb over the nearby farm wall. That farm, incidentally, is *Burnhead B&B* (Map 25; ☎ 01434-320841, 🖳 www.burnheadbedandbreakfast.co.uk; 2T, en suite), built with Roman stones. Rates start at £35pp; packed lunches (£5) are available if requested in advance.

Soon afterwards, round the back of a neighbouring farm, lies the buried remains of **Great Chesters Fort** (not to be confused with Chesters Fort in Chollerford, see p124), known to the Romans as **Aesica**. It is known that the Dalmatae from the Yugoslav mountains were garrisoned here during Hadrian's reign and later the Hamii from Syria, who were famous archers.

There have been some important finds at Great Chesters, for example, one of the few tombstones of a legionary soldier (as opposed to an auxiliary). Archaeologists also found evidence of an aqueduct that once supplied the fort – bringing water from the head of Haltwhistle Burn, some six miles away! What's more, before the fort, which was built to guard Caw Gap, this farmyard was the home of Milecastle 43. This is yet further evidence that the Wall and its accompanying defences were built in two stages, with the decision to move the forts up to the Wall taken only after the Wall itself and its accompanying milecastles and turrets had already been built; see p11 for details. Indeed, where the Haltwhistle Burn crosses the Stanegate the remains of an early Roman fort have been discovered – presumably the one that was abandoned when Aesica was built, its garrison moved to the new premises.

Alas, there's little remaining of small, three-acre (1.2-hectare) Aesica except for some outer walls and an **altar** to the east of its south gate; heavily eroded, it is nevertheless the only original altar remaining in situ on the Wall and still inspires many a trekker to leave a small fiscal donation on its top, presumably for luck. The path to Haltwhistle leaves from near the altar, heading down the slopes.

Back on the trail, leave the wood (Map 26) to the west of the fort, making sure you check out the gatepost on the right as you descend from the stile – large

65 MINS FROM WALLTOWN QUARRY CAFÉ (MAP 27) TO GREAT CHESTERS FORT (MAP 25) ⟶

BITS OF WALL CAN BE SEEN HERE & THERE; MUCH OF IT IN RUINS BUT PARTS HAVE BEEN RESTORED

NOTE ROMAN MILESTONE NOW USED AS A GATE POST

COCKMOUNT HILL

WALLTOWN CRAGS

CLIMB TO TOP OF CRAG

TURRET 44B (KING ARTHUR'S TURRET)

WALLTOWN FARM   065

NOTE HOW THE VALLUM IS FAR FROM THE WALL HERE, BEYOND THE ROAD

LOOK EAST FOR GREAT VIEWS OF WHERE YOU'VE COME FROM... OR YOU'RE GOING TO

MAP 26

0   ¼ mile
0   APPROX SCALE   500m

trailblazer

← 60 MINS TO WALLTOWN QUARRY CAFÉ (MAP 27) FROM GREAT CHESTERS FORT (MAP 25)

ROUTE GUIDE AND MAPS

and cylindrical, it was clearly once a **Roman milestone**. The only other sign of Roman construction is the defensive ditch which appears intermittently along this section; the Wall itself disappears from the top of the ridge, while the Vallum lies some way to the south.

Dropping steeply down past **Turret 44B** (King Arthur's Turret), the trail continues along the **Walltown Crags** to the excellently preserved **Turret 45A** (Map 27) and the start of an impressive section of Wall, ended abruptly by a regular farm wall that leads south down to **Walltown Quarry**. It is believed to be one of the few remaining parts of the Wall that hasn't undergone any 19th-century restoration. Once a working quarry, the land around here is now a country park and already plays host to a variety of ducks and other birdlife.

On bright sunny days the benches outside the small café here, *Walltown Refreshments* (Easter to end Oct, daily 10am-5pm), are pleasant places to hang out and soak up the sun, though if the weather's less than perfect but you still want to rest there are *tearooms* at the **Roman Army Museum** (☎ 016977-47485, 🖳 www.vindolanda.com; daily Apr-Sep 10am-6pm, Mar & Oct 10am-4.30pm, closed Nov-Feb; £5 adult, £4.25 senior/student, £2.75 child, £14 family, see also p155 for details of combined entry tickets), just 100m or so down the road. The museum was refurbished over the winter of 2010-11; new features include a 3D film of a visualisation of the top of the wall from here to Vindolanda and additional exhibits about life in the Roman army. The museum is situated by the site of the Roman fort, Magna ('Rocks') at **Carvoran**.

The fort lay to the south of the Vallum by the Stanegate so, presumably, was not a Wall fort, despite its proximity to the Wall. The museum itself has a reasonable collection, though it comes a distant second compared to its sister museum at Vindolanda (see p155). It does, however, have a wonderful **video** featuring a bird's-eye view of the Wall, including computer-generated reconstructions of how the Wall must have looked almost 2000 years ago.

The Roman Army Museum is a terminus for some of the AD122 buses from Hexham, with others continuing onto Carlisle; see pp56-8 for further information and pp212-15 for the timetable. Telford's No 185 also calls in here on its way between Haltwhistle and Carlisle.

Opposite the Museum is *Walltown Lodge* (☎ 016977-47514, 🖳 www.wall townlodge.com; 1T/2D, all en suite), one of the few B&Bs that lie right on the trail. A smart and relatively new place that charges £30-40pp (£10 single occupancy supplement); they offer evening meals for £15 and packed lunches for £5, and even dog kennels (£5) – though all by prior arrangement only.

As you continue on the trail, the Vallum, for so long a stranger, once again becomes your companion as you stroll down to the bridge. Before it stands one of the more popular B&Bs on the route: *Holmhead* (Map 27; ☎ 016977-47402, 🖳 www.bandbhadrianswall.com; 2T or D/2D, all en suite). Right in the shadow of enigmatic Thirlwall Castle, right on the line of the Wall, and actually *built* from Hadrian's Wall stones (which, with delicious irony, were nicked from Thirlwall Castle which had nicked them from the Wall in the first place) this delightful farmhouse, surrounded on two sides by pretty streams, is under new ownership but still provides accommodation for all budgets. **B&B** is £65-75 (single occupancy £50). They have wi-fi. The **camping barn** (£12.50pp plus £3.50 to hire a sleeping bag) sleeps five and has a kitchenette. There is also a **bunk barn** (£8) which sleeps up to seven people. Both barns have shower/toilet facilities. However, reservations are recommended as the barns are often booked by groups. They also have a small area where you can **camp** for £10 per pitch (basic toilet/shower facilities are available).

❏ **The Elizabethan wall that never was**
Much of the millennium and a half between the departure of the Romans and the ordination of the Wall as a UNESCO World Heritage Site was characterised by the practice of border reiving, where gangs would attack their rivals and neighbours to raid, rustle and rape.

While these days this 'hidden history' of the Wall receives scant attention, there is no doubt that at the time the problem was a serious one, serious enough for a protection racket to be established and a new word, 'blackmail', to be coined (see box p194). Indeed, the raiding reached such a height in Elizabethan times that in 1587 a proposal was made to revive and rebuild the Wall in order to keep some sort of semblance of order. If that wasn't practical, the proposal declared, a new wall, constructed on similar lines to the Roman version, should be built, with *sconces* (castles) at every mile. Unfortunately, the cost was estimated to be a prohibitive £30,000 and was never taken up.

MAP 27

70 MINS FROM GILSLAND (MAP 28) →

← WALLTOWN QUARRY CAFÉ

65 MINS TO GREAT CHESTERS FORT (MAP 25) →

LONGBYRE

ROMAN DITCH

CHECK THE BUMPS & RIDGES IN THIS FIELD!

Four Wynds

☐ 068

WATCH OUT FOR TRAIN!

BIT OF WALL

PENNINE WAY

☐ 069

THIRLWALL CASTLE

TIPALT BURN

HOLMHEAD B&B

TURN LEFT FOR DETOUR TO GREENHEAD

PATH KEEPS TO THE NORTH OF THE ROMAN DITCH

IGNORE STILE

PATH NOT VERY CLEAR HERE, PARTICULARLY IF COMING FROM EAST BUT STICK TO THE TOP OF THE RIDGE

26

WALLTOWN CRAGS

TURRET 45A

FANTASTIC BIT OF WALL UP TO 13 COURSES HIGH

PATH ROUND CRAGS

BENCH

WALLTOWN QUARRY – NOW A POND

☐ 066

WALLTOWN REFRESHMENTS (& TOILETS)

CP

WALLTOWN LODGE

AD122 BUS STOP

☐ 067

CARVORAN (MAGNA)

ROMAN ARMY MUSEUM; REMAINS OF ROMAN FORT & TEAROOMS

GREENHEAD

Greenhead Hostel

BUS STOP

Greenhead Hotel

SCHOOL

TO A69 ↓

Old Forge Tearoom

GOLF COURSE

28

B6318

APPROX SCALE

0 ¼ mile

0 500m

65 MINS TO GILSLAND (MAP 28) →

WALLTOWN QUARRY CAFÉ →

60 MINS FROM GREAT CHESTERS FORT (MAP 25) →

If that's not enough, Holmhead also possesses two Roman inscriptions. The first lies besides the kitchen door and says *Civitas Dumnoni*, commemorating the work of a tribe from Devonshire which was drafted up here for Wall construction and repairs. It's quite a rare inscription, for the Wall was built almost entirely by regular Roman troops and manned by auxiliaries from Spain, Bavaria etc; the British rarely got a look in, so why these troops were asked to undertake work on the Wall here is unknown. A second inscription can be found in the wall of the bunkhouse, and tells how the Roman centurion Julius Ianalis oversaw the construction of this section of the Wall. You'll have to ask the owners to point it out to you – it's not easy to locate.

As for the 14th-century **Thirlwall Castle** (Map 27), Thirlwall means 'Gap in the Wall' in the local dialect and the castle was built in a gap in the Wall where it was crossed by the Tipalt Burn. A typically strong, defensible home, Thirlwall was built to protect the owners from the cross-border reiving raids (see box p194) that were rife at this time.

The Thirlwall family (they adopted the name of the local area when they bought the land for the castle) had made their fortune in military campaigns in France. It is one thing to earn a fortune, however, and quite another to keep it, particularly in this part of the world in the 14th century. Hence the extravagant fortifications to their family home, built using whatever material lay close at hand – which, of course, meant the Wall. The castle lasted for 300 years before the family moved to Hexham and the castle was sold to the Earl of Carlisle for £4000. Already in possession of one large country pile, the earl was interested only in Thirlwall's land and allowed the castle to fall into disrepair and, eventually, ruin. There's little to see today except the shell of the keep but it remains an atmospheric and charmingly dilapidated place.

Opposite the castle, a path leads alongside a stream to a railway, where you have a choice. Turn left before the railway, head over the bridge, and you arrive at ...

GREENHEAD [MAP 27, p165]

Though well-known to Wall walkers thanks to its proximity to the trail and its facilities, there's little to Greenhead beyond a school, church, the *Old Forge Tearoom* (Tue-Fri 9.30am-4.30pm, Sat & Sun to 5pm), which serves homemade dishes, a **pub/hotel**, **hostel** and **B&B**.

Greenhead Hotel (☎ 016977-47411, 🖳 www.greenheadhotelandhostel.co.uk; 1T/1D/2D, T or F, all en suite, bath available) has a bar and a restaurant and is the focus of the village. Rates start at £70 (around £40 for single occupancy). Food is served daily noon-8.30pm. They also have free wi-fi. Dogs are welcome by prior arrangement but have to stay in kennels outside.

The hostel is *Greenhead Hostel* (see Greenhead Hotel for contact details; open all year; 40 beds), housed in a converted Methodist church. Once in danger of closure, it's now owned by Greenhead Hotel. Strangely, though not affiliated with the YHA any more, they still charge £13.50 for YHA members, £15 for non-members.

The AD122 and Telford's No 185 **buses** stop regularly by the hotel/village hall and if you walk to the road end (A69), a few minutes away, you can catch Arriva's/Stagecoach's No 685 service. See pp56-8 for further information.

... or continue straight on to the main road where, turning right and then left, you pass a decent chunk of Wall that's been shored up to allow the B6318 to bisect it. For B&B stay on the road for *Four Wynds Guest House* (☎ 01697-747972, 🖳 www.four-wynds-guest-house.co.uk; 2T/1D or F, all en suite); it has rooms for £68 based on two sharing (£38-40 single occupancy). Dogs are welcome as long as the proprietors have advance notice.

The path follows the line of the Wall past the undulations of the Vallum, Military Way and the Wall itself. Continuing to Gap Farm (named after the Tyne Gap which runs nearby and which marks the watershed of Britain), you soon arrive at the friendly town/village of Gilsland.

GILSLAND   [MAP 28, p169]

An unprepossessing town by the lofty standards of this part of the trail, Gilsland is nevertheless an important place on the walk. It is here that we find the border between Northumberland and Cumbria; Gilsland is actually still in Northumberland but is the last place that is on this trail. Here, too, we cross the watershed and the Red Rock Fault.

It's also here that we find **Poltross Burn Milecastle** (No 48), one of the most important on the Wall. In excellent nick, the ruins include a series of steps in their north-east corner; by estimating their direction, archaeologists were able to determine the height of the walkway on the Wall at 12ft (3.66m). It is also, alas, one of the last Roman milecastles we see, providing further evidence that we are leaving the wild, windswept lands of Northumberland behind us to enter the more rural, cosy scenery of Cumbria, where the land has been ploughed and cultivated for centuries, destroying much of the Wall in the process.

In the village itself the post office has now closed but the small **shop** (Mon-Wed & Fri 7.30am-12.30pm & 1.30-5.30pm, Thu & Sat 7.30am-12.30pm), is still struggling on. It sells hot tea, coffee and a few snacks and has its own **ATM** that, unusually, doesn't charge a fee.

A better option for food, however, is to walk 50 yards further on to *House of Meg*

(☎ 016977-47777; Apr/May-Oct Mon-Sat 9.30am-4.30pm, Sun 10am-4pm, Nov-Apr/May Thur-Sat 9.30am-4pm, Sun 10am-4pm), a smart little café named after a character from Walter Scott's *Waverley*, which was set around here.

Of Gilsland's three pubs, neither the Bridge Inn nor Station Hotel, immediately below the trail, offers food or accommodation, leaving only the *Samson Inn* (☎ 016977-47220; 1T en suite/1D, T or F private bathroom) to feed and shelter walkers. Food (summer daily noon-9pm, Oct-Mar Mon-Fri 6-9pm, Sat & Sun noon-9pm) is served: highlights include rabbit pie (£9.95). They also offer B&B (£35-40pp, £40-50 single occupancy) in a building next door to the pub.

At the very end of the village and right on the Wall, *Willowford Farm* (☎ 016977-47962, 🖳 www.willowford.co.uk; 1D/4D or T, all en suite, bath available; Mar-Oct) has rooms in a converted barn. With digital radios in the rooms, a free-range organic breakfast in the morning and a whacking great bit of Wall right outside, this is a great place. Dogs are welcome subject to prior arrangement. Another bonus is that they offer evening meals (from £18; book at least 24 hours in advance) and are licensed. B&B costs £75-80 (£50 single occupancy).

Bush Nook (☎ 016977-47194, 🖳 www.bushnook.co.uk; 1S/3D/2T, all en

❏ **Walk side by side and on healthy grass** Don't walk in single file or on worn areas. Protect our heritage!

suite, bath available) is an 18th-century stone-built former farm constructed, at least in part, from Hadrian's Wall stone. Most of the rooms have open-beamed ceilings, there's a delightful conservatory and they are licensed. B&B in the house costs £35-40pp; they also have a self-catering cottage (1D) which can be used on a B&B basis (£45-50pp) if available. They can also make a packed lunch (£5.50) if requested in advance. Dogs are welcome but they are not permitted in the bedrooms; however, they have an enclosed area where they can stay. The only problem is that it is a walk of at least a mile (and nearer 1½ miles) from the path; if you prefer not to walk this contact them and they will help to arrange transport. To reach Bush Nook, turn left upon hitting the road after the Poltross Burn Milecastle, and another left at the next junction.

A little out of town but very much part of its history, *Gilsland Spa Hotel* (☎ 016977-47203, ☐ www.gilslandspa.co.uk; 94 rooms including single, double, twin and family, all en suite, bath available) dates back to a time when Gilsland was still a smart town where visitors would flock to take the waters. Set in 140 acres (56 hectares) of park and woodland overlooking the town from the north, it remains an impressive place. B&B starts at £45pp (£55 for single occupancy). They have a *restaurant* where residents can have an evening meal (6.30pm) and Galloways bar (food served daily noon-2pm & 6-8pm) which is open to anyone.

Not too far away, *Brookside Villa* (☎ 016977-47300, ☐ www.brooksidevilla.com; 4T or D or F, en suite, bath available) is an even older institution, having first provided good-quality accommodation to weary travellers in 1888! Recommended by more than one reader, B&B costs from £40pp (£55 for single occupancy). Dogs are welcome, subject to prior arrangement. They offer a 'trail walkers package' for people staying more than one night; contact them for details. They also serve evening meals (from £15.50) and are fully licensed, offering locally brewed ales from Geltsdale Brewery in Brampton.

Also worth considering is *The Hill on the Wall* (☎ 016977-47214, ☐ www.hillonthewall.co.uk; 1D/1T en suite, 1T private bathroom, bath available; Feb-Nov), an award-winning B&B housed in a fortified 16th-century house, or bastle (see p208). It's a beautiful place – perhaps the best-looking accommodation on the entire trail – with wonderful old furniture including a large pine table hewn from the wood of a 17th-century mill. To make you feel right at home, all the rooms are named after Roman celebrities such as Hadrian's Retreat and Caligula's Chamber. They also have wi-fi. Rates start at £37.50-42.50pp (£50-62.50 for single occupancy).

The AD122 and Telford's No 185 **buses** leave from opposite the Bridge Inn/Village Hall. Arriva's/Stagecoach's No 685 also calls in on its way to Newcastle or to Carlisle. See pp56-8 for further details.

From the Poltross Burn Milecastle, the trail crosses the train tracks to a field where a rather remarkable sight awaits: an extensive and well-preserved piece of Roman Wall clearly going into, and under, a rather dilapidated old house. This, I presume, was the Romanway Guest House (aka the Old Vicarage), mentioned by Hunter Davies (see p50) and others, which used to have two Roman altars on its porch. Unfortunately, they don't seem to be accepting guests these days and the Wall is out of bounds.

Across the road you rejoin the Wall, again a decent chunk, this one leading from one farmhouse on the outskirts of Gilsland to another in the middle of a field. This Wall section has its own turrets too, Nos **48A** and **48B**, the latter near Willowford Farm (see p167). Look back from the second turret to the first and, given that the Romans built their turrets at equal intervals between their mile-

MAP 28

GILSLAND

Hill on the Wall

B6318

Turret 48A

Turret 48B

Willowford Farm B&B – look for copy of Roman inscription on plaque on barn wall

THIS SECTION OF WALL IS A GOOD EXAMPLE OF A NARROW WALL ON BROAD FOUNDATIONS – AND THE LAST EXAMPLE IF HEADING WEST

Brookside Villa

Bridge Inn

TO GILSLAND SPA HOTEL, ½MILE/1KM

BUS STOP

ATM & SHOP

House of Meg

Parking

CATTLE GRID

TO BUSH NOOK B&B

072

SCHOOL

WATCH OUT FOR THE TRAIN!

WALL GOES TO SIDE OF OLD HOUSE

Samson Inn

ROUND SOMEBODY'S BACK GARDEN

THE GAP

WALKING IN ROMAN DITCH HERE

Station Hotel

POST BOX

071

BRIDGE OVER POLTROSS BURN

Poltross Burn Milecastle 48

070

CHAPEL HOUSE FARM, AKA FOULTOWN (!)

STILES

GARDEN FILLED WITH CARTOON CHARACTER GNOMES

27

29

trailblazer

1/4 mile

APPROX SCALE

500m

castles, you get an idea of what one-third of a Roman mile looked like – and thus can imagine roughly what one Roman mile looked like.

Negotiating the various gates and barriers of the second farmhouse (check out the 'Roman-style' plaque stuck to the side of the barn wall), the trail – and Wall – continues down to the Irthing and the **Willowford Bridge** foundations, where the Wall and Military Way crossed the river (Map 29). Note how the river has changed its course down the centuries, for this abutment would once have been on the riverbank. There were a number of bridges at this spot, the first being built around the same time as the Wall in AD122-8. The latest, **Irthing Bridge**, one of the most beautiful on the trail, is made of weathered steel and lies just a few metres away.

The Willowford crossing also holds quite an important place in the history of the Wall. It was here that the stone Wall, which the Romans started to construct in Newcastle and extended westwards, finally met up with the turf Wall from Bowness-on-Solway. In other words, this was the last section of Wall to have been built; once they'd done this bit and joined the two sections together, their ambition to build a barrier across Britain had been realised. Any construction done after this – moving the forts up to the Wall, for example, or converting the turf Wall into a stone one – were mere refinements carried out when their infrastructure improved and allowed them to transport limestone this far west. It was also here that the broad Wall foundations ran out. Presumably, by the time the stone wall to the west of the Irthing was being constructed, to replace the original turf and timber one, the Romans had settled on a narrow Wall so built narrow foundations to suit it.

After the bridge, it's a bit of a schlep up to Milecastle 49, followed by a lengthy section of Wall leading up to Birdoswald. Don't be in too much of a hurry to get there: there are estimated to be half a dozen or so engravings on this section of the Wall. Two of the best known include a dedication stone, just over halfway between the milecastle and the fort (look for the large brown stone near the top of the Wall) and, best of all, a great phallic symbol near Birdoswald itself. To find the latter, look for where a 'modern' stone wall hits Hadrian's Wall at a 90° angle on its northern side, not far before you enter into Birdoswald itself. You'll notice that at this point there is a hole in the foot of the Wall – presumably a culvert to allow the water to drain properly. Facing this hole, look to the left of it and a few metres away you'll see a second, smaller hole in the foot of the Wall. Almost directly above this, at about chest height, is the symbol.

Once at Birdoswald Fort a number of choices present themselves: either keep on going, remembering to **stamp your passport** before you go; or stay (see below), or catch the **Hadrian's Wall bus AD122** (see pp56-8 for further information, pp212-15 for the timetable) or, of course, you can visit the fort.

If you decide to stay in the area there is the *Birdoswald YHA Hostel* (Map 29; ☎ 0845-371 9551, 🖳 birdoswald@yha.org.uk; open daily mid-July to mid-Sep to walkers; 36 beds; from £15pp including entrance to the site; self-catering only), set within the ruins of the fort. There are six rooms (2 x 4-bed, 2 x 6-bed, 2 x 8-bed).

MAP 29

55 MINS FROM BANKS (MAP 30)

40 MINS TO GILSLAND (MAP 28)

BIRDOSWALD

45 MINS FROM GILSLAND (MAP 28)

BIRDOSWALD

50 MINS TO BANKS (MAP 30)

¼ mile

APPROX SCALE

500m

trailblazer

28

ORIGINAL ROMAN WALL

ROMAN BRIDGE ABUTMENT

ROMAN INSCRIPTION ON SOUTH SIDE OF WALL HERE

MODERN WILLOWFORD/ IRTHING BRIDGE

MILECASTLE 49

STEEP

YHA Hostel

073

TURRET 49B

BIRDOSWALD

Irthing River

2 GATES

HIGH HOUSE

FOLLOWING THE LINE OF THE TURF WALL HERE NOTE NO VISIBLE SIGN, JUST LOTS OF UNUSUALLY UNDULATING GROUND

Wall Burn

074

30

DROP INTO VALLUM BRIEFLY AFTER BRIDGE

ROUTE GUIDE AND MAPS

BIRDOSWALD [see map p171]

(☎ 016977-47602; Apr-Sep daily 10am-5.30pm; Oct 10am-4pm; £5/4.50/3 adults/concs; English Heritage members free)

The Roman name for Birdoswald was **Banna**, meaning 'Spur' and the fort does indeed sit on a spur above the River Irthing. It's a lovely position up here, with views in every direction best appreciated, perhaps, from the picnic area set up at the southern end of the fort. Unfortunately, the ruins themselves fail to live up to their setting.

But no matter, for the beauty of Birdoswald lies mainly in the details. There are the carvings on the Wall leading up to Birdoswald, as mentioned on p170; the pleasant **farmhouse** which dominates the site, with Roman stones clearly visible in the fabric of its walls which actually date back to the early 17th century; the remains of a **granary**, the only extensive set of ruins that have thus far been excavated in this fort that once held a thousand soldiers; and the **excavated Roman gates**, one of which, on the east side, is said to be one of the best preserved on the Wall, with the *voussoir* (arch stone) and the impost stone (the stone that supported the arch) still extant.

The **museum** is one of the smartest, too, and deals not only with the Roman occupation of the site but with the location's entire history. There is also a *café* here.

Perhaps the most remarkable discoveries, however, were the 19 or so religious altars, all but one dedicated to Jupiter, that were found in the same area to the east of the fort. The theory is that these altars were deliberately buried there as part of some elaborate ritual, possibly on Jupiter's day on January 1 after the annual parade. (The only altar not dedicated to Jupiter was dedicated instead to the Cumbrian war god, Codicus.) We can assume only that, to whomever they were dedicated, they were all put up by the Dacians from Romania who occupied the fort in the 3rd and 4th centuries AD.

After Birdoswald, the Wall continues for a little longer until the trail deserts both it and the road to follow what appears to be either the line of the Vallum or the ditch, a clear topographical feature for the next few miles. But it's a little more complicated than that. Remember, west of the Irthing the Wall was originally built of turf and these clear, steep undulations in the earth are the remnants of this, the turf Wall (the only obvious turf section left on the entire trail), which would later be replaced by stone.

What you are actually following for the next few fields (until you hit the path to Lanercost) is, immediately to your left, the ditch and the Vallum, with the two separated by the remains of the turf Wall. But note how the turf Wall is *not* on the same line as the later stone Wall you followed from Birdoswald, which is down near the road.

There's one other point of interest about this stretch: neither the stone nor the turf Wall have particularly good views to the north, unlike the Wall of the previous two stages which insisted on following the tops of ridges and crags. Why this is so is unclear, though a popular theory is that the local Brigante tribe in this area were more trouble than the Caledones to the north, so the Romans decided to locate the Wall with good views to the south rather than north.

The turf Wall peters out altogether as you progress down the hill past Turret 50B (which is actually not on the trail). After crossing over the farm track and **Wall Burn** you continue following the line of the Vallum, rejoining the road and the route of the stone Wall after a short stretch through woodland (Map 30).

Passing **Piper Sike Turret** (No 51A), the trail continues on or near the road to **Pike Hill Signal Tower** – the only signal tower on the Wall. A pre-Hadrian construction, the tower was possibly built for the Roman campaigns in Scotland under Agricola, where other such towers have been found, to give early warning of any movements by the Caledones. As these campaigns came to an end and the Wall was built, the tower was integrated into the Wall defences. Note how the Wall kinks to incorporate the tower – proof, if it were needed, that the tower came first. As you'd imagine, the views from the signal tower are pretty extensive.

BANKS [MAP 30, p173]

A semi-circular huddle of houses, there's not much to Banks at all, though there is a post box, telephone box, and a B&B: *Quarry Side* (☎ 01697-72538, 🖳 beth.harding@btinternet.com; 1T/1D share bathroom, 1D en suite) on the west side of the semi-circle, charges £60-65 (£35-40 single occupancy) for **B&B**. Dogs are welcome subject to prior arrangement. From 2011 they will also have a **campsite** (25 pitches, £5pp) with toilet and washing-up facilities. If booked in advance packed lunches (£5) are available and, if there is space, campers can have breakfast (about £6).

The AD122 **bus** stops here (see pp56-8 for further information and pp212-15 for the timetable).

BANKS TO CARLISLE [MAPS 30-38]

Introduction

Today we finally say goodbye to the last remnants of the Wall itself. By the time we reach Walton there is nothing left save for the odd trace of Vallum and ditch. The depredations of man on this side of the Pennines have served to destroy the Wall completely; odd, when one considers that Newcastle, the largest of all settlements on the route, still manages to muster two or three remaining sections of its own (see pp88-9 and box pp90-1). But though central Carlisle has much olde-worlde charm, there is nothing left of Roman Britain outside the museums.

Still, no matter, for the walking is no less pleasant on this **14¹/₂-mile (23.3km; 6-6¹/₄hrs)** stage and the scenery, in places at least, just as interesting. And occasionally, just occasionally, you do get proof that the trail is still following the line of the Wall and its associated defences.

❏ **Lanercost Priory**
Lanercost Priory (Map 31), founded in 1166 by Sir Robert de Vaux and built, like so much else, from masonry taken from the Wall which has been combined with the local sandstone. A wealth of Roman stones and remains are housed within, including one of the 19 altars found at Birdoswald (see p172). The AD122 bus stops at Lanercost (see timetable pp212-15).

The route

The various pieces of Wall on this stage occur quite early on. The first is **Hare Hill** (Map 31), just ten minutes or so of road walking from Banks. Once thought to be the highest remaining piece of Wall left on the trail, it is now widely believed to be little more than a 19th-century reconstruction that used original Roman stones. That's not to dismiss it altogether, however, for if you walk around the side of the Wall facing away from the road you should be able to find, at approximately head height, a small Roman inscription indicating that Primus Pilus, a senior centurion of the First Cohort, built it. In fact, this stone was taken from a site called Moneyholes, some distance to the west.

The next feature on the Wall is ***Haytongate Farm*** (☎ 016977-41119, 💻 www .haytongate.co.uk; 1D/1T or D/1F with three single beds, all with private facilities) where a 'snack hut' (daily 7am-11pm) sits by the path. As with all such huts – and you'll find others near Crosby-on-Eden and at Drumburgh – the owners are relying on your honesty to pay for anything you consume; don't betray their trust. The hut even has its own website now – 💻 www.itrod.co.uk – where you can buy some neat Hadrian's Wall themed T-shirts, though you can also buy them here. By the time you get here they may also have a portaloo. From May 2011 they are offering B&B for £35pp (£55 single occupancy). Guests will also have access to a kitchen to heat meals up.

Having crossed Burtholme Beck, beneath the trees on your right you'll see an original piece of Wall, untampered and unreconstructed, with the original mortar still *in situ*. It's good to see how the Wall is still marking a boundary, showing a continuity across the ages.

The last major piece of Roman masonry occurs just before the village of Walton, itself reached by a delightfully pleasant stroll through fields, across bridges and along roads. The Roman ruins in this case were once the abutment to a bridge and lie just above where the 'modern' Dovecote Bridge sits today. Unfortunately, being made of sandstone, the abutment and the Wall which once led up to it have since been backfilled to prevent them eroding away completely, though you can find a description of them in Hunter Davies's travelogue *A Walk along the Wall* (see p50).

The path used to follow the line of this Wall to the river (a tributary of the Irthing) but for the last few years walkers have been encouraged to take what they say is a 'temporary' diversion along the road. However, it would appear that this has become a permanent path and the prettier, riparian option is now, alas, closed to the public.

WALTON [MAP 32]

Walton is not an unattractive little place but there's little of interest for Wall walkers, particularly now the Centurion Inn, once the quintessential Wall pub, has closed – hopefully just temporarily while new owners are found. There's an old church with **phone-** and **post-boxes** opposite.

Low Rigg Farm (☎ 016977-3233, 💻 www.lowriggfarm.co.uk; 1T shared bathroom/1D, T or F, en suite; Apr-Oct), a 125-acre (5-hectare) dairy farm, makes its own bread and preserves and uses them as ingredients for breakfast. B&B here is £35-50pp. *(continued on p178)*

ROUTE GUIDE AND MAPS

ROUTE GUIDE AND MAPS

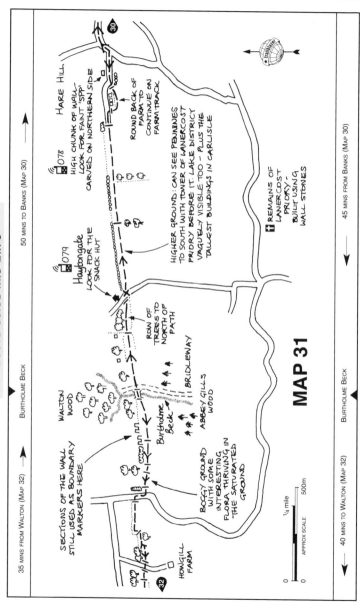

35 MINS FROM WALTON (MAP 32) →   BURTHOLME BECK   50 MINS TO BANKS (MAP 30) →

SECTIONS OF THE WALL STILL USED AS BOUNDARY MARKERS HERE

WALTON WOOD

HOWGILL FARM

BOGGY GROUND WITH SOME INTERESTING FLORA THRIVING IN THE SATURATED GROUND

Burtholme Beck

ABBEY GILLS WOOD

BRIDLEWAY

ROW OF TREES TO NORTH OF PATH

Haytongate LOOK FOR THE SNACK HUT

079

078

HARE HILL

HIGH CHUNK OF WALL — LOOK FOR FAINT 'SPP' CARVED ON NORTHERN SIDE

ROUND BACK OF FARM TO CONTINUE ON FARM TRACK

HIGHER GROUND: CAN SEE PENNINES TO SOUTH WITH TOWER OF LANERCOST PRIORY BEFORE IT. LAKE DISTRICT VAGUELY VISIBLE TOO – PLUS THE TALLEST BUILDINGS IN CARLISLE

REMAINS OF LANERCOST PRIORY BUILT USING WALL STONES

MAP 31

BURTHOLME BECK

BURTHOLME BECK

40 MINS TO WALTON (MAP 32)   45 MINS FROM BANKS (MAP 30)

¼ mile
APPROX SCALE
0   500m
0

MAP 32

50 MINS FROM NEWTOWN (MAP 33) →   WALTON   →   35 MINS TO BURTHOLME BECK (MAP 31) →

← 50 MINS TO NEWTOWN (MAP 33)   WALTON   ← 40 MINS FROM BURTHOLME BECK (MAP 31)

IGNORE STILE

OVERHEAD CABLE

35

080
ABUTMENT TO RIGHT, JUST AFTER BRIDGE

DOVECOTE BRIDGE

TO WALTON HIGH RIGG B&B

WALTON

WALTON GREEN & BUS STOP

"ROMAN HOUSE"

CENTURION INN (CLOSED AT TIME OF WRITING) OCCUPYING SITE OF A FORMER MILECASTLE

↓ LOOK SOUTH FOR VIEWS OF PENNINES

TO LOW RIGG FARM B&B

FOOTBALL FIELD

POST BOX

PUBLIC PHONE

081

SWAINSTEADS FARM

GATE & CATTLE GRID

Sandysike

MUDDY

WEIR – GREAT PLACE FOR A PICNIC AND GOOD VIEWS OF FALLS

082

Cam Beck

33

¼ mile   500m
APPROX SCALE

ROUTE GUIDE AND MAPS

(continued from p175) A mile to the north of the village, ***Walton High Rigg*** (☎ 016977-2117, 🖥 www.waltonhighrigg.co .uk; 1D, T or F, private bathroom; Easter-Oct) is a Georgian listed farmhouse with great views over the Pennines and Lake District. B&B costs £30pp (£40 for single occupancy). Packed lunches are available if requested in advance.

Walton seems rather cut off from the rest of the world – even the AD122 Hadrian's Wall bus doesn't call in here. There is a fragmented **bus** service, however, with Stagecoach's No 97 leaving from Walton Green on Wednesdays and Fridays.

From Walton, one couple wrote in to say that they got slightly lost; follow the signs carefully. The trail drops through more farmyards following, approximately, the line of the Roman ditch. Crossing a small stream, the path climbs through woods to ***Sandysike*** (☎ 016977-2330, 🖥 sandysike@talk21.com; 1S private bathroom, separate toilet/1D shared facilities), a working farm where B&B in the gorgeous Georgian farmhouse costs £30pp, and there's also an equally charming eight-bed **bunkhouse** (£10pp; plus £6pp if bedding is required). They also allow **camping** (£5pp; shower/toilet facilities in the bunkhouse). Dogs are welcome by prior arrangement; packed lunches and evening meals can be provided. However, debit/credit cards are not accepted. Overall, a cracking place.

From Sandysike, the path follows the farm track, taking a first left through the cow field before the farm buildings (there should be a signpost there), then drops again to a bridge over a second, slightly larger stream with a series of little waterfalls: this is **Cam Beck**. A 3¾-acre (1.5-hectare) Roman fort, **Castlesteads**, lies just a few hundred metres to the south, unfortunately it's out of bounds. Unusually, **Camboglanna** (as the Romans knew it; the name means 'Crooked Glen') lay between the Wall and the Vallum and not actually on the Wall. At different times it was garrisoned by troops from Spain, Gaul and Tungria. In his book, *A Walk along the Wall,* Hunter Davies (see p50) mentions visiting the house that now occupies the site and finding Roman altars lying around in the summerhouse.

One more stream and a whole patchwork of fields are crossed as you make your way towards Carlisle, a city whose highest buildings start to appear on the horizon as you progress westwards. It can start to feel, as you cross field after field, that this part of the walk is some sort of treadmill. But there are some things of interest on the way. There are also some small hamlets, such as aptly named **Newtown**, home to ***Newtown Farm*** (☎ 016977-2768, 🖥 www.new townfarmbedandbreakfast.co.uk; 1T or F/1D, both en suite, 1D private bathroom) where B&B costs £25-30pp (£40 single occupancy). Evening meals and packed lunches are available if requested in advance.

❑ **Walk side by side and on healthy grass** Don't walk in single file or on worn areas. Protect our heritage!

NEWTOWN   50 MINS TO WALTON (MAP 32)

PATH GOES
THROUGH FARM

TO CASTLESTEADS
CAMBOGLANNA
FORT - NO ENTRY!

AFTER BRIDGE TURN RIGHT
FOR 20M THEN FOLLOW SIGNS
CLOSELY

STONE
STEPS

GATE IN CORNER
OF FIELD

HORSE FIELD

A6071

BACK
GARDEN

BETWEEN CORRUGATED
IRON FENCES

VILLAGE
GREEN

Newtown Farm B&B

PUBLIC PHONE

TO BRAMPTON
SEE TOWN PLAN

NEWTOWN

KISSING GATE BY THE
LAST HOUSE IN NEWTOWN

TO IRTHINGTON

MAP 33

NEWTOWN   50 MINS FROM WALTON (MAP 32)

ROUTE GUIDE AND MAPS

BRAMPTON   [See map p181]

Brampton's a lovely little market town sitting snugly in the Irthing Valley, reasonably convenient for the trail and with virtually every second building either a pub, hotel or tearoom. Granted a Market Charter in 1252, the main market day is Wednesday.

The main sight is **St Martin's Church** (9.30am-4.30pm), the only church designed by architect Philip Webb, with some wonderful stained-glass windows by his fellow pre-Raphaelite Edward Burne-Jones.

Services

The **tourist information centre** (☎ 016977-3433; Easter-Aug Mon-Sat 10am-5pm, Sep & Oct to 4pm) is in the Moot Hall at the eastern end of Front St, the main street in the town. They will do accommodation booking (see box p52).

The library (Mon 2-5pm, Wed 10am-noon & 2-5pm, Thur & Fri 2-5pm, Sat 10am-1pm) has **internet access**; if you have your own laptop, you'll find the White Lion (see Where to eat) has a faster and more reliable internet service. There's a Co-op **supermarket** (daily 7am-10pm) behind Market Place, with a Spar (Mon-Sat 7am-10pm, Sun 8am-10pm) across the road from the TIC.

Just a couple of doors down is the H Jobson **pharmacy** (Mon, Wed, Fri 9am-6pm, Tue & Thur to 5.30pm, Sat to 5pm), and next door is a **bank** (HSBC) with ATM (with a Barclays a little further down on the opposite side). Next door is the **post office** (Mon-Fri 9am-5.30pm, Sat to 12.30pm), while opposite the HSBC there's a **camping/trekking shop**, Off The Wall (☎ 016977-41600, 🖳 www.offthe wall-web.co.uk; Mon-Sat 9am-5pm), in the centre of town.

Transport
[See pp56-8] The AD122 (see pp212-15) and Telford's No 185 buses stop on Front St; Arriva's/Stagecoach's No 685 calls in here as do Stagecoach's Nos 94 & 97 and Telford's/Wright's No 680.

Note that, while Brampton does boast a **train station**, it's 1¹/₂ miles out of town. The walk takes you through woods and is pleasant – but it's still the most inconvenient station on the walk by some distance.

Where to stay
Oakwood Park (☎ 016977-2436, 🖳 www.oakwoodparkhotel.co.uk; 1D/2T/1D, T or F, all en suite, bath available; Mar-Nov), Longtown Rd, is a Victorian pile set in ten acres of grounds about a mile north of town on the way to the Wall. B&B starts at £30pp (from £38 for single occupancy; £65 for three people in the family room). Evening meals and packed lunches are available if requested in advance.

On Station Rd and east of the town centre *Sands House* (☎ 016977-3085, 🖳 www.thesandshouse.co.uk; 2D/2T/1D, T or F, most en suite, bath available) is a 17th-century coaching inn with comfy rooms from £60 (£40 for single occupancy, £75 for the family room).

In town the Georgian *Oval House* (☎ 016977-2106, 🖳 www.ovalhouse.demon .co.uk; 1T private facilities/1D/2D or F, all en suite, bath available) offers B&B for £70 (£40-70 single occupancy). *Howard Arms Hotel* (☎ 016977-42758; 1S/2T/5D, all en

suite, bath available) charges £85 per room for B&B, £65 for the single.

The White Lion (☎ 016977-42272; 4T/4D, most en suite, bath available) is a friendly old place in the heart of town. Once again in the process of changing ownership, they charge £50 (£35pp single occupancy) plus £5.95pp for breakfast. Well-behaved dogs are welcome subject to prior arrangement.

Where to eat and drink
During the day *Capon Tree Café* (☎ 016977-3649; Mon-Sat 9.15am-4.30pm) is good value with their diverse range of scones for just £1-1.30 each. However, note that they are closed for one week in August, usually the week leading up to the bank holiday.

Virtually next door, *Jacobites* (☎ 016977-3535; summer Mon-Thur 8.30am-5pm, Fri & Sat 8.30am-8pm, winter Mon-Sat 8.30am-5pm) is another popular spot with a similar menu, with jacket spuds from £4.50 to £5.25; they serve tapas on Friday and Saturday evenings in the summer.

The *Sandwich Shop* (☎ 016977-42888; Mon-Sat 7am-3.30pm) serves breakfasts, sandwiches and baguettes, all at rock-bottom prices (sandwiches £1.40-2.30, jacket potatoes £2.40). The *White Lion* (see Where to stay; food served Mon-Fri noon-3pm & 6-9pm, Sat & Sun noon-4pm), does a great-value Sunday lunch for £5.95. Its closest rival is *Howard Arms Hotel* (see Where to stay; daily Mon-Thur noon-3pm & 6-9pm; Fri & Sat noon-9pm, Sun noon-6pm) which is looking spruce after its renovation and has mains, such as gammon steak, starting at £10.95.

Round behind the tourist office, *Huntington's Informal Dining* (☎ 016977-3481, 🖳 www.huntingtonsinformaldining .co.uk; Wed-Sat from 5pm, Sun May-Oct only) is, as its name suggests, a relaxed, unpretentious place with an interesting menu, including local butcher's Cumberland sausage with mash and onion gravy (£9.95) and a seafood special every Friday.

There is the usual abundance of takeaways in Brampton too, including *Brampton Tandoori* (☎ 016977-2600/1;

Sun-Fri 6-11pm, Sat 4-11pm); *Hoi Sun Chinese* (☎ 016977-2090; Tue-Thur 5-10.30pm, Fri-Sun 5-11pm); *Berti's Fish & Chips* (☎ 016977-2218; Mon, Wed-Fri 11.30am-1.30pm & 5-9.30pm) on Front St; *Golden Palace* (☎ 016977-2232; Wed-Mon

5-11pm); and *Roosters* (☎ 016977-42471; Mon-Sat 11am-10pm) another chippie with haddock and chips for £4.20. Incidentally, this place may deliver up to Sandysike (see p178) near Walton.

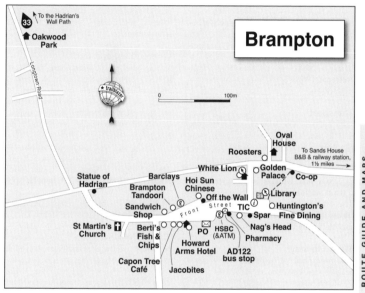

ROUTE GUIDE AND MAPS

From Newtown, follow both the Vallum and ditch. A short-cut path leads from the grassy track off north to **Laversdale** (off Map 34), home to the pleasant little *Stonewalls Campsite* (☎ 01228-573666), where a pitch costs £5pp; shower (£2) and toilet facilities are available and they have a neat little shed-cum-kitchen where you can make your own breakfast (an honesty box is provided). If you don't want to cook your own food in the evening, just up the road is the *Sportsman Inn* (☎ 01228-573255; bar Mon-Thur 5-11pm, Fri & Sat 4-11pm, Sun noon-11pm; food served Wed-Sat 6-9pm, Sun noon-3pm & 6-8pm). Stagecoach's No 97 **bus** service stops in Laversdale; see pp56-8 for further details.

The trail eventually meets up with a road at **Oldwall**, where you share the path with some free-range chickens and maybe the odd sheep or two. If you are planning to stay in Laversdale and missed the short-cut path turn right onto the road here; it's a 20-minute walk.

After **Bleatarn Farmhouse** you walk past the tarn itself – with Carlisle Airport hidden away to the south – on a slightly raised, arrow-straight path. This

MAP 34

40 MINS FROM TURN FOR SANDY LANE (MAP 35)

OLDWALL

30 MINS TO NEWTOWN (MAP 33)

40 MINS TO TURN FOR SANDY LANE (MAP 35)

OLDWALL

30 MINS FROM NEWTOWN (MAP 33)

AFTER STILE TAKE A
LEFT THROUGH KISSING GATE

POWER
CABLES

DITCH AND TREES
ACCOMPANYING
THE PATH HERE

VALLUM

SHORTCUT PATH TO
LAVERSDALE, THE
SPORTSMAN INN &
STONEWALLS
CAMPSITE (15 MINS)

LOOK FOR THE
CHICKENS AND SHEEP

CARLISLE
AIRPORT

OLDWALL

085

TO LAVERSDALE,
THE SPORTSMAN INN
& STONEWALLS CAMPSITE

BUS
STOP

SHEEP
FIELD

BRIDGE
& GATES

FENCE &
HAWTHORNS

WHEAT
FIELD

STILL FOLLOWING
THE COURSE OF
HADRIAN'S WALL

IGNORE THIS
PATH TO RIGHT

FIVE GATES GOING
ROUND BACK OF FARM

TOILET

BLEATARN
FARMHOUSE

PATH BRUSHES
EDGE OF TARN

BLEA
TARN

¼ mile

500m

APPROX SCALE

0

0

is actually the Wall you are walking upon. The minor road that follows also marks out the course of the Wall, though you leave it after half a mile (1km) or so to join a *clarty* (the local word for muddy) bridleway, Sandy Lane (Map 35), down to **Crosby-on-Eden**. Here, again, the Romans intrude on the modern world: the road you join at Crosby is actually part of the Stanegate. Just before the road is a refreshment stall with hot and cold drinks and snacks. Don't forget to use the honesty box!

CROSBY-ON-EDEN [MAPS 35 & 36]

A village split into two parts connected by the A689, Crosby-on-Eden lies an hour or two from Carlisle on the trail and thus is a perfect place to take the weight off your feet, get yourself a drink and gird your loins for that final push into the city. As with many of the minor villages encountered in this western half of the walk, Crosby is built around, and consists of little more than, the main road. It's here you'll find the

30 MINS FROM CROSBY-ON-EDEN (MAP 36) ▶ TURN FOR SANDY LANE   40 MINS TO OLDWALL (MAP 34) ⟶

MAP 35

34

WALKING ON WALL! OR AT LEAST ON THE LINE OF IT

📱086

LOW WELLHEAD FARM

BRIDLEWAY KNOWN LOCALLY AS SANDY LANE - THOUGH MORE MUDDY THAN SANDY

0   ¼ mile
0   APPROX SCALE   500m

SERIES OF GATES THROUGH A FARM, FENCES EITHER SIDE

📱087

STILE & GATE

📱088

CROSBY MANSION

BRIDGE OVER THE A689

Bluebell Camping Barn

REFRESHMENTS

36

ROAD RUNNING ALONG LINE OF STANEGATE

Crosby Lodge Country House Hotel

TREES WITH DITCH BETWEEN THEM AND ROAD

⋆ trailblazer

ROUTE GUIDE AND MAPS

◀ 30 MINS TO CROSBY-ON-EDEN (MAP 36)   TURN FOR SANDY LANE ◀   40 MINS FROM OLDWALL (MAP 34)

START OF BRIDLEWAY   25 MINS   CROSBY-ON-EDEN

CROSBY-ON-EDEN
(LOW CROSBY)

MAP 36

*trailblazer

PHONE   POST   SCHOOL
BOX   BOX
                        ST JOHN'S
The Stag
Inn
                                    35

A PROLIFERATION OF   BIG   GREEN   BUS STOP
WILD FLOWERS CROWD   PORTICOED   LANE
IN ON BOTH SIDES AS   HOUSE
THE RIVER AND PATH   089
SEPARATE

TO WALLFOOT   POWER
HOTEL &   LINES
RESTAURANT
(4-5 MINS)   PATH UNCLEAR –
                                  JUST FOLLOW RIVER

37   TREES AND AN
                  EMBANKMENT
        SHED   SEPARATE YOU
                  FROM THE RIVER

MUDDY   0   1/4 mile
BRIDLEWAY   090
                                     0   APPROX SCALE   500m
   RIVERSIDE
   ROUTE BETTER   River
   BUT OVERGROWN   Eden

START OF BRIDLEWAY   25 MINS   CROSBY-ON-EDEN

Church of St John, on the way into Low
Crosby village, erected in 1864 on the site
of a much older edifice.

At the start of the village, *Crosby
Lodge Country House Hotel* (Map 35; ☎
01228-573618, 🖳 www.crosbylodge.co
.uk; 3D/8D or T; all en suite, bath available)
is a lovely Georgian pile built in 1805, surrounded by parkland and with the Eden
flowing not too far away. It's good to see
smart establishments such as this viewing
trekkers as potential customers rather than
mud-splattered nuisances that bring the
tone of the place down. Subject to prior
arrangement dogs can stay in two of the

rooms in the stable block. They serve
drinks and sandwiches (£4.20-6.95)
throughout the day for guests and non-residents alike; meals are available daily noon-
1.30pm and 7-8.45pm though for residents
only on Sunday evenings. B&B starts from
£80pp (single occupancy £90); expect to
pay about £40 for a three-course meal
including coffee.

Along the main road, in Low Crosby,
you'll find *The Stag Inn* (Map 36; ☎
01228-573210; bar daily 11am-11pm), otherwise known by exhausted trekkers as *The
Stagger In*. This 17th-century inn has
recently been taken over by new owners

and is classed as a 'gastro-pub'. Hot food is served daily year-round (noon-3pm & 6-9pm), with sandwiches and salads available 3-6pm.

Just one minute from the trail, **Bluebell** (☎ 01228-573600, or ☎ 0777-841 7999, 💻 www.bluebellcamping.co.uk) is a new **camping barn** set in the grounds of a Georgian country house just a minute or two from the path. The barn itself also dates back to the 18th century and has space for 16 people (£13pp) as well as smart kitchens, dining areas and showers. It may be booked by groups so it is worth contacting them in advance.

About half an hour outside Crosby, but only five minutes from the path, newly refurbished **Wallfoot Hotel and Restaurant** (☎ 01228-573696, 💻 www.wallfoot.co.uk; 2S/1D or T/2D/2D, T or F, all en suite, bath available) lies on the A689, is licensed and serves meals (daily noon-2pm & 5-9pm) in the restaurant, which is open to non residents as well. B&B is £70-75 (£45-60 for single occupancy). Dogs (£5 per dog) are welcome; booking is preferred. If arranged in advance they are happy to pick guests up in Carlisle or take them there.

Transport-wise, the AD122 and Telford's No 185 buses stop by the Stag Inn; Stagecoach's No 94 also stops in Crosby. See pp56-8 for more information and pp212-15 for the timetable.

From Crosby-on-Eden, you now forsake the line of the Wall altogether to indulge, as you did on the first stage from Newcastle, in a little bit of riverside strolling. It's a pleasant walk, curtailed by a diversion to Linstock to cross the M6.

The remains of **Linstock Castle** (Map 37), an old fortified house and pele tower now incorporated into a modern farm, lies to the right of the trail as you enter the village. After the M6 another lengthy piece of road-walking follows before the trail joins a cycle route, separated from the road by a hedge.

This cycle route takes you round the back of **Rickerby** (Map 38), an entire hamlet that, with all its towers and turrets, resembles one enormous Victorian folly. There's even a tower to the north of the trail in a field of rape. This eccentric architecture was the work of a presumably eccentric man with an undoubtedly eccentric name: George Head Head.

Crossing a pleasant park at the end of Rickerby, the trail crosses an iron bridge and continues past a school and golf course and then follows the water's edge to the **Sands Sports Centre** which has a *café* (daily 9am-9.30pm), a **passport-stamping point** (see box p49) as well as a decent eatery. Turn left here to head into Carlisle.

❏ **The Wall's first tourist?**
According to the Venerable Bede, in AD685 St Cuthbert came to Carlisle to visit an English queen staying in a nunnery in town. Whilst there, Cuthbert was taken by the citizens of Carlisle to look at the town walls and the 'remarkable fountain, formerly built by the Romans'. Thus, with this brief mention by Bede, Cuthbert becomes the first recorded tourist to visit the Wall. The 'remarkable fountain', incidentally, has never been found, though in the 1930s a building was excavated with a fountain in its central courtyard, which dated back to AD78 and the reign of Vespasian. Could this be the fountain Cuthbert was shown?

MAP 37

LINSTOCK

MUDDY SECTION WITH
OVERPOWERING SMELL OF
THE COUNTRY FROM THE
NEARBY FARM

LINSTOCK
CASTLE

BENCH

ROAD BRIDGE OVER
THE M6 MOTORWAY

POST
BOX

POWER
LINES

BENCH

A DULL BUT
QUIET STRETCH
OF ROAD
WALKING

091
THE
BEECHES

THE PATH GOES ROUND THE
BACK OF THE VILLAGE ON
A CYCLE TRACK

River
Eden

0 ¼ mile

0 APPROX SCALE 500m

25 MINS TO START OF BRIDLEWAY (MAP 36)

25 MINS FROM START OF BRIDLEWAY (MAP 36)

THE BEECHES

THE BEECHES

40 MINS FROM A7 BRIDGE (MAP 38)

40 MINS TO A7 BRIDGE (MAP 38)

ROUTE GUIDE AND MAPS

❑ Important note – walking times

Unless otherwise specified, **all times in this book refer only to the time spent walking**. You will need to add 20-30% to allow for rests, photography, checking the map, drinking water etc. When planning the day's hike count on 5-7 hours' actual walking.

40 MINS FROM DISUSED RAIL BRIDGE (MAP 39) →

A7 BRIDGE

40 MINS TO THE BEECHES (MAP 37) →

37

FOLLY IN FIELD

PUBLIC PHONE

POST BOX

RICKERBY, STRANGE VILLAGE-ESTATE-COUNTRY HOUSE!

BRIDGE & KISSING GATE

012

River Eden

WAR MEMORIAL

RICKERBY PARK

IRON BRIDGE

SCHOOL

GOLF COURSE

OUTSKIRTS OF CARLISLE

SANDS SPORTS CENTRE - STAMPING POINT

093

BOULDER 'SCULPTURES'

RIVERSIDE TRAIL

THIS WAY TO CITY CENTRE (SEE CARLISLE CITY PLAN)

A7

TARMAC 'ROAD' THROUGH PARK IS THE PROPER TRAIL

PATH ON RIVERSIDE SURROUNDED BY WILD FLOWERS

MONKEY BARS

ATHLETICS TRACK

SPORTS CENTRE

CAR PARK

SHORTCUT TO YHA HOSTEL

TREE LINED AVENUE THROUGH PARK

RAIL BRIDGE

TWO PATHS RUN PARALLEL — TAKE THE ONE NEAREST THE RIVER

39

MAP 38

¼ mile

0   APPROX SCALE   500m

0

40 MINS TO DISUSED RAIL BRIDGE (MAP 39) ←

A7 BRIDGE

40 MINS FROM THE BEECHES (MAP 37) ←

ROUTE GUIDE AND MAPS

CARLISLE

Though it cannot compare, in scale, fame or importance with that other Wall city, Newcastle, Carlisle is a pleasant place with a fair bit to see and do and a compactness and modest size that, unlike its Geordie rival, is never intimidating.

The most remarkable thing about Carlisle today, however, is the lack of any significant Roman remains within the city boundaries. Sure, there are Roman stones in the fabric of Carlisle Castle but it's only at **Tullie House Museum**, see p192 – in our opinion, the only essential port of call in Carlisle for anyone interested in the Romans and their Wall – that one gets any real recognition and celebration of the city's Roman past.

The lack of anything Roman is even more remarkable when one considers two salient facts. Firstly, St Cuthbert visited the city in AD685 and was taken to see a 'remarkable' Roman fountain (see box p185). Secondly, that 2000 years ago this city was the headquarters for the whole Wall and the home of two forts, one of which was the largest of them all. This was **Uxelodunum**, commonly known as **Stanwix** after the suburb that exists today in this location on the north side of the Eden, measuring 9.3 acres (3.72 hectares) in total and garrisoned by the 1000-strong Ala Petriana cavalry.

Stanwix was not the first fort in town, however. That was **Lugovalium**, stretching from Botchergate (near the train station) to the Castle – in other words, pretty much the whole of the city centre. This first fort was built around AD72 by governor Cerialis to defend the Stanegate. (There is some evidence that Agricola had a turf fort here around AD80.)

Despite the presence of Stanwix, built around 50 years later when the Wall was constructed, Lugovalium (the name is derived from the sun god, Lug) continued to be used until the 4th century or so, although it filled a role that was less military and more civic as time went on.

The local tribe, the Carvetii, saw the presence of such a large garrison not as a threat but an opportunity, and began trading with the Romans and inhabiting the land near the Lugovalium fort. This continued until the Carvetii's settlement became their unofficial capital – and Carlisle was born (though the name, Caerluel, is a post-Roman invention meaning 'Castle of Luel'), rising to provincial capital status by the end of the 4th century.

But apart from the essential and absorbing Tullie House Museum, and perhaps a visit to the Castle, see p192, and its Roman dig exhibition, there's nothing that demands your time in Carlisle, leaving you free to enjoy the shops, restaurants and cheery atmosphere of this interesting little city.

Services

The focus of the city centre is Market Cross, the cobbled pedestrian-only junction where you'll find the Old Town Hall, now home to the **tourist information centre** (TIC; ☎ 01228-625600, 💻 www.historic-carlisle.org.uk; Jul-Aug Mon-Sat 9.30am-5.30pm, May-Aug Sun 10.30am-4pm, Mar-June & Sep-Oct Mon-Sat 9.30am-5.30pm, Nov-Feb Mon-Sat 10am-4pm, bank holiday Mondays 9.30am-4pm). They will do accommodation booking (see box p52).

The **post office** (Mon-Sat 9am-5.30pm) has moved to WH Smith at 51-53 English St.

For **internet access**, the library (Mon, Wed & Fri 9.30am-5.30pm, Tue & Thur to 7pm, Sat to 4pm, Sun noon-4pm), upstairs in the Lanes Shopping Centre, charges £1 for 30 minutes. If you have your own laptop you're better off going to a bar or café that advertises free wi-fi, such as Foxes (see Where to Eat), the bar at the Crown & Mitre Hotel on the Market Square or William Rufus on Botchergate. There's a Boots **pharmacy** on English St.

Those looking for some last-minute **trekking gear** have plenty of choices, with Trespass, Cotswolds on English St, Mountain Warehouse on Scotch St, and Freetime on West Tower St. Jessops, the national **photography** chain, have a branch on Devonshire St.

ROUTE GUIDE AND MAPS

Carlisle

Where to stay
1 Carlisle YHA Hostel
9 Brooklyn House
10 Cartref
11 Ashleigh Guest House
12 Derwentlea
13 Langleigh Guest House
14 Cornerways Guest House
15 Howard Lodge Guest House

Where to eat and drink
2 La Pergola
3 Sandwich Place
4 Bells Bakery
5 Bon Appétit
6 Franco's
7 The Fryery
8 Turf Tavern
16 Alexandros
17 Davids
18 Yummy's
19 La Mezzaluna
20 Pizza Base
21 Home & Away

190 Banks to Carlisle

Transport

[See pp56-8] Though Wall walkers usually turn off the trail into the city at Eden Bridge, those arriving by public transport will alight either at the **bus station** on Lonsdale St, home to both local and National Express buses, or at the **railway station**, just to the south of the city centre off Botchergate.

The AD122 (see timetable pp212-15) and Telford's No 185 **buses** leave from English St and also stop in West Tower St (convenient for Tullie House and the Castle). Telford's No 680 leaves from English St but Wright's No 680 leaves from Warwick St. Arriva's/Stagecoach's No 685 is another useful service, leaving from the bus station for Newcastle; Stagecoach's No 94 and 97 stop on The Crescent and depart from English St; while, perhaps of most interest of all is Stagecoach's No 93/71 service from Carlisle Bus Station to Bowness-on-Solway.

Train services run hourly to Newcastle via Brampton, Haltwhistle, Hexham and Corbridge.

If you need a **taxi** try City Taxis (☎ 01228-520000).

Where to stay

Finding somewhere to stay in Carlisle is not as easy as it should be. B&Bs are relatively plentiful but often book up quickly, while the city's only hostel is open only in high summer and, for the moment at least; the nearest campsite is in Grinsdale (see p196).

The hostel is *Carlisle YHA Hostel* (☎ 0845-371 9510) on Bridge Lane, Caldewgate, housed in the halls of residence of Carlisle's university and thus open only when the students have returned home at the end of the scholarly year (ie July and August). If that doesn't sound too charming, do remember that these halls were converted from a Theakston's brewery, and the conversion has been a sensitive one; indeed, it's won awards. The Old Brewery Residences has 56 beds (seven single rooms in each flat) as well as kitchens (it's self-catering only).

If staying here it would be quicker to take the short cut shown on Map 38, p187,

than to follow the A7 (main route) into town. Being a student hall of residence, it must be said that it's a little tatty but it does have two distinct advantages: a location across the river from the castle near the heart of the city and, wonderfully, you get your own single room. Rates start at £23pp.

For a B&B, the first area to look is Victoria Place, just a five-minute walk from Eden Bridge and the trail, where three listed buildings stand next to each other: *Cartref* (☎ 01228-522077; 2S shared facilities/6D or T, all en suite), at No 44, is perhaps the smartest of these, a large and attractively furnished place. The owners work really hard to make this place as comfy as possible and they succeed. Rates are £27.50-30pp with their award-winning breakfast included. Packed lunches (£5) are available. Dogs (£5) are welcome if booked in advance. Next door, at No 46, *Ashleigh Guest House* (☎ 01228-521631; 1S/2D/2T/3D, T or F, all en suite) is one of the more established places in town. B&B starts at £30pp (single/single occupancy £30-40).

On the other side of *Cartref*, at No 42, is *Brooklyn House* (☎ 01228-590002; 3S/3D or T/2D, T or F, most en suite, bath available), B&B costs £25-30pp.

At 107 Warwick Rd, *Cornerways Guest House* (☎ 01228-521733, 🖳 www .cornerwaysbandb.co.uk; 4S/2D/2T/3D, T or F, most en suite, others share facilities) is a cosy, friendly place, despite the rather charmless exterior, with B&B for £35-45pp. Nearby, at No 90, *Howard Lodge Guest House* (☎ 01228-529842, 🖳 www .howard-lodge.co.uk; 1S/1D/4D or T/2D, T or F, most en suite) prides itself on its large breakfasts and charges £30pp in a twin, £35 for the single. Dogs are welcome if arranged in advance.

A little further on, at 6 Howard Place, *Langleigh Guest House* (☎ 01228-530440, ☎ 0781-045 6650, 🖳 www.langleigh house.co.uk; 3S/1D/3D,T or F/1D, T or F, all with private facilities, bath available) has smart rooms and charges £36pp. The owners have another place, *Derwentlea* (☎ 01228-409706, 🖳 www.derwentlea.co.uk; 2S/4D or T/1D, T or F, all en suite, bath available), 14 Howard Place, where rooms are also £36pp. Evening meals (£15-25) are available at both establishments if requested at least 24 hours in advance.

Down in Botchergate, the road running south from near the station, are several larger hotels. They include *Ibis Hotel* (☎ 01228-518000, 🖳 www.ibishotel.com; 102 rooms, most are doubles but some are twin/family, all en suite), a depressingly ugly place on the outside but comfortable inside; rates start at £58 (room only; breakfast is £7.50pp). Dogs are welcome subject to prior arrangement.

Where to eat and drink
Unlike the accommodation situation, you'll have no trouble finding food in the city.

The first place to look for takeaway food is The Crescent, near the station. Here you'll find plenty of places with late opening hours including *Home & Away* (☎ 01228-512615; Sun-Thur 11am-midnight, Fri & Sat 11am-3am), a chippie; *Pizza Base* (☎ 01228-591800; daily 4.30pm to 'late') near the centre of The Crescent, which does kebabs as well as pizzas; and, next-door, *La Mezzaluna* (☎ 01228-534472, 🖳 www .lamezzalunacarlisle.co.uk; Mon & Wed-Sat 10am-10pm, Sun 11am-9pm), an Italian restaurant which also offers a take-out service. Not too far away, *Yummys* (☎ 01228-598800; Sun-Thur 5pm-midnight, Fri & Sat 5pm-2am) provides for those looking for Chinese food to take away.

For lunch, on Fisher St the *Sandwich Place* (☎ 01228-514550; Mon-Fri 9am-3pm, Sat 10am-2pm) is a great spot for takeaway sandwiches and baguettes; it also does a packed lunch offer of £3 for baguette, crisps and a drink or chocolate bar.

Further up, *Bells Bakery* (Mon-Fri 7.30am-4pm, Sat 8am-4pm) does similar fare with a similar offer.

There are also a couple of cafés that are worth mentioning. *Foxes* (☎ 01228-536439; 🖳 www.foxescafelounge.co.uk; Tue-Sat 9am-4.30pm, also Fri & Sat 7.30-11.30pm), round the back of the museum, is a lovely place with wi-fi, friendly staff and delicious food.

One of the first eateries you'll see as you walk into town from Eden Bridge is *Turf Tavern* (☎ 01228-515367; bar 11am-11pm, food served daily noon-9pm), offering basic but filling and good-value pub fare; they have lots of special deals – Mon-Sat before 8pm two people can have a main course each for just £8, for example.

For more upmarket dining there's *Davids* (☎ 01228-523578; Tue-Sat noon-1.30pm & 6.30-9pm), a cracking little place on Warwick Rd. The food's the thing here: the menu changes regularly but if available check out the loin of Lakeland lamb with a herb and pistachio crust in redcurrant and red wine glaze (£17.95). They close for about a fortnight sometime in both January and August so contact them to check.

Just a few doors down, *Alexandros* (☎ 01228-592227, 🖳 www.thegreek.co.uk; Mon 5.30-9.30pm, Tue-Sat noon-1.30pm & 5.30-9.30pm) is a Greek eatery. If you're unsure whether you'll like Greek food, try their mini-meze (available at lunch and 5.30-6.30pm) for just £10.50pp (though don't be fooled by the term 'mini'– you'll still find there's more food on the table than you can possibly manage to eat in one sitting).

There are several good Italian places in town, two of which deserve a mention: *La Pergola* (☎ 01228-534084; Mon 5.30-9.45pm, Tue-Fri noon-1.45pm & 5.30-9.45pm, Sat noon-1.45pm & 6-9.45pm), at 28 Castle St, just up from the museum, is notable for its exceptional happy-hour prices (every lunchtime and until 6.45pm in the evening; all evening on Mon) where many dishes are virtually halved in price (eg pizzas normally from £7.80 are £5-6). Its charms don't end with its prices, however, for this is an enjoyable place with some quality food.

A second noteworthy Italian place is *Franco's* (☎ 01228-512305; Mon-Fri 11.30am-2.30pm & 5.30-10pm, Sat 11.30am-10pm, Sun noon-10pm) on Market Square behind the TIC, Carlisle's oldest Italian restaurant having been founded here in 1974. They too have a happy hour special (Mon-Sat 5.30-6.30pm, Sun 6-6.30pm) where any pizza or pasta dish is £5.

ROUTE GUIDE AND MAPS

ROUTE GUIDE AND MAPS

What to see and do

The only must-see sight is housed in one of Carlisle's most historic buildings, the Jacobean **Tullie House Museum** (☎ 01228-618700, 🖥 www.tulliehouse.co.uk; April-June & Sep-Oct Mon-Sat 10am-5pm, Sun noon-5pm, July & Aug Mon-Sat 10am-5pm, Sun 11am-5pm, Nov-Mar Mon-Sat 10am-4pm, Sun noon-4pm; £5.20/3.60/free adults/concs/children) on Castle St.

As interesting as the 16th-century townhouse that forms part of the museum (and which gives it its name) may be, the main reason for calling in is the chance to see their Roman display. It's a wonderful run-through of the Roman story in this area and includes many hands-on exhibits (including a reconstructed section of the turf wall that really gives you a good idea of how imposing and formidable a barrier it was).

Though the collection is possibly slightly less impressive than that held by Newcastle's Great North Museum: Hancock, the presentation is infinitely superior and will appeal to young and old alike. They also have a sunken Roman shrine in the grounds of the house – for a long time the only Roman ruins discovered in situ in the city. The Tullie Museum has long been recognised by this book as the most educational, relevant and enjoyable museum for Wall walkers with its sections on Romans and reivers. But by the time you read this their Roman collection may have got even better! A permanent 'Roman Gateway' exhibition, in partnership with the British Museum (from whom, presumably, some of the exhibits will be borrowed), is being installed and should open in June 2011. Details are still a little sketchy but it is believed that the £1.36 million Roman Gallery will include a program that allows you to create your own Roman avatar.

From Tullie House a curious subway – called the Millennium Gallery – leads under the ring road. At the other end of it is Carlisle's other main attraction in Carlisle: its large **Castle** (☎ 01228-591922; Apr-Sep daily 9.30am-5pm, Oct-Mar 10am-4pm; £5/4/3 adults/concs/children; free for English Heritage members). Now sandwiched between the park and the noisy ring-road, a castle was originally built on this site by William Rufus in 1092, though this earth-and-wood construction was replaced in 1122 under orders of Henry I. It still looks impressive and imposing. Inside, the main part of interest is the exhibition of the latest Roman finds from Carlisle.

❏ High tide in the Solway Estuary

For the final section (Carlisle to Bowness-on-Solway) it is vital that you check beforehand to see when the high tides occur in the Solway Estuary!

You can do this in a number of ways: many B&Bs and hostels have a **booklet** of tide times; there are **noticeboards** at Bowness-on-Solway and Dykefields with the times printed on; or you can check on the internet.

Visit the website 🖥 http://easytide.ukho.gov.uk, then click on Predict then Area, choose 1-4 for Europe, then choose England in Country/regions and then look down the list and choose Silloth.

If walking during British Summer Time (late Mar to late Oct) you will need to **add two hours** to the high-tide times given (one hour in winter) as Silloth, while the nearest port to the trail, is not located on the path. You need to avoid being on this walk an hour either side of the high-tide point, as the trail will still be flooded.

(Opposite) Top: Carlisle town centre and market hall. **Bottom**: The trig point at Green Slack (see p153), at 345m the highest point on the path.

(Overleaf): Looking back towards Housesteads and beyond along a fine piece of Clayton Wall (see p150). Note the turf top.

CARLISLE TO BOWNESS-ON-SOLWAY   [MAPS 38-45]
Introduction
This is an unusual end to the walk. There are no ruins, neither of Wall nor fort, and only occasional glimpses of Vallum and ditch. There are no moors either, nor crags, nor even really any gradients.

Nevertheless, there are some delights in store on this **14-mile (22.5km; 4³/₄-5hrs)** stage, including a couple of cute villages, some great views over the River Eden to Scotland and a stroll through an Area of Outstanding Natural Beauty; and if the weather holds, the walk is both a peaceful, gentle pleasure and the perfect way to finish and reflect upon the epic journey you've just undertaken.

There are a couple of mysteries surrounding this last stage. The first is why the Wall dodges around so much? In all, it changes direction 34 times over the 14 miles between Carlisle and Bowness (the trail is, as usual, a little longer). By comparison, on the way into Carlisle there were just 19 changes in 17 miles. One theory, and it's the only one we have at the moment, is that *(continued on p196)*

35 MINS FROM GRINSDALE (MAP 40) ⟶   DISUSED RAIL BRIDGE ⟶

0   ¹/₄ mile
0   APPROX SCALE   500m

★ trailblazer

River Eden

MAP 39

094
DISUSED RAIL BRIDGE-
NOTE 'SLANTED'
BRICKWORK UNDERNEATH

PATH GOES UNDER
POWER LINES

PATH HERE
ABOVE THE RIVER

INDUSTRIAL ESTATE &
SEWERAGE WORKS ON
OUTSKIRTS OF CARLISLE

⟵ 35 MINS TO GRINSDALE (MAP 40)   DISUSED RAIL BRIDGE ⟵

ROUTE GUIDE AND MAPS

(**Opposite**) **Top**: The peaceful sands by the Solway. **Middle**: Yet another pretty bridge on the path, this one over Cam Beck (see p178), west of Walton. **Bottom**: Some of the residents of Hillside Farm, Boustead Hill (see p198).

❏ The reivers

The Middle Ages, particularly the 300 years or so between the War of Scottish Independence c1315 and the Union of the Crown in 1603, was a tempestuous and bloody time for the Wall region. The almost constant warring between Scotland and England meant that those poor souls who chose to live in the borderlands between the two were subject to frequent harassment by one side or another. Their crops were regularly destroyed or appropriated by the troops and their livestock slaughtered to feed the army. As a result, many locals chose to engage in sheep and cattle rustling, a practice known as **reiving**, in order to eke out a living and ensure their survival.

Such was the ubiquity of this practice that reiving eventually became a way of life and one that local borderers regarded as a profession rather than a crime. Nor was it merely English families raiding Scottish ones and vice versa, for often they stole from their fellow compatriots. Nor, for that matter, was reiving confined merely to the destitute and desperate – local nobles condoned and occasionally even indulged in the practice themselves, as did the Wardens of the Marches, the very people who were supposed to be upholding the rule of law in the region!

As the reiving continued through the generations, various strange (or so it seems to us now) laws were put in place to try to regulate the situation. For example, a victim of a reive had two courses of action open to him. The first was to file a complaint with the warden who would then be compelled to investigate. Or, and this was by far the more common choice, the victim could raise a raiding party of his own and pursue the reivers himself. It became enshrined in Border Law that anybody conducting this counter-raid was compelled to ride along with them and offer such help as they could, or else stand accused of being complicit in the original raid. If this counter-attack caught the reivers within 24 hours they could fight to retrieve their livestock. If, however, the 24 hours passed without any encounter with the thieves, the reivers could keep their booty. Eventually, to try to combat the worst excesses of reiving, the two countries decided to set up armies, known as Borderers, as a first line of defence against raiding parties from across the border. Heavily armed, the Borderers were recruited from local families and travelled on horseback, using their intimate knowledge of the local area to launch guerrilla attacks on local reiving parties.

The whole phenomenon of reiving effectively ended with the accession of James VI of Scotland to the English throne. His attempts to unify the two countries included appropriating the land of reiver families, the introduction of a ban on weapons and a drive to arrest and execute notorious reivers. There was even talk of rebuilding Hadrian's Wall to limit and control cross-border movement. Whereas before the reivers could raid in one country then cross into another for safety, with the two countries unified no such safe haven existed and the reivers could be pursued relentlessly. The construction of the Military Road in the mid-18th century also helped the authorities police the region more efficiently.

But though the phenomenon of reiving no longer exists, echoes of this troubled period in the region's history can still be heard. The terms 'kidnapping' (a favourite pastime of the reivers), 'blackmail' (originally protection money paid to the reivers, as opposed to legitimate rent paid to a landowner which was called 'greenmail') and 'bereaved' (which originally meant to lose a loved one by the hand of the reivers) are all words that come from this period. Imposing fortifications, now just ruins – for instance bastle (see p208) houses such as Drumburgh Castle in the village of the same name, pele towers (such as the ones at Burgh-by-Sands and Linstock, as well as off the Wall in Corbridge's churchyard) and larger fortifications such as the wonderful Thirlwall Castle – were built by well-to-do families to protect themselves from reivers.

MAP 40

GRINSDALE

BEAUMONT

45 MINS

River Eden

097 BEAUMONT

NOW ABOVE RIVER FOLLOWING UNDULATING PATH LARGELY ON WOODEN WALKWAY WITH STEPS & 'BRIDGES' OVER SMALL GULLIES. PATH THROUGH WOODS FILLED WITH GARLIC, BLUEBELLS, RED CAMPION, PRIMROSES & RED CAMPION IN SPRING

STEPS DOWN TO AND ALONG RIVER BANK

STEPS NOT CURRENTLY PART OF PATH THOUGH ARE PLANNED TO BE IN NEAR FUTURE

DUCKPOND

096 SOURMILK FOOTBRIDGE

STEPS UP THE STEEP EMBANKMENT

VALLUM

POWER LINES

JOIN TRACK

GRINSDALE

BARN

PUBLIC PHONE

095

39

TO WEST VIEW CAMPSITE

COW FIELD

GATE

ROUND BACK OF GARDENS

HORSE FIELD

VERY SLIPPERY BANK; PAVING STONES HAVE BEEN PUT DOWN HERE AND THERE

BLACK & WHITE HOUSE

TO MONKHILL & DROVERS REST

41

BEAUMONT

45 MINS

¼ mile

0   500m

APPROX SCALE

(continued from p193) 2000 years ago the Eden, which the Wall roughly follows on this last leg, was itself full of kinks and changes in direction. (It is interesting to note, too, that the Vallum strays from the line of the Wall after leaving Carlisle – again nobody is entirely sure why.)

The other mystery, of course, is why there are so few ruins, especially when one considers that this stage was bookended by the two largest Roman forts on the entire Wall (with Carlisle's Stanwix being the largest, Bowness the second) with a third fort at Burgh-by-Sands and a fourth at Drumburgh. Part of the answer can be found in a number of the public buildings, including the churches at Burgh-by-Sands and Bowness which both used Roman stones in their construction. But this just leads to a further question: why did the Romans feel it necessary to pack this side of the country with more troops than the other side?

The route
The stage begins where the last one left off, with a stroll by the Eden through the outskirts of Carlisle. Eventually the trail forsakes the river near the village of **Grinsdale** (Map 40) which has a **campsite**, *West View* (☎ 01228-526336; Easter to Oct), just under a mile from the trail. It costs £5pp including the use of shower/toilet facilities. Booking is appreciated.

Note that although the river is the dominant feature, the trail still follows the line of the Wall where it can, invisible though it is. Proof of this is in the reappearance of the Vallum, the dip in the field to your left as you cross the little **Sourmilk footbridge** (where a sandstone head of Minerva, goddess of wisdom and warfare, was found in the 19th century; it's now in Carlisle's Tullie Museum). Then there's **Beaumont** and its church, situated at the top of the 'beautiful mountain' that gives the village its name; unsurprisingly, it's largely built with stones from the Wall. Stagecoach's No 93/71 **bus** service calls here; see pp56-8 for further details. St Michael's Church (Map 41; see also below) is about 1½ miles further on and is passed on the way into Burgh-by-Sands.

BURGH-BY-SANDS   [MAP 41]
Burgh-by-Sands is the largest settlement on today's walk, a village that stretches out along the road.

The 13th-century **St Michael's Church** is the main focus for Romanophiles here, its walls largely made from Wall stones and its location at the centre of what was once a five-acre (2-hectare) Roman fort. This was **Aballava**, garrisoned for much of its history by auxiliary troops of Moors from North Africa. Comparatively little is known of Aballava, though we do know that the bathhouse (which, as is typical, would have been outside the fort) was located where the vicarage is today, and excavations have revealed a number of Roman artefacts, including glassware and metalwork, and in

1928 a section of Wall foundations was uncovered in the graveyard.

There's more evidence of Roman occupation within the church itself, where the face of a pagan god can clearly be discerned on the east wall of the chancel behind the altar, emerging from the blank plaster that covers the rest of the wall.

Presumably the builders of the church weren't fussy about which Roman stones they used, hence the pagan face. Isn't it curious how it hasn't been removed, especially as, when the faithful face the altar and bow, they are also bowing to this pagan god? At the opposite end of the aisle, note how the church tower has no exterior door and only tiny slit windows, presumably because it was once a pele tower used to

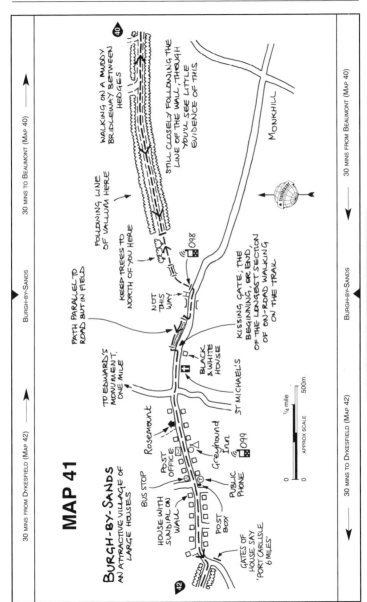

MAP 41

BURGH-BY-SANDS
AN ATTRACTIVE VILLAGE OF LARGE HOUSES

HOUSE WITH SUNDIAL ON WALL

BUS STOP

ROSEMOUNT

POST OFFICE

POST BOX

GREYHOUND INN

PUBLIC PHONE

1099

GATES OF HOUSE SAY 'PORT CARLISLE 6 MILES'

TO EDWARD'S MONUMENT, ONE MILE

ST MICHAEL'S

BLACK & WHITE HOUSE

KISSING GATE; THE BEGINNING, OR END, OF THE LONGEST SECTION OF ON-ROAD WALKING ON THE TRAIL

PATH PARALLEL TO ROAD BUT IN FIELD

NOT THIS WAY

KEEP TREES TO NORTH OF YOU HERE

FOLLOWING LINE OF VALLUM HERE

1098

WALKING ON A MUDDY BRIDLEWAY BETWEEN HEDGES

STILL CLOSELY FOLLOWING THE LINE OF THE WALL, THOUGH YOU'LL SEE LITTLE EVIDENCE OF THIS

MONKHILL

¼ mile

0   500m

0

APPROX SCALE

ROUTE GUIDE AND MAPS

ROUTE GUIDE AND MAPS

protect the locals against raiders. Virtually opposite the church, a road leads up to the **Edward I monument**, marking the spot where the so-called Hammer of the Scots died from dysentery while waiting to cross the Solway Firth on 7 July 1307. There's an impressive statue by The Greyhound pub in Burgh, which commemorates the same event.

Other than these sights there's little reason to dally in Burgh, except perhaps to call in at *The Greyhound Inn* (☎ 01228-576579, 🖳 http://thegreyhoundinn-burgh .co.uk; bar daily 11am-11pm; food served Tue-Sun noon-2pm & 6-8pm), where the local and ambitious new owners are really making a fine go of the place. There is space for some people to **camp** (£15 per

Statue of Edward I

tent including breakfast, £10 without breakfast); campers can use the shower/toilet facilities in the pub. Booking is advised. There's also a B&B, *Rosemount* (☎ 01228-576440, 🖳 www.rosemount cottage.co.uk; 2T/2D, all en suite, bath available) on the main road; rates are £35pp (£45 single occupancy). Packed lunches are available (£2.50-5). Dogs are welcome if booked in advance.

If you're lucky enough to be here when it's open, the friendly **post office** (Tue & Thur 9am-noon & 3-5pm) has a small supply of chocolates, drinks and snacks.

Finally, leaving Burgh, Stagecoach's Nos 93/71 **buses** come through the village on their way to Bowness or Carlisle; see pp56-8 for further information and the public transport map.

After Burgh, the path continues along the road. It also still follows the line of the Vallum, though the only suggestion that this is the case is the name of one of the houses – 'Vallum' – along the way.

Continuing your tarmac travails, you come next to **Dykesfield** (Map 42) and on, over the cattle grid, to the area of the trail that is liable to flooding at certain times of the year; see box p192. It's also one of the most interminable stretches, a wearying trek over flat terrain with a floodbank blocking your views to the south and the wind whipping off the shore to chill your marrow from the north. You can vary the walk slightly by walking atop the embankment to the south of the road – one of the last vestiges of the old railway that ran through here to Port Carlisle – where at least you can get a better view of Skiddaw and the Lake District peaks to the south (though watch your step as the embankment is precarious in places). But even this thrill palls after a while, probably even before you reach, on your left, a road leading to the small village of Boustead Hill.

BOUSTEAD HILL   [MAP 42]

Most people whizz through this last section from Carlisle to Bowness, hurrying along to make sure they arrive at the end of the trail to catch the last bus back. But those who take their time are rewarded with some very pleasant accommodation, good food and lovely people; and Boustead Hill, at approximately halfway between Carlisle and the end of the walk, is a logical place to

stop. True, it's little more than a row of rather grand houses, amongst which are two **B&Bs**. But the accommodation, the people and the views across the marshes to the estuary are reason enough to stop for a night.

Of the B&Bs, *Hillside* (☎ 01228-576398, 🖳 www.hadrianswalkbnb.co.uk; 1T/2D shared bath; Apr-Oct) is a welcoming place charging £25-30pp. They also

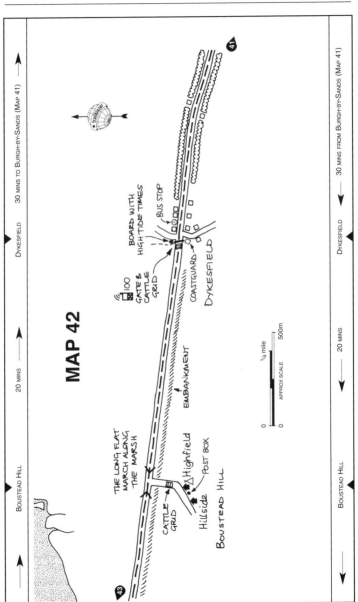

MAP 42

THE LONG FLAT MARCH ALONG THE MARSH

EMBANKMENT

BOARD WITH HIGH-TIDE TIMES

GATE & CATTLE GRID

BUS STOP

COASTGUARD

DYKESFIELD

CATTLE GRID

△Highfield

POST BOX

Hillside

BOUSTEAD HILL

¼ mile

0

0   500m

APPROX SCALE

have a **bunk barn** (open all year; sleeps about 12) with its own kitchen (including microwave, crockery, cutlery and gas cooker), shower and toilet; they charge £10pp. The owner is typical of the sort of person one meets at this end of the trail – chatty, friendly, and oh so helpful in a very unfussy way. Breakfasts are also available to guests of the barn if requested in advance, though aren't included in the price. Dogs are welcome subject to prior arrangement. Oh, and the wi-fi is excellent here too. All in all, thoroughly recommended.

The other B&B, just down the hill and the first you come to, is *Highfield* (☎ 01228-576060, 🖥 www.highfield-holidays

.co.uk; 1D or T en suite /1D or F with a Jacuzzi), a smarter affair where B&B starts at £60 (£38 single occupancy) – great value considering the quality of the accommodation. They even have their own family of barn owls living on their 300 acres of land and a **campsite** (Mar-Oct) out back charging £10 per pitch with one person (plus £4 for an extra person), including use of showers, hot and cold water and kitchen facilities. If arranged in advance breakfast (about £6) is available for campers and packed lunches (£5) for anyone.

Stagecoach's No 93/71 **bus** service calls here; see pp56-8 for further details.

At the end of this long marsh-side stretch is the small hamlet of Drumburgh.

DRUMBURGH   [MAP 43]

Drumburgh, an unassuming little farming community, resides where once a small Roman fort stood. This fort was known as Concavata, built to watch over the salt flats nearby. Today the hamlet's highlight is **Drumburgh Castle**, a bastle (see p208) house built in 1307 to provide protection against reivers (see box p194). The livestock would be housed on the ground floor, with the family living upstairs. Note the heraldic crest above the door and the griffins perched on the roof.

Drumburgh has little else to interest the trekker except, and this is lovely, a **serve-yourself tuckshop** called, mysteriously, *Laal Bite* (Easter to Oct, daily 8am-6pm) at The Grange (☎ 01228-576551, 🖥 www.thegrangecottage.co.uk), opposite where the trail turns left off the road. They sell ice creams and snacks and have drinks machines and a toilet. They also have a cottage which can be rented on a weekly basis.

Stagecoach's No 93/71 **bus** service calls here; see pp56-8 for further details.

From Drumburgh the trail takes a deviation away from the road to pass through a few farms, emerging eventually at **Glasson** (Map 44), whose appeal for trekkers starts and finishes with the *Highland Laddie Inn* (☎ 016973-51839; bar daily noon-midnight; food served daily (noon-2.30pm, to 2pm on Sun, & 6.30-8.45pm in summer but not on one day a week in the winter months so check in advance then). Stagecoach **Bus** No 93/71 calls in at Glasson on its way to Bowness and Carlisle; see pp56-8 for further information. Opposite the Inn, a bridleway heads off north-west, following the line of the Vallum (though you'll have trouble spotting any evidence of this), before dodging back to the shoreline, emerging back onto the road at the end of Port Carlisle.

20 MINS TO BOUSTEAD HILL (MAP 42)

TURN FOR EASTON

10 MINS

DRUMBURGH

42

CATTLE GRID

EMBANKMENT

EASTON MARSH

MAP 43

TO EASTON

River Eden

EMBANKMENT SWINGS NORTH OF DRUMBURGH TO AVOID HILL

HOUSE

DEAD FLAT ROAD ALONG MARSH. EASY WALKING BUT EXPOSED IN BAD WEATHER

TOILETS

LAAL BITE TUCKSHOP

PUBLIC PHONE

DRUMBURGH CASTLE

THE GRANGE

CROFT FARM

DRUMBURGH

WIDE TRACK

44

¼ mile

APPROX SCALE

0   500m

0

20 MINS FROM BOUSTEAD HILL (MAP 42)

TURN FOR EASTON

10 MINS

DRUMBURGH

BENCH OVERLOOKING ESTUARY-
A GOOD PLACE FOR A FINAL REST

River Eden

TRAIL MADE FOR
THE HADRIAN'S WALL PATH-
FORMERLY A RAILWAY
TRACK

105

COTTAGE &
GLENDALE
HOLIDAY PARK

FOLLOWING LINE
OF VALLUM

PUBLIC
PHONE

BUS STOP

Highland
Laddie Inn 104

MILL
ROAD

POST
BOX

GLASSON

103

THREE KISSING GATES,
VERY MUDDY

DITCH, FENCE
& HAWTHORNS

PAVING SLABS OVER
MUDDY SECTION

WALKER HOUSE - AN
APPROPRIATE NAME

PATHS LEFT &
RIGHT, BUT GO
STRAIGHT ON

102

43

★ trailhazer

TO DRUMBURGH
MOSS NNR

0   1/4 mile

0   APPROX SCALE   500m

MAP 44

30 MINS TO PORT CARLISLE (MAP 45)

GLASSON

30 MINS FROM DRUMBURGH (MAP 43)

30 MINS FROM PORT CARLISLE (MAP 45)

GLASSON

30 MINS TO DRUMBURGH (MAP 43)

ROUTE GUIDE AND MAPS

MAP 45

BOWNESS-ON-SOLWAY

PORT CARLISLE

River Eden

Bowness Marsh

BRIDGE OVER THE OLD PORT CARLISLE CANAL

THE FORMER CUSTOMS HOUSE

OLD DOCKS / BREAKWATER

BLACK POOL OF WATER

KIRKLAND SCAR

Chapel Side Campsite

STRANGE LITTLE ALLOTMENT-CUM-COTTAGE

PUBLIC PHONE

Hesket House

PORT CARLISLE BOWLING CLUB & WATER TAP

Hope & Anchor

THREE GATES GOING ROUND THE BACK OF SOME WATERFRONT HOUSES - FORMERLY WAREHOUSES

PLEASANT WATERSIDE PATH SEPARATED FROM ROAD BY HIGH HEDGE

PARKING SPOT

GREY HAVEN

Shore Gate

Maia Lodge

The Old Chapel

GAZEBO & HERB GARDEN - THE END OF THE PATH! (OR THE START)

Kings Arms

BUS STOP

Lindow Hall & TOILETS

Wallsend House (The Old Rectory)

25 MINS

¼ mile

500m

APPROX SCALE

ROUTE GUIDE AND MAPS

PORT CARLISLE   [MAP 45, p203]

The path chooses to ignore Port Carlisle, preferring to hug the shore and turn onto the road only at the end of the village, one of the more interesting on this stage. For one thing, at one time there were big plans for Port Carlisle, with both a railway line and a canal terminating here – both of which followed the line of the Wall. Stephenson's *Rocket* actually travelled along the line in 1829, and indeed it was hoped that the village would become a major port for goods to and from Scotland and Ireland. However, factors conspired against Port Carlisle and the railway line shut after 100 years of use, while the canal was abandoned after just 30 years.

Thereafter, Port Carlisle slipped back into the sleepy backwaters of the British Isles. Today, you can see the remains of the lock and port, and you cross the last vestiges of the canal on the walk. Look out across the water too and, just a few metres away, are the remains of the harbour walls.

Today the village is home to the Port Carlisle Bowling Club which has a **water tap** on the wall of its clubhouse that you can use; and the *Hope and Anchor* (☎ 016973-51460; bar Easter-Sep daily noon till late; Oct to Easter closed 3-6pm; food served daily noon-2pm & 6-8pm), opposite. As with so many places around here, the owners are as accommodating as possible and, particularly if you book ahead, will open for breakfast upon request and serve food outside of their 'official' hours.

This is also the last place where you can get **cashback** (as long as you buy

something, plus there's a 50p charge) from your debit card – there's nothing in Bowness – and they have installed wi-fi (and have a computer terminal for those without laptops) too!

Hesket House (☎ 016973-51876, ☎ 0790-033 5361, 🖳 www.heskethouse.com; 1T or D private bathroom/2D, T or F en suite, bath available), the last house in the village, was formerly the *Steam Packet Inn* and has three smart rooms with B&B starting for £60-65 (£45 single occupancy) and £85 for three in a family room. Since the rooms are large they can add more beds if necessary. Incidentally, above the door is a small grey stone **altar**, distinctly Roman, set into the brickwork. It fits in rather well. Dogs (£5) are welcome if booked in advance and packed lunches are available (about £5).

Half a mile or so up the road at Kirkland House Farm, *Chapel Side Campsite* (☎ 016973-51400; Apr-Oct) has pitches for £6 per tent with two people (including the use of cold showers and toilets; £3 per additional person). They're converting a barn into a camping barn (£10pp); it should sleep about 12 people and will have a toilet, coin-operated shower and basic cooking facilities. However, at the time of writing, the many delays meant that the work still hadn't been completed but they are hoping it will be open in 2011 so contact them for further details.

Stagecoach's No 93/71 **bus** service calls here; see pp56-8 for further details.

From Port Carlisle it's an uneventful 20-minute stroll along the coastal road to Bowness where you can get a pint, food, possibly some accommodation or maybe a bus back to Carlisle. As you enter the village the trail takes a sudden and unexpected turn right towards the coast, where a small shelter and pretty garden mark the end of the trail. In the shelter you can find the final **passport stamp**, as well as a seat to rest upon.

And that's it. The walk is done.

You're done.

Well done!

BOWNESS-ON-SOLWAY
[MAP 45, p203]

Bowness is a lovely, peaceful place to finish the walk. Indeed, it's almost eerily quiet and one gets the sense that the outside world has little to do with Bowness – and vice versa.

The name Bowness comes from the bow-shaped corner of the *ness*, or peninsula here. As the last place where the Solway is fordable, it is understandable why the Romans decided to finish their Wall here, and a large 7-acre (2.8-hectare) fort was built where the village now stands. This was **Maia**, the second largest fort on the Wall (indeed, 'Maia' can be translated as 'Larger'). Originally, the Wall was supposed to continue a little way beyond the fort at Bowness, for the Romans were wary that the Caledones and Irish could sneak by the Wall and land on Cumbria's west coast. However, the Romans soon decided to build a series of towers on that coastline instead, including one at Maryport – now known as the Western Sea Defences.

Today, there's very little evidence of the Romans, though there is said to be an inscription above a barn door somewhere in the village; I have to say, I've never found it. There are also some purloined stones from the Wall in the fabric of the Norman church, which stands on the site of the fort. Yet the destruction of the Wall around here seems to be quite a recent event: in 1801 there were said to be 500 yards of Wall standing just outside the village.

In the absence of much in the way of Wall or fort remains it's fair to say that Bowness is a little lacking in tourist attractions, though the church has a couple of bells inside at the back behind the font which were nicked from villages across the Solway in the 17th century – yet another manifestation of the antipathy that simmered for centuries between neighbours in this part of the world. It is apparently a tradition for every new vicar across the water to formally ask the parish for the bells back.

It's fair to say that some of the locals are a little worried that this end of the walk is being ignored. It was bad enough that the AD122 bus no longer comes here; but when the helicopter failed to fly anywhere west of Carlisle during the Lighting of the Wall (see box p38) some villagers began to get worried that they were slowly, inexorably, being separated from the rest of the walk – with a view to being removed altogether from the official path, perhaps because of the lack of much evidence of the Wall around here. As anyone who has finished their walk in the convivial atmosphere in the King's Arms will testify, this would be a *big* shame.

Speaking of which, the **King's Arms** (☎ 016973-51426, ☐ www.kingsarmsbowness.co.uk; 3T, shared facilities; bar open daily Easter to Sep 11am-11pm, rest of year 5.30-11pm, longer if walkers are around) has become the spiritual, if not the official, end of the trail. As if to cement this position the pub issues Wall certificates (50p) for those who've finished the trail (to be fair, they were the ones who thought of the certificates first), sells souvenir T-shirts and has a Wall walkers' visitors book that usually contains a few useful recommendations for those about to start their walk – in addition to lots of comments about the weather/hardships suffered/joy they now feel from those who've just finished. On the outside wall they also have a map showing where the original Roman fort would have stood, with the pub lying almost at its heart. **B&B** costs £22.50pp (£25 single occupancy) and dogs are welcome, subject to prior arrangement. Note that they do not accept credit/debit cards. They also serve massive meals (food served Mon-Fri 5.30-8.30pm, Sat noon-2pm & 5.30-8.30pm, Sun noon-2pm & 7-8.30pm). However, they only cook on Wednesdays if people are staying, either here or at local B&Bs so check/book in advance.

Accommodation-wise, at the start of the village is a lovely new place: **Shore Gate** (☎ 016973-51308, ☐ www.shoregate house.co.uk; 3D or T en suite/1D, T or F private bathroom) is right at the beginning of the village and offers really sumptuous views of the estuary. Add to this some smart – and, unusually, 'modern' rooms, and eager-to-please owners and you have a really welcome addition to the B&B scene at this end of the trail. Prices are £57 (£40 single occupancy). Packed lunches are available if requested in advance.

The smartest and most established B&B in town is *Wallsend House* (☎ 016973-51055, 🖳 www.wallsend.net; 2S/1D/1T/1D, T or F, all en suite, bath available), which charges £35pp for two sharing (£38 in a single) and is housed in a lovely building, the Old Rectory, at the western end of the village. New owners took over in November 2010; they have dogs but welcome other dogs (£4) subject to prior arrangement. They also plan to serve Staffordshire oatcakes at breakfast as they come from Staffordshire.

The Old Chapel (☎ 016973-51126, 🖳 www.oldchapelbownessonsolway.com; 1S/2T share shower facilities/1D, T or F en suite with bath) is a converted sandstone Wesleyan chapel from 1872 that lies on the route. The family room upstairs sleeps four people. They also, unusually, give guests access to a modern kitchen area complete with cooker, microwave, fridge – and washing machine! Dogs are welcome subject to prior arrangement. Rates are from £27.50pp including a continental breakfast.

There is one more accommodation option: *Lindow Hall*, just up from the church and the home of the village's public toilets, can *with prior arrangement* be hired out; call ☎ 016973-51322 for further details and to make a booking. Costs are £10 per head, though do bring a sleeping bag as you'll be on a mat on the hall floor. The hall has a shower and a kitchen and can sleep up to 40 people though they will take reservations from groups of any size.

To get back to Carlisle can be tricky, depending on what day you arrive. **If it's a Sunday or a Bank Holiday, there is no public transport.** At other times there's Stagecoach's No 93/71 which calls in at the bus stop just down and opposite the *King's Arms* and departs at 7.30am (Mon-Fri only; 7.52am on Sat), 10.20am, 2.10pm, 5.12pm, 6.50pm (Mon-Fri only), 7.20pm (Sat), 9.50pm (Fri/Sat only) and 11.48pm (Fri/Sat only), taking about 42 minutes to reach Carlisle. Always check the times as they may have changed from those printed above. See pp56-8 for further information.

Alternatively, ask your B&B owner or the landlord of the King's Arms and they may be able to sort you out a lift for around £25; if that fails the only other option is a **taxi** – though expect to pay about £36 for a trip to Carlisle.

❑ Haaf netting

If you're lucky, when visiting Bowness you may come across the strange sight of half a dozen men standing chest-deep in the waters of the Solway holding large nets secured to wooden frames. This practice, known as haaf netting, is the traditional means of fishing in the estuary. The practice is believed to have come from the Vikings in around the 10th century AD, and indeed the very word 'haaf' comes from the Norse word for channel. The haaf net itself is a wooden frame, or 'beam', 5.5m long which is said to be the length of an old Viking oar without the blade. The net is then suspended from this beam, and the fishermen, usually in groups of half a dozen or so, form a line across the channel to catch any fish, usually sea trout and Atlantic salmon, that pass their way.

MAP KEY

Map key

♠	Where to stay	📖	Library/bookstore	●	Other
○	Where to eat and drink	◐	Internet	CP	Car park
△	Campsite	🏛	Museum/gallery	◷	Bus station
⊠	Post Office	✝	Church/cathedral	◴	Bus stop
Ⓔ	Bank/ATM	☎	Telephone	⎯▭⎯	Rail line & station
ⓘ	Tourist Information	☑	Public toilet	▦	Park
		□	Building	📱082	GPS waypoint

⟋	Walking Track	⟋	Gate	≈	Stream
⟋⟋	Minor Track	⟋	Bridge	∿	River
⟋⟋	4WD Track	⋯	Fence	🌳	Forest / Wood
⫽	Road	⟋	Stone Wall	⅄ ⅄ ⅄	Boggy Ground
⫽	Steps	⟋	Hedge	⌐⌐	Hadrian's Wall
↗	Slope	▨	Water	⫱⫱	Vallum
↗	Steep Slope	⋰	Sand	⫽⫽	Ditch
⟋	Stile	∘∘	Stones	🅰43	Map Continuation

APPENDIX A: GLOSSARY

Antonine Wall Turf wall built to the north of Hadrian's construction by his successor, Antoninus Pius

Bastle House A fortified house built during the Middle Ages in the border region to protect the owner and his family from bandits

Brigantes The main tribe whose land was crossed by the Wall

Caledones The collective name for the tribes living north of the Wall

Gask Frontier The first border separating the conquered lands in the south from the 'Barbarians' in the north. Established by Domitian (AD81-96), it was also built to watch over the glens but was quickly withdrawn further south when troops were required elsewhere in the empire

Milecastle A series of 'mini-castles' spaced 1000 paces apart (or one Roman mile) along the entire length of the Wall. Built to house troops, they could hold an estimated 32 men each

Military Road Now the B6318, the Military Road was an 18th-century thoroughfare built on the orders of General Wade to thwart further attacks from Bonnie Prince Charlie

Military Way A Roman thoroughfare built around AD160 between the Stanegate and the Wall, often along the northern earthwork of the Vallum (which had by then been largely decommissioned)

Pele tower A square defensive tower built by wealthier families in the 16th century in the border counties of England and Scotland to defend themselves against the trepidations of reivers. The layout would typically follow the same design, with a storeroom on the ground floor, from which a staircase would lead upstairs to the living quarters. On the roof the family would light a beacon to summon help during a raid.

Reivers Bandits and cattle rustlers during the Middle Ages

Stanegate The east–west road that ran between the Roman settlements of Carlisle and Corbridge which was one of the major reasons for the construction of the Wall

Turret Stone observation posts, 161 in total, spaced evenly along the Wall to watch for movements to the north of the Wall

Vallum Roman earthwork, consisting of a deep ditch running between two high mud or earth walls, that ran to the south of and parallel to the Wall

Norse words

Squashed between the Saxons and the Scots, the area of the Borders and the Lake District has kept many Norse words that you'll find today in the local place names. Amongst them:

Norse	Meaning
fell	upper slope of hill
beck/burn	stream
haugh	flat land beside river
holm	island in river
hope	sheltered valley
moss	peat bog

APPENDIX B: GPS WAYPOINTS

MAP	WAYPOINT	OS GRID REF	DESCRIPTION
1	001	N54 59.313 W1 31.846	Segedunum
1	002	N54 58.431 W1 32.376	Wincomblee Bridge
2	003	N54 57.722 W1 32.737	Top of steps
2	004	N54 58.017 W1 34.658	St Lawrence Rd
3	005	N54 58.280 W1 35.370	Ouseburn
3	006	N54 58.215 W1 35.993	Millennium Bridge
3	007	N54 57.965 W1 36.755	Copthorne Hotel
4	008	N54 57.731 W1 39.035	Car park
4	009	N54 57.831 W1 39.372	Riverside path joins road
4	010	N54 57.927 W1 39.866	Cross A695
5	011	N54 58.130 W1 41.204	Milepost
5	012	N54 58.364 W1 41.571	Path leaves road for Denton Dene
5	013	N54 58.611 W1 41.886	Bridge across A1
5	014	N54 58.459 W1 42.143	Join road (Ottringham Close)
6	015	N54 58.613 W1 42.902	Path goes under bridge
6	016	N54 58.807 W1 43.962	Over A6085 at Newburn
6	017	N54 58.900 W1 44.649	Boathouse
7	018	N54 58.884 W1 45.938	Gate at Ryton Island
7	019	N54 59.013 W1 45.985	Join the Wylam waggonway
7	020	N54 59.067 W1 47.485	Leave the Wylam waggonway
8	021	N54 59.273 W1 48.207	Bend in track
8	022	N54 59.463 W1 48.213	Shortcut path to Houghton North Farm
8	023	N54 59.815 W1 47.322	Heddon Roman wall
8	024	N55 00.005 W1 48.629	Path leaves road and joins bridleway
9	025	N55 00.094 W1 49.482	Cross road by Rudchester
9	026	N55 00.217 W1 50.375	Join B6318 by Two Hoots
9	027	N55 00.284 W1 50.989	Cross B6318
10	028	N55 00.468 W1 52.160	Cross road to Albemarle Barracks
11	029	N55 00.590 W1 55.415	Robin Hood Inn
11	030	N55 00.680 W1 56.604	Walking in Roman ditch
11	031	N55 00.692 W1 56.977	Cross B6318
12	032	N55 00.745 W1 59.128	Over stile off road
13	033	N55 00.670 W1 59.764	Stile by B6318
13	034	N55 00.642 W2 00.355	Path to Corbridge
13	035	N55 00.767 W2 01.232	Port Gate
14	036	N55 01.091 W2 03.854	Off road onto path by Roman ditch
14	037	N55 01.161 W2 04.591	Track
15	038	N55 01.153 W2 05.742	St Oswald's Hill Head
15	039	N55 01.155 W2 06.050	Path to Acomb
15	040	N55 01.259 W2 06.669	Cross road by track to quarry
15	041	N55 01.335 W2 07.151	Join road at end of wood
16	042	N55 01.420 W2 07.605	Path to Brunton Turret
16	043	N55 01.564 W2 07.459	Join road to Chollerford
16	044	N55 01.723 W2 08.297	Chesters entrance
16	045	N55 01.763 W2 09.203	Walwick junction
16	046	N55 01.946 W2 09.159	Leave road; enter farm

MAP	WAYPOINT	OS GRID REF	DESCRIPTION
Corbridge–Hexham–Acomb alternative			
13a	*110*	*N55 00.122 W2 00.375*	*Junction of tracks*
13a	*111*	*N55 00.050 W2 00.647*	*Junction of roads*
13a	*112*	*N54 59.882 W2 00.870*	*Leazes Lane*
13a	*113*	*N54 59.023 W2 00.885*	*Under A69*
13b	*114*	*N54 58.276 W2 01.174*	*Join Tyneside path off road*
13b	*115*	*N54 58.141 W2 02.416*	*Bridge*
13b	*116*	*N54 58.001 W2 02.422*	*Cross river by A69*
13b	*117*	*N54 57.952 W2 02.657*	*Cross track*
13c	*118*	*N54 57.940 W2 03.090*	*Signpost to Duke's House*
13c	*119*	*N54 57.785 W2 03.897*	*Junction of paths*
13d	*120*	*N54 57.730 W2 04.803*	*Signpost to Hexham*
13d	*121*	*N54 57.911 W2 05.273*	*Signpost to Duke's House*
13e	*122*	*N54 59.103 W2 06.098*	*Junction of roads below Acomb*
13e	*123*	*N54 59.230 W2 06.327*	*Leave road*
13e	*124*	*N54 59.369 W2 06.350*	*Gate by mill*
13e	*125*	*N54 59.582 W2 06.452*	*Acomb*
13e	*126*	*N54 59.939 W2 06.515*	*Left across stile*
Main route			
17	047	N55 02.182 W2 11.043	Cross track to Green Carts Farm
17	048	N55 02.301 W2 11.558	Trig point
18	049	N55 02.183 W2 12.857	Stile to Brocolitia
18	050	N55 02.034 W2 13.366	Mithras Temple
18	051	N55 02.122 W2 13.624	Cross road
19	052	N55 01.861 W2 15.978	Milecastle 33
19	053	N55 01.685 W2 17.660	Grindon Turret 34a
20	054	N55 01.540 W2 18.395	Milecastle 35
20	055	N55 01.474 W2 18.844	Trig point
21	056	N55 00.880 W2 19.715	Knag Burn Gate
22	057	N55 00.731 W2 20.258	Milecastle 37
22	058	N55 00.229 W2 22.528	Castle Nick (Milecastle 39)
23	059	N55 00.092 W2 23.281	Gates at Peel Rigg leading down to Once Brewed
23	060	N55 00.120 W2 24.282	Green Slack (trig point)
23	061	N55 00.099 W2 24.433	Path to Winshields Farm
24	062	N54 59.809 W2 25.522	Bogle Hole
24	063	N54 59.629 W2 26.819	Hole Gap
25	064	N54 59.585 W2 27.117	Stile at Burnhead
Walking to and from Haltwhistle			
25	*130*	*N54 59.585 W2 27.117*	*Gate onto road by bridge over Haltwhistle Burn*
25	*131*	*N54 59.262 W2 26.959*	*Gate onto B6318*
25	*132*	*N54 59.232 W2 27.119*	*Gate off B6318*
25	*133*	*N54 58.645 W2 27.501*	*Bridge by Old Brickworks*
25	*134*	*N54 58.769 W2 27.746*	*Gate*
25	*135*	*N54 59.179 W2 27.516*	*B6318*

MAP	WAYPOINT	OS GRID REF	DESCRIPTION
Main route			
26	065	N54 59.598 W2 30.057	Stile by track to Walltown Farm
27	066	N54 59.205 W2 31.163	Walltown Refreshments
27	067	N54 59.268 W2 31.223	Path north by Roman ditch
27	068	N54 59.301 W2 32.050	Gate opposite Thirlwall Castle
27	069	N54 59.281 W2 32.353	Path leaves road; cross stile
28	070	N54 59.325 W2 33.365	Stile
28	071	N54 59.368 W2 34.156	Cross road leading to Samson Inn
28	072	N54 59.375 W2 34.720	Cross road near Turret 48A
29	073	N54 59.375 W2 36.245	Gate at Birdoswald
29	074	N54 58.961 W2 37.893	Drop into Vallum
30	075	N54 58.845 W2 38.486	Track to Comb Crag
30	076	N54 58.604 W2 39.602	Stile off road at Pike Hill
30	077	N54 58.468 W2 40.171	Back onto road
31	078	N54 58.462 W2 40.952	Hare Hill Wall
31	079	N54 58.462 W2 40.813	Haytongate
32	080	N54 58.296 W2 44.435	Roman bridge abutment
32	081	N54 58.146 W2 45.362	Gate into woods
32	082	N54 58.118 W2 45.651	Gate heading into second field
33	083	N54 57.812 W2 46.431	Bridge over a stream
33	084	N54 57.219 W2 47.361	Gate leaving Newton
34	085	N54 56.805 W2 48.853	Gate by bus stop at Oldwall
35	086	N54 56.334 W2 51.308	Join bridleway known as Sandy Lane
35	087	N54 55.901 W2 51.053	Stile and gate off Sandy Lane
35	088	N54 55.755 W2 51.169	Onto road
36	089	N54 55.452 W2 52.510	Bridge over stream
36	090	N54 55.194 W2 52.922	Turn away from Eden River
37	091	N54 54.395 W2 54.431	Path off road by The Beeches
38	092	N54 54.273 W2 55.208	Bridge and kissing gate
38	093	N54 54.007 W2 56.091	Sands Sports Centre
39	094	N54 53.946 W2 57.775	Go under bridge over Eden
40	095	N54 54.752 W2 59.179	Grinsdale
40	096	N54 54.806 W2 59.883	Cross Sourmilk Footbridge
40	097	N54 55.517 W3 00.925	Gate into Beaumont
41	098	N54 55.287 W3 02.522	Join road
41	099	N54 55.301 W3 03.413	Greyhound Inn
42	100	N54 55.351 W3 05.013	Cattle grid at Dykesfield
43	101	N54 55.639 W3 08.904	Drumburgh
44	102	N54 55.346 W3 09.452	To Drumburgh Moss SSSI
44	103	N54 55.932 W3 10.198	Path onto road at Glasson
44	104	N54 56.052 W3 10.045	Junction by Highland Laddie Inn
44	105	N54 56.397 W3 10.708	Entry to Glendale Holiday Park
45	106	N54 56.983 W3 11.317	Port Carlisle
45	107	N54 57.240 W3 12.773	Start/end of path by gazebo at herb garden

HADRIAN'S WALL COUNTRY BUS SERVICE§   (see also pp56-8)

	185≠	AD122	AD122	AD122	185≠
Newcastle Central Station	–	–	09.30	–	–
Heddon-on-the-Wall, Towne Gate	–	–	09.57	–	–
Harlow Hill	–	–	10.00	–	–
Robin Hood Inn (East Wallhouses)	–	–	10.02	–	–
Errington Arms (The Portgate)	–	–	10.06	–	–
Corbridge, Hill St	–	–	10.13	–	–
Corbridge Roman site (roadside)	–	–	10.15	–	–
Hexham TIC (Wentworth car park)	–	09.00	10.30	12.15	–
Hexham Rail Station	–	09.03	10.33	12.18	–
Acomb	–	09.08	10.38	12.23	–
Wall Village	–	09.10	10.40	12.25	–
Chollerford	–	09.12	10.42	12.27	–
Chesters Roman Fort (roadside)	–	09.13	10.43	12.28	–
Housesteads Car Park	–	09.29	10.59	12.44	–
Once Brewed, Nat Park Centre	–	09.34	11.04	12.49	–
Vindolanda	–	09.39	11.09	12.54	–
Once Brewed, Nat Park Centre	–	09.44	11.14	12.59	–
Twice Brewed Inn	–	09.45	11.15	13.00	–
Milecastle Inn (for Cawfield)	–	09.49	11.19	13.04	–
Shield Hill, Herding Hill	–	09.51	11.21	13.06	–
Haltwhistle, Market Place	–	09.55	11.25	13.10	–
Haltwhistle Rail Station	09.18	09.58	11.28	13.13	12.23
Roman Army Museum (Walltown)	09.27	10.06	11.36	13.21	12.32
Greenhead	09.30	10.10	–	13.25	12.35
Longbyre	–	10.12	–	13.27	–
Gilsland, Bridge Inn	09.36	10.15	–	13.30	12.41
Birdoswald Roman Fort	–	10.22	–	13.37	–
Banks	–	10.30	–	13.45	–
Lanercost Priory	–	10.34	–	13.49	–
Brampton, Front St	10.00	10.41	–	13.56	13.05
Crosby-on-Eden, Stag Inn	10.09	10.51	–	14.06	13.14
Carlisle, West Tower St (for Tullie House/Castle)	10.20	11.03	–	14.18	13.25
Carlisle, English St for railway station	10.23	11.06	–	14.21	13.28

§ Note that the AD122 service runs daily from 22 April to 30 October in 2011.
≠ Service No 185 operates Monday (**but not** Bank Holiday Mondays) to Saturday.

AD122	AD122	185≠	AD122	AD122	
–	–	–	–	–	**Newcastle Central Station**
–	–	–	–	–	**Heddon-on-the-Wall, Towne Gate**
–	–	–	–	–	**Harlow Hill**
–	–	–	–	–	**Robin Hood Inn, East Wallhouses**
–	–	–	–	–	**Errington Arms, The Portgate**
–	–	–	–	–	**Corbridge, Hill St**
–	–	–	–	–	**Corbridge Roman site (roadside)**
13.15	14.20	–	16.00	17.25	**Hexham TIC**
13.18	14.23	–	16.03	17.28	**Hexham Rail Station**
13.23	14.28	–	16.08	17.33	**Acomb**
13.25	14.30	–	16.10	17.35	**Wall Village**
13.27	14.32	–	16.12	17.37	**Chollerford**
13.28	14.33	–	16.13	17.38	**Chesters Roman Fort (roadside)**
13.44	14.49	–	16.29	17.54	**Housesteads, Car Park**
13.49	14.54	–	16.34	17.59	**Once Brewed, Nat Park Centre**
13.54	14.59	–	16.39	18.04	**Vindolanda**
13.59	15.04	–	16.44	18.09	**Once Brewed, Nat Park Centre**
14.00	15.05	–	16.45	18.10	**Twice Brewed Inn**
14.04	15.09	–	16.49	18.14	**Milecastle Inn**
14.06	15.11	–	–	18.16	**Shield Hill, Herding Hill**
14.10	15.15	–	–	18.20	**Haltwhistle, Market Place**
14.13	15.18	14.38	–	18.23	**Haltwhistle Rail Station**
14.21	15.26	14.47	16.50	18.31	**Roman Museum (Walltown Quarry)**
–	15.30	14.50	–	18.35	**Greenhead**
–	15.32	–	–	18.37	**Longbyre**
–	15.35	14.56	–	18.40	**Bridge Inn, Gilsland**
–	15.42	–	–	18.47	**Birdoswald Roman Fort**
–	15.50	–	–	18.55	**Banks**
–	15.54	–	–	18.59	**Lanercost Priory**
–	16.01	15.20	–	19.06	**Brampton, Front St**
–	16.11	–	–	19.16	**Crosby-on-Eden, opp Stag Inn**
–	16.23	–	–	19.28	**Carlisle, West Tower St (for Tullie House/Castle)**
–	16.26	–	–	19.31	**Carlisle, English St (The Courts) for railway station**

HADRIAN'S WALL COUNTRY BUS SERVICE§				(see also pp56-8)
	AD122	185≠	AD122	185≠	AD122
Carlisle, English St (The Courts) for railway station	–	–	09.20	10.30	–
Carlisle, West Tower St (for Tullie House/Castle)	–	–	09.23	10.33	–
Crosby-on-Eden, Stag Inn	–	–	09.36	10.47	–
Brampton, Front St	07.55	08.39	09.46	11.03	–
Lanercost Priory	–	–	09.53	–	–
Banks	–	–	09.57	–	–
Birdoswald Roman Fort	–	–	10.05	–	–
Gilsland, opp Village Hall	–	08.56	10.11	11.20	–
Longbyre	–	–	10.14	–	–
Greenhead, Village Hall	08.10	09.01	10.16	11.25	–
Roman Army Museum (Walltown)	08.14	09.05	10.20	11.29	11.37
Haltwhistle Railway Station	–	09.12	10.30	11.36	–
Haltwhistle, Market Place	–	–	10.32	–	–
Shield Hill, Herding Hill	–	–	10.36	–	–
Milecastle Inn (for Cawfield)	08.16	–	10.38	–	11.39
Twice Brewed Inn	08.19	–	10.42	–	11.42
Once Brewed, Nat Park Centre	08.20	–	10.43	–	11.43
Vindolanda	–	–	10.48	–	11.48
Once Brewed, Nat Park Centre	08.20	–	10.53	–	11.53
Housesteads Roman fort Car Park	08.26	–	10.59	–	11.59
Chesters Roman Fort (roadside)	08.41	–	11.14	–	12.14
Chollerford	08.42	–	11.15	–	12.15
Wall Village	08.44	–	11.17	–	12.17
Acomb	08.46	–	11.19	–	12.19
Hexham Rail Station	08.52	–	11.25	–	12.25
Hexham TIC, Wentworth Car park	08.56	–	11.28	–	12.28
Corbridge Roman site (roadside)	–	–	–	–	–
Corbridge, Hill St	–	–	–	–	–
Errington Arms (The Portgate)	–	–	–	–	–
Robin Hood Inn (East Wallhouses)	–	–	–	–	–
Harlow Hill	–	–	–	–	–
Heddon-on-the-Wall, Towne Gate	–	–	–	–	–
Newcastle Central Station	–	–	–	–	–

§ Note that the AD122 service runs daily from 22 April to 30 October in 2011
≠ Service No 185 operates Monday (**but not** Bank Holiday Mondays) to Saturday.

AD122	185≠	AD122	AD122	AD122	
11.55	13.30	–	14.30	–	**Carlisle, English St (The Courts) for railway station**
11.58	13.33	–	14.33	–	**Carlisle, West Tower St (for Tullie House/Castle)**
	–	–			
12.11	13.47	–	14.46	–	**Crosby-on-Eden, opp Stag Inn**
12.21	14.03	–	14.56	–	**Brampton, Front St**
12.28	–	–	15.03	–	**Lanercost Priory**
12.32	–	–	15.07	–	**Banks**
12.40	–	–	15.15	–	**Birdoswald Roman Fort**
12.46	14.20	–	15.21	–	**Gilsland, opp Village Hall**
12.49	–	–	15.24	–	**Longbyre**
12.51	14.25	–	15.26	–	**Greenhead, Village Hall**
12.55	14.29	14.22	15.30	16.55	**Roman Museum (Walltown Quarry)**
13.05	14.36	–	15.40	17.05	**Haltwhistle Rail Station**
13.07	–	–	15.42	17.07	**Haltwhistle, Market Place**
13.11	–	–	15.46	17.11	**Shield Hill, Herding Hill**
13.13	–	14.24	15.48	17.13	**Milecastle Inn (for Cawfield)**
13.17	–	14.27	15.52	17.17	**Twice Brewed Inn**
13.18	–	14.28	15.53	17.18	**Once Brewed, Nat Park Centre**
13.23	–	14.33	15.58	17.23	**Vindolanda**
13.28	–	14.38	16.03	17.28	**Once Brewed, Nat Park Centre**
13.34	–	14,44	16.09	17.34	**Housesteads Roman Fort Car Park**
13.49	–	14.59	16.24	17.49	**Chesters Roman Fort (roadside)**
13.50	–	15.00	16.25	17.50	**Chollerford**
13.52	–	15.02	16.27	17.52	**Wall Village**
13.54	–	15.04	16.29	17.54	**Acomb**
14.00	–	15.10	16.35	18.00	**Hexham Rail Station**
14.03	–	15.13	16.38	18.03	**Hexham TIC**
–	–	–	–	18.13	**Corbridge Roman site (roadside)**
–	–	–	–	18.15	**Corbridge, Hill St**
–	–	–	–	18.19	**Errington Arms, The Portgate**
–	–	–	–	18.21	**Robin Hood Inn, East Wallhouses**
–	–	–	–	18.25	**Harlow Hill**
–	–	–	–	18.31	**Heddon-on-the-Wall, Towne Gate**
–	–	–	–	18.57	**Newcastle Central Station**

INDEX

Page references in **bold** type refer to maps

222 Other walking guides from Trailblazer

Kilimanjaro – the trekking guide to Africa's highest mountain
Henry Stedman, 3rd edn, £12.99
ISBN 978-1-905864-24-9, 368pp, 40 maps, 30 photos
At 19,340ft the world's tallest freestanding mountain, Kilimanjaro is one of the most popular destinations for hikers visiting Africa. It's possible to walk up to the summit: no technical skills are necessary. Includes town guides to Nairobi and Dar-Es-Salaam, and a colour guide to flora and fauna. Includes Mount Meru.

The Inca Trail, Cusco & Machu Picchu
Alex Stewart, 4th edn, £12.99
ISBN 978-1-905864-15-7, 352pp, 74 maps, 40 colour photos
The Inca Trail, from Cusco to Machu Picchu, is South America's most popular trek. Practical guide including detailed trail maps, plans of Inca sites, plus guides to Cusco and Machu Picchu. Route guides to other trails in the area: the Santa Teresa Trek and the Choquequirao Trek as well as the Vilcabamba Trail plus the routes linking them. Includes a new history of the Incas by Hugh Thomson.

Dolomites Trekking Alta Via 1 & Alta Via 2 *Henry Stedman*
2nd edn, 192pp, 52 trail maps, 7 town plans, 38 colour photos
ISBN 978-1-873756-83-6, £11.99   AV1 (9-13 days) & AV2 (10-16 days) are the most popular long-distance hikes in the Dolomites. Numerous shorter walks also included. Places to stay, walking times plus detailed guides to Cortina and six other towns.

Tour du Mont Blanc *Jim Manthorpe* 1st edn, £11.99
ISBN 978-1-905864-12-6, 208pp, 60 maps, 30 colour photos
At 4810m (15,781ft), Mont Blanc is the highest mountain in western Europe, and one of the most famous mountains in the world. The trail (105 miles, 168km) that circumnavigates it, passing through France, Italy and Switzerland, is the most popular long distance walk in Europe. Includes Chamonix and Courmayeur guides.

The Walker's Haute Route – Mt Blanc to the Matterhorn
*Alexander Stewart,*1st edn, 256pp, 60 maps, 30 colour photos
ISBN 978-1-905864-08-9, £12.99
From Mont Blanc to the Matterhorn, Chamonix to Zermatt, the 180km (113-mile) Walkers' Haute Route traverses one of the finest stretches of the Pennine Alps – the range between Valais in Switzerland and Piedmont and Aosta Valley in Italy. Includes Chamonix and Zermatt guides.

TRAILBLAZER GUIDES – TITLE LIST

Adventure Cycle-Touring Handbook	2nd edn out now
Adventure Motorcycling Handbook	5th edn out now
Australia by Rail	5th edn out now
Australia's Great Ocean Road	1st edn out now
Azerbaijan	4th edn out now
Coast to Coast (British Walking Guide)	4th edn out now
Cornwall Coast Path (British Walking Guide)	3rd edn out now
Corsica Trekking – GR20	1st edn out now
Cotswold Way (British Walking Guide)	1st edn out now
Dolomites Trekking – AV1 & AV2	2nd edn out now
Inca Trail, Cusco & Machu Picchu	4th edn out now
Indian Rail Handbook	1st edn Oct 2011
Hadrian's Wall Path (British Walking Guide)	3rd edn out now
Himalaya by Bike – a route and planning guide	1st edn out now
Japan by Rail	2nd edn out now
Kilimanjaro – the trekking guide (includes Mt Meru)	3rd edn out now
Mediterranean Handbook	1st edn out now
Moroccan Atlas – The Trekking Guide	1st edn out now
Morocco Overland (4WD/motorcycle/mountainbike)	1st edn out now
Nepal Trekking & The Great Himalaya Trail	1st edn out now
New Zealand – The Great Walks	2nd edn out now
North Downs Way (British Walking Guide)	1st edn out now
Norway's Arctic Highway	1st edn out now
Offa's Dyke Path (British Walking Guide)	3rd edn July 2011
Overlanders' Handbook – worldwide driving guide	1st edn out now
Peddars Way & Norfolk Coast Path (British Walking)	1st edn out now
Pembrokeshire Coast Path (British Walking Guide)	3rd edn out now
Pennine Way (British Walking Guide)	3rd edn out now
The Ridgeway (British Walking Guide)	2nd edn out now
Sahara Overland – a route and planning guide	2nd edn out now
Scottish Highlands – The Hillwalking Guide	2nd edn out now
The Silk Roads – a route and planning guide	3rd edn out now
South Downs Way (British Walking Guide)	3rd edn out now
Tibet Overland – mountain biking & jeep touring	1st edn out now
Tour du Mont Blanc	1st edn out now
Trans-Canada Rail Guide	5th edn out now
Trans-Siberian Handbook	8th edn July 2011
Trekking in the Annapurna Region	5th edn Sep 2011
Trekking in the Everest Region	5th edn out now
Trekking in Ladakh	3rd edn out now
Trekking in the Pyrenees	3rd edn out now
The Walker's Haute Route – Mont Blanc to Matterhorn	1st edn out now
West Highland Way (British Walking Guide)	4th edn out now

www.trailblazer-guides.com

TRAILBLAZER'S LONG-DISTANCE PATH (LDP) WALKING GUIDES

We've applied to destinations which are closer to home Trailblazer's proven formula for publishing definitive practical route guides for adventurous travellers. Britain's network of long-distance trails enables the walker to explore some of the finest landscapes in the country's best walking areas. These are guides that are user-friendly, practical, informative and environmentally sensitive.

'The same attention to detail that distinguishes its other guides has been brought to bear here'.
THE SUNDAY TIMES

● **Unique mapping features** In many walking guidebooks the reader has to read a route description then try to relate it to the map. Our guides are much easier to use because walking directions, tricky junctions, places to stay and eat, points of interest and walking times are all written onto the maps themselves in the places to which they apply. With their uncluttered clarity, these are not general-purpose maps but fully edited maps drawn by walkers for walkers.

● **Largest-scale walking maps** At a scale of just under 1:20,000 (8cm or 3⅛ inches to one mile) the maps in these guides are bigger than even the most detailed British walking maps currently available in the shops.

● **Not just a trail guide – includes where to stay, where to eat and public transport** Our guidebooks cover the complete walking experience, not just the route. Accommodation options for all budgets are provided (pubs, hotels, B&Bs, campsites, bunkhouses, hostels) as well as places to eat. Detailed public transport information for all access points to each trail means that there are itineraries for all walkers, for hiking the entire route as well as for day or weekend walks.

Coast to Coast *Henry Stedman* ISBN 978-1-905864-30-0, £11.99
4th edition, 256pp, 109 maps & town plans, 40 colour photos

Cornwall Coast Path *Edith Schofield* ISBN 978-1-905864-19-5, £9.99
3rd edition, 256pp, 112 maps & town plans, 40 colour photos

Cotswold Way *Tricia & Bob Hayne* ISBN 978-1-905864-16-4, £9.99
1st edition, 192pp, 60 maps & town plans, 40 colour photos

Hadrian's Wall Path *Henry Stedman* ISBN 978-1-905864-37-9, £11.99
3rd edition, 224pp, 59 maps & town plans, 40 colour photos

Offa's Dyke Path *Keith Carter* ISBN 978-1-905864-06-5, £9.99
2nd edition, 208pp, 88 maps & town plans, 40 colour photos

North Downs Way *John Curtin* ISBN 978-1-873756-96-6, £9.99
1st edition, 192pp, 60 maps & town plans, 40 colour photos

Peddars Way & Norfolk Coast Path *A Stewart* ISBN 978-1-905864-28-7, £11.99
1st edition, 192pp, 60 maps & town plans, 40 colour photos

Pembrokeshire Coast Path *Jim Manthorpe* ISBN 978-1-905864-27-0, £9.99
3rd edition, 224pp, 96 maps & town plans, 40 colour photos

Pennine Way *Keith Carter & Chris Scott* ISBN 978-1-905864-34-8, £11.99
3rd edition, 272pp, 138 maps & town plans, 40 colour photos

The Ridgeway *Nick Hill* ISBN 978-1-905864-17-1, £9.99
2nd edition, 192pp, 53 maps & town plans, 40 colour photos

South Downs Way *Jim Manthorpe* ISBN 978-1-905864-18-8, £9.99
3rd edition, 192pp, 60 maps & town plans, 40 colour photos

West Highland Way *Charlie Loram* ISBN 978-1-905864-29-4, £9.99
4th edition, 192pp, 53 maps, 10 town plans, 40 colour photos

TRAILBLAZER
British Walking Guides

SCOTTISH HIGHLANDS Hillwalking Guide

WEST HIGHLAND WAY

PENNINE WAY

HADRIAN'S WALL PATH

COAST TO COAST

PENNINE WAY

OFFA'S DYKE PATH

COTSWOLD WAY

THE RIDGEWAY

PEDDARS WAY & NORFOLK COAST PATH

PEMBROKESHIRE COAST PATH

CORNWALL COAST PATH

NORTH DOWNS WAY

SOUTH DOWNS WAY

Coast to Coast PATH

Hadrian's Wall PATH

Pennine Way

Cotswold Way

South Downs WAY

THE Ridgeway

Cornwall Coast PATH

Offa's Dyke PATH

Pembrokeshire COAST PATH

Peddars Way and NORFOLK COAST PATH

Scottish Highlands THE HILLWALKING GUIDE

West Highland WAY

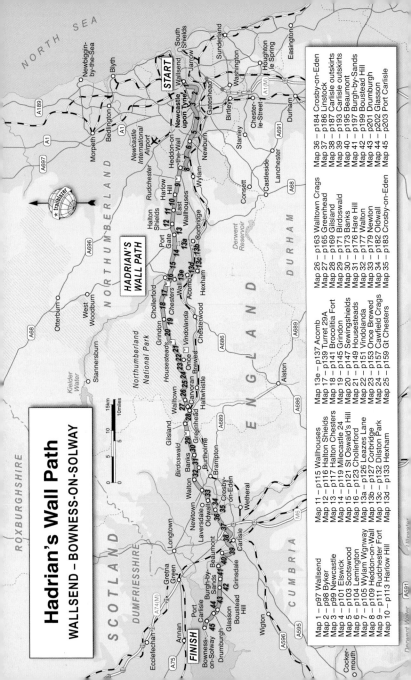

Hadrian's Wall Path
WALLSEND – BOWNESS-ON-SOLWAY

HADRIAN'S WALL PATH

START — Newcastle upon Tyne

FINISH — Bowness-on-Solway